MAKE IT STICK

make it stick
The Science of Successful Learning

Peter C. Brown
Henry L. Roediger III
Mark A. McDaniel

THE BELKNAP PRESS *of* HARVARD UNIVERSITY PRESS

Cambridge, Massachusetts

London, England

2014

Printed in the United States of America

Library of Congress Cataloging-in-Publication Data
Brown, Peter C.
Make it stick : the science of successful learning / Peter C. Brown,
Henry L. Roediger, Mark A. McDaniel.
pages cm
Includes bibliographical references and index.
ISBN 978-0-674-72901-8
1. Learning—Research.   2. Cognition—Research.   3. Study skills.
I. Title.
LB1060.B768 2014
370.15'23—dc23
2013038420

Memory is the mother of all wisdom.

Aeschylus
Prometheus Bound

Contents

Preface

PEOPLE GENERALLY ARE going about learning in the wrong ways. Empirical research into how we learn and remember shows that much of what we take for gospel about how to learn turns out to be largely wasted effort. Even college and medical students—whose main job is learning—rely on study techniques that are far from optimal. At the same time, this field of research, which goes back 125 years but has been particularly fruitful in recent years, has yielded a body of insights that constitute a growing science of learning: highly effective, evidence-based strategies to replace less effective but widely accepted practices that are rooted in theory, lore, and intuition. But there's a catch: the most effective learning strategies are not intuitive.

Two of us, Henry Roediger and Mark McDaniel, are cognitive scientists who have dedicated our careers to the study of learning and memory. Peter Brown is a storyteller. We have teamed up to explain how learning and memory work, and we do this less by reciting the research than by telling stories of people who have found their way to mastery of complex knowledge and skills. Through these examples we illuminate the principles of learning that the research shows are highly effective. This book arose in part from a collaboration among eleven cognitive psychologists. In 2002, the James S. McDonnell Foundation of St. Louis, Missouri, in an effort to better bridge the gap between basic knowledge on learning in cognitive psychology and its application in education, awarded a research grant "Applying Cognitive Psychology to Enhance Educational Practice" to Roediger and McDaniel and nine others, with Roediger as the principal investigator. The team collaborated for ten years on research to translate cognitive science into educational science, and in many respects this book is a direct result of that work. The researchers and many of their studies are cited in the book, the notes, and our acknowledgments. Roediger's and McDaniel's work is also supported by several other funders, and McDaniel is the co-director of Washington University's Center for Integrative Research in Learning and Memory.

Most books deal with topics serially—they cover one topic, move on to the next, and so on. We follow this strategy in the sense that each chapter addresses new topics, but we also apply two of the primary learning principles in the book: spaced repetition of key ideas, and the interleaving of different but related topics. If learners spread out their study of a topic, returning to it periodically over time, they remember it better. Similarly, if they interleave the study of different topics, they learn each better than if they had studied them one at a time in sequence. Thus we unabashedly cover key ideas more than once, repeating principles in different contexts across the book.

The reader will remember them better and use them more effectively as a result.

This is a book about what people can do for themselves right now in order to learn better and remember longer. The responsibility for learning rests with every individual. Teachers and coaches, too, can be more effective right now by helping students understand these principles and by designing them into the learning experience. This is not a book about how education policy or the school system ought to be reformed. Clearly, though, there are policy implications. For example, college professors at the forefront of applying these strategies in the classroom have experimented with their potential for narrowing the achievement gap in the sciences, and the results of those studies are eye opening.

We write for students and teachers, of course, and for all readers for whom effective learning is a high priority: for trainers in business, industry, and the military; for leaders of professional associations offering in-service training to their members; and for coaches. We also write for lifelong learners nearing middle age or older who want to hone their skills so as to stay in the game.

While much remains to be known about learning and its neural underpinnings, a large body of research has yielded principles and practical strategies that can be put to work immediately, at no cost, and to great effect.

MAKE IT STICK

1

Learning Is Misunderstood

EARLY IN HIS CAREER as a pilot, Matt Brown was flying a twin-engine Cessna northeast out of Harlingen, Texas, when he noticed a drop in oil pressure in his right engine. He was alone, flying through the night at eleven thousand feet, making a hotshot freight run to a plant in Kentucky that had shut down its manufacturing line awaiting product parts for assembly.

He reduced altitude and kept an eye on the oil gauge, hoping to fly as far as a planned fuel stop in Louisiana, where he could service the plane, but the pressure kept falling. Matt has been messing around with piston engines since he was old enough to hold a wrench, and he knew he had a problem. He ran a mental checklist, figuring his options. If he let the oil pressure get too low he risked the engine's seizing up. How much further could he fly before shutting it down? What would happen when he did? He'd lose lift on the right side, but could he stay aloft? He reviewed the tolerances he'd memorized for the Cessna 401. Loaded, the best you could do on one engine was slow your descent. But he had a light load, and he'd burned through most of his fuel. So he shut down the ailing right engine, feathered the prop to reduce drag, increased power on the left, flew with opposite rudder, and limped another ten miles toward his intended stop. There, he made his approach in a wide left-hand turn, for the simple but critical reason that without power on his right side it was only from a left-hand turn that he still had the lift needed to level out for a touchdown.

While we don't need to understand each of the actions Matt took, *he* certainly needed to, and his ability to work himself out of a jam illustrates what we mean in this book when we talk about learning: we mean acquiring knowledge and skills and having them readily available from memory so you can make sense of future problems and opportunities.

There are some immutable aspects of learning that we can probably all agree on:

First, to be useful, learning requires memory, so what we've learned is still there later when we need it.

Second, we need to keep learning and remembering all our lives. We can't advance through middle school without some mastery of language arts, math, science, and social studies. Getting ahead at work takes mastery of job skills and difficult colleagues. In retirement, we pick up new interests. In our dotage, we move into simpler housing while we're still able to adapt. If you're good at learning, you have an advantage in life.

Third, learning is an acquired skill, and the most effective strategies are often counterintuitive.

Claims We Make in This Book

You may not agree with the last point, but we hope to persuade you of it. Here, more or less unadorned in list form, are some of the principal claims we make in support of our argument. We set them forth more fully in the chapters that follow.

Learning is deeper and more durable when it's *effortful*. Learning that's easy is like writing in sand, here today and gone tomorrow.

We are *poor judges* of when we are learning well and when we're not. When the going is harder and slower and it doesn't feel productive, we are drawn to strategies that feel more fruitful, unaware that the gains from these strategies are often temporary.

Rereading text and *massed practice* of a skill or new knowledge are by far the preferred study strategies of learners of all stripes, but they're also among the *least productive*. By massed practice we mean the single-minded, rapid-fire repetition of something you're trying to burn into memory, the "practice-practice-practice" of conventional wisdom. Cramming for exams is an example. Rereading and massed practice give rise to feelings of fluency that are taken to be signs of mastery, but for true mastery or durability these strategies are largely a waste of time.

Retrieval practice—recalling facts or concepts or events from memory—is a more effective learning strategy than review by rereading. Flashcards are a simple example. Retrieval strengthens the memory and interrupts forgetting. A single, simple quiz after reading a text or hearing a lecture produces better learning and remembering than rereading the text or reviewing lecture notes. While the brain is not a muscle that gets stronger with exercise, the neural pathways that make up a body of learning do get stronger, when the memory is retrieved and the learning is practiced. Periodic practice arrests forgetting, strengthens retrieval routes, and is essential for hanging onto the knowledge you want to gain.

When you *space out practice* at a task and get a little rusty between sessions, or you interleave the practice of two or more subjects, retrieval is harder and feels less productive, but the effort produces longer lasting learning and enables more versatile application of it in later settings.

Trying to solve a problem *before being taught the solution* leads to better learning, even when errors are made in the attempt.

The popular notion that you learn better when you receive instruction in a form consistent with your preferred *learning style,* for example as an auditory or visual learner, is *not supported by the empirical research.* People do have multiple forms of intelligence to bring to bear on learning, and you learn better when you "go wide," drawing on all of your aptitudes and resourcefulness, than when you limit instruction or experience to the style you find most amenable.

When you're adept at extracting the *underlying principles or "rules"* that differentiate types of problems, you're more successful at picking the right solutions in unfamiliar situations. This skill is better acquired through *interleaved and varied practice* than massed practice. For instance, interleaving practice at computing the volumes of different kinds of geometric solids makes you more skilled at picking the right solution when a later test presents a random solid. Interleaving the identification of bird types or the works of oil painters improves your ability both to learn the unifying attributes within a type and to differentiate between types, improving your skill at categorizing new specimens you encounter later.

We're all *susceptible to illusions* that can hijack our judgment of what we know and can do. Testing helps calibrate our judgments of what we've learned. A pilot who is responding to a failure of hydraulic systems in a flight simulator discovers quickly whether he's on top of the corrective procedures or not. In virtually all areas of learning, you build better mastery when you use testing as a tool to identify and bring up your areas of weakness.

All new learning requires a *foundation of prior knowledge.* You need to know how to land a twin engine plane on two engines before you can learn to land it on one. To learn trigonometry, you need to remember your algebra and geometry. To learn cabinetmaking, you need to have mastered the properties of wood and composite materials, how to join boards, cut rabbets, rout edges, and miter corners.

In a cartoon by the *Far Side* cartoonist Gary Larson, a bug-eyed school kid asks his teacher, "Mr. Osborne, can I be excused? My brain is full!" If you're just engaging in mechanical repetition, it's true, you quickly hit the limit of what you can keep in mind. However, if you practice *elaboration,* there's no known limit to how much you can learn. Elaboration is the process of giving new material meaning by expressing it in your own words and connecting it with what you already know. The more you can explain about the way your new learning relates to your prior knowledge, the stronger your grasp of the new learning will be, and the more connections you create that will help you remember it later. Warm air can hold more moisture than cold air; to know that this is true in your own experience, you can think of the drip of water from the back of an air conditioner or the way a stifling summer day turns cooler out the back side of a sudden thunderstorm. Evaporation has a cooling effect: you know this because a humid day at your uncle's in Atlanta feels hotter than a dry one at your cousin's in Phoenix, where your sweat disappears even before your skin feels damp. When you study the principles of heat transfer, you understand conduction from warming your hands around a hot cup of cocoa; radiation from the way the sun pools in the den on a wintry day; convection from the life-saving blast of A/C as your uncle squires you slowly through his favorite back alley haunts of Atlanta.

Putting new knowledge into a *larger context* helps learning. For example, the more of the unfolding story of history you know, the more of it you can learn. And the more ways you give that story meaning, say by connecting it to your understanding of human ambition and the untidiness of fate, the better the story stays with you. Likewise, if you're trying to learn an abstraction, like the principle of angular momentum, it's easier when you ground it in something concrete that you already know, like the way a figure skater's rotation speeds up as she draws her arms to her chest.

People who learn to *extract the key ideas from new material and organize them into a mental model* and connect that model to prior knowledge show an advantage in learning complex mastery. A mental model is a mental representation of some external reality.[1] Think of a baseball batter waiting for a pitch. He has less than an instant to decipher whether it's a curveball, a changeup, or something else. How does he do it? There are a few subtle signals that help: the way the pitcher winds up, the way he throws, the spin of the ball's seams. A great batter winnows out all the extraneous perceptual distractions, seeing only these variations in pitches, and through practice he forms distinct mental models based on a different set of cues for each kind of pitch. He connects these models to what he knows about batting stance, strike zone, and swinging so as to stay on top of the ball. These he connects to mental models of player positions: if he's got guys on first and second, maybe he'll sacrifice to move the runners ahead. If he's got men on first and third and there is one out, he's got to keep from hitting into a double play while still hitting to score the runner. His mental models of player positions connect to his models of the opposition (are they playing deep or shallow?) and to the signals flying around from the dugout to the base coaches to him. In a great at-bat, all these pieces come together seamlessly: the batter connects with the ball and drives it through a hole in the outfield, buying the time to get on first and advance his men. Because he has culled out all but the most important elements for identifying and responding to each kind of pitch, constructed mental models out of that learning, and connected those models to his mastery of the other essential elements of this complex game, an expert player has a better chance of scoring runs than a less experienced one who cannot make sense of the vast and changeable information he faces every time he steps up to the plate.

Many people believe that their intellectual ability is hardwired from birth, and that failure to meet a learning challenge is an indictment of their native ability. But every time you learn something new, *you change the brain*—the residue of your experiences is stored. It's true that we start life with the gift of our genes, but it's also true that we become capable through the learning and development of mental models that enable us to reason, solve, and create. In other words, the elements that shape your intellectual abilities lie to a surprising extent within your own control. Understanding that this is so enables you to see failure as a badge of effort and a source of useful information—the need to dig deeper or to try a different strategy. The need to understand that when learning is hard, you're doing important work. To understand that striving and setbacks, as in any action video game or new BMX bike stunt, are essential if you are to surpass your current level of performance toward true expertise. Making mistakes and correcting them builds the bridges to advanced learning.

Empirical Evidence versus Theory, Lore, and Intuition

Much of how we structure training and schooling is based on learning theories that have been handed down to us, and these are shaped by our own sense of what works, a sensibility drawn from our personal experiences as teachers, coaches, students, and mere humans at large on the earth. How we teach and study is largely a mix of theory, lore, and intuition. But over the last forty years and more, cognitive psychologists have been working to build a body of evidence to clarify what works and to discover the strategies that get results.

Cognitive psychology is the basic science of understanding how the mind works, conducting empirical research into how people perceive, remember, and think. Many others have their hands in the puzzle of learning as well. Developmental and educational psychologists are concerned with theories of human development and how they can be used to shape the tools of education—such as testing regimes, instructional organizers (for example topic outlines and schematic illustrations), and resources for special groups like those in remedial and gifted education. Neuroscientists, using new imaging techniques and other tools, are advancing our understanding of brain mechanisms that underlie learning, but we're still a very long way from knowing what neuroscience will tell us about how to improve education.

How is one to know whose advice to take on how best to go about learning?

It's wise to be skeptical. Advice is easy to find, only a few mouse-clicks away. Yet not all advice is grounded in research—far from it. Nor does all that passes as research meet the standards of science, such as having appropriate control conditions to assure that the results of an investigation are objective and generalizable. The best empirical studies are experimental in nature: the researcher develops a hypothesis and then tests it through a set of experiments that must meet rigorous criteria for design and objectivity. In the chapters that follow, we have distilled the findings of a large body of such studies that have stood up under review by the scientific community before being published in professional journals. We are collaborators in some of these studies, but not the lion's share. Where we're offering theory rather than scientifically validated results, we say so. To make our points we use, in addition to tested science, anecdotes from people like Matt Brown whose work requires mastery of complex knowledge and skills, stories that illustrate the underlying principles of how we learn and remember. Discussion of the research studies themselves is kept to a minimum, but you will find many of them cited in the notes at the end of the book if you care to dig further.

People Misunderstand Learning

It turns out that much of what we've been doing as teachers and students isn't serving us well, but some comparatively simple changes could make a big difference. People commonly believe that if you expose yourself to something enough times— say, a textbook passage or a set of terms from an eighth grade biology class—you can burn it into memory. Not so. Many teachers believe that if they can make learning easier and faster, the learning will be better. Much research turns this belief on its head: when learning is harder, it's stronger and lasts longer. It's widely believed by teachers, trainers, and coaches that the most effective way to master a new skill is to give it dogged, single-minded focus, practicing over and over until you've got it down. Our faith in this runs deep, because most of us see fast gains during the learning phase of massed practice. What's apparent from the research is that gains achieved during massed practice are transitory and melt away quickly.

The finding that rereading textbooks is often labor in vain ought to send a chill up the spines of educators and learners, because it's the number one study strategy of most people—including more than 80 percent of college students in some surveys—and is central in what we tell ourselves to do during the hours we dedicate to learning. Rereading has three strikes against it. It is time consuming. It doesn't result in durable memory. And it often involves a kind of unwitting self-deception, as growing familiarity with the text comes to feel like mastery of the content. The hours immersed in rereading can seem like due diligence, but the amount of study time is no measure of mastery.[2]

You needn't look far to find training systems that lean heavily on the conviction that mere exposure leads to learning. Consider Matt Brown, the pilot. When Matt was ready to advance from piston planes, he had a whole new body of knowledge to master in order to get certified for the business jet he was hired to pilot. We asked him to describe this process. His employer sent him to eighteen days of training, ten hours a day, in what Matt called the "fire hose" method of instruction. The first seven days straight were spent in the classroom being instructed in all the plane's systems: electrical, fuel, pneumatics, and so on, how these systems operated and interacted, and all their fail-safe tolerances like pressures, weights, temperatures, and speeds. Matt is required to have at his immediate command about eighty different "memory action items"—actions to take without hesitation or thought in order to stabilize the plane the moment any one of a dozen or so unexpected events occur. It might be a sudden decompression, a thrust reverser coming unlocked in flight, an engine failure, an electrical fire.

Matt and his fellow pilots gazed for hours at mind-numbing PowerPoint illustrations of their airplane's principal systems. Then something interesting happened.

"About the middle of day five," Matt said, "they flash a schematic of the fuel system on the screen, with its pressure sensors, shutoff valves, ejector pumps, bypass lines, and on and on, and you're struggling to stay focused. Then this one instructor asks us, 'Has anybody here had the fuel filter bypass light go on in flight?' This pilot across the room raises his hand. So the instructor says, 'Tell us what happened,' and suddenly you're thinking, Whoa, what if that was me?

"So, this guy was at 33,000 feet or something and he's about to lose both engines because he got fuel without antifreeze in it and his filters are clogging with ice. You hear that story and, believe me, that schematic comes to life and sticks with you. Jet fuel can commonly have a little water in it, and when it gets cold at high altitude, the water will condense out, and it can freeze and block the line. So whenever you refuel, you make good and sure to look for a sign on the fuel truck saying the fuel has Prist in it, which is an antifreeze. And if you ever see that light go on in flight, you're going to get yourself down to some warmer air in a hurry."[3] Learning is stronger when it matters, when the abstract is made concrete and personal.

Then the nature of Matt's instruction shifted. The next eleven days were spent in a mix of classroom and flight simulator training. Here, Matt described the kind of active engagement that leads to durable learning, as the pilots had to grapple with their aircraft to demonstrate mastery of standard operating procedures, respond to unexpected situations, and drill on the rhythm and physical memory of the movements that are required in the cockpit for dealing with them. A flight simulator provides retrieval practice, and the practice is spaced, interleaved, and varied and involves as far as possible the same mental processes Matt will invoke when he's at altitude. In a simulator, the abstract is made concrete and personal. A simulator is also a series of tests, in that it helps Matt and his instructors calibrate their judgment of where he needs to focus to bring up his mastery.

In some places, like Matt Brown's flight simulator, teachers and trainers have found their way to highly effective learning techniques, yet in virtually any field, these techniques tend to be the exception, and "fire hose" lectures (or their equivalent) are too often the norm.

In fact, what students are advised to do is often plain wrong. For instance, study tips published on a website at George Mason University include this advice: "The key to learning something well is repetition; the more times you go over the material the better chance you have of storing it permanently."[4] Another, from a Dartmouth College website, suggests: "If you intend to remember something, you probably will."[5] A public service piece that runs occasionally in the *St. Louis Post-Dispatch* offering study advice shows a kid with his nose buried in a book. "Concentrate," the caption reads. "Focus on one thing and one thing only. Repeat, repeat, repeat! Repeating what you have to remember can help burn it into your memory."[6] Belief in the power of rereading, intentionality, and repetition is pervasive, but the truth is you usually can't embed something in memory simply by repeating it over and over. This tactic might work when looking up a phone number and holding it in your mind while punching it into your phone, but it doesn't work for durable learning.

A simple example, reproduced on the Internet (search "penny memory test"), presents a dozen different images of a common penny, only one of which is correct. As many times as you've seen a penny, you're hard pressed to say with confidence which one it is. Similarly, a recent study asked faculty and students who worked in the Psychology Building at UCLA to identify the fire extinguisher closest to their office. Most failed the test. One professor, who had been at UCLA for twenty-five years, left his safety class and decided to look for the fire extinguisher closest to his office. He discovered that it was actually right next to his office door, just inches from the doorknob he turned every time he went into his office. Thus, in this case, even years of repetitive exposure did not result in his learning where to grab the closest extinguisher if his wastebasket caught fire.[7]

Early Evidence

The fallacy in thinking that repetitive exposure builds memory has been well established through a series of investigations going back to the mid-1960s, when the psychologist Endel Tulving at the University of Toronto began testing people on their ability to remember lists of common English nouns. In a first phase of the experiment, the participants simply read a list of paired items six times (for example, a pair on the list might be "chair—9"); they did not expect a memory test. The first item in each pair was always a noun. After reading the listed pairs six times, participants were then told that they would be getting a list of nouns that they would be asked to remember. For one group of people, the nouns were the same ones they had just read six times in the prior reading phase; for another group, the nouns to be learned were different from those they had previously read. Remarkably, Tulving found that the two groups' learning of the nouns did not differ—the learning curves were statistically indistinguishable. Intuition would suggest otherwise, but prior exposure did not aid later recall. Mere repetition did not enhance learning. Subsequent studies by many researchers have pressed further into questions of whether repeated exposure or longer periods of holding an idea in mind contribute to later recall, and these studies have confirmed and elaborated on the findings that repetition by itself does not lead to good long-term memory.[8]

These results led researchers to investigate the benefits of rereading texts. In a 2008 article in *Contemporary Educational Psychology,* Washington University scientists reported on a series of studies they conducted at their own school and at the University of New Mexico to shed light on rereading as a strategy to improve understanding and memory of prose. Like most research, these studies stood on the shoulders of earlier work by others; some showed that when the same text is read multiple times the same inferences are made and the same connections between topics are formed, and others suggested modest benefits from rereading. These benefits had been found in two different situations. In the first, some students read and immediately reread study material, whereas other students read the material only once. Both groups took an immediate test after reading, and the group who had read twice performed a bit better than the group who had read once. However, on a delayed test the benefit of immediate rereading had worn off, and the rereaders performed at the same level as the one-time readers. In the other situation, students read the material the first time and then waited some days before they reread it. This group, having done spaced readings of the text, performed better on the test than the group who did not reread the material.[9]

Subsequent experiments at Washington University, aimed at teasing apart some of the questions the earlier studies had raised, assessed the benefits of rereading among students of differing abilities, in a learning situation paralleling that faced by students in classes. A total of 148 students read five different passages taken from textbooks and *Scientific American*. The students were at two different universities; some were high-ability readers, and others were low-ability; some students read the material only once, and others read it twice in succession. Then all of them responded to questions to demonstrate what they had learned and remembered.

In these experiments, multiple readings in close succession did not prove to be a potent study method for either group, at either school, in any of the conditions tested. In fact, the researchers found no rereading benefit at all under these conditions.

What's the conclusion? It makes sense to reread a text once if there's been a meaningful lapse of time since the first reading, but doing multiple readings in close succession is a time-consuming study strategy that yields negligible benefits at the expense of much more effective strategies that take less time. Yet surveys of college students confirm what professors have long known: highlighting, underlining, and sustained poring over notes and texts are the most-used study strategies, by far.[10]

Illusions of Knowing

If rereading is largely ineffective, why do students favor it? One reason may be that they're getting bad study advice. But there's another, subtler way they're pushed toward this method of review, the phenomenon mentioned earlier: rising familiarity with a text and fluency in reading it can create an illusion of mastery. As any professor will attest, students work hard to capture the precise wording of phrases they hear in class lectures, laboring under the misapprehension that the essence of the subject lies in the syntax in which it's described. Mastering the lecture or the text is not the same as mastering the ideas behind them. However, repeated reading provides the illusion of mastery of the underlying ideas. Don't let yourself be fooled. The fact that you can repeat the phrases in a text or your lecture notes is no indication that you understand the significance of the precepts they describe, their application, or how they relate to what you already know about the subject.

Too common is the experience of a college professor answering a knock on her office door only to find a first-year student in distress, asking to discuss his low grade on the first test in introductory psychology. How is it possible? He attended all the lectures and took diligent notes on them. He read the text and highlighted the critical passages.

How did he study for the test? she asks.

Well, he'd gone back and highlighted his notes, and then reviewed the highlighted notes and his highlighted text material several times until he felt he was thoroughly familiar with all of it. How could it be that he had pulled a D on the exam?

Had he used the set of key concepts in the back of each chapter to test himself? Could he look at a concept like "conditioned stimulus," define it, and use it in a paragraph? While he was reading, had he thought of converting the main points of the text into a series of questions and then later tried to answer them while he was studying? Had he at least rephrased the main ideas in his own words as he read? Had he tried to relate them to what he already knew? Had he looked for examples outside the text? The answer was no in every case.

He sees himself as the model student, diligent to a fault, but the truth is he doesn't know how to study effectively.

The illusion of mastery is an example of poor metacognition: what we know about what we know. Being accurate in your judgment of what you know and don't know is critical for decision making. The problem was famously (and prophetically) summed up by Secretary of State Donald Rumsfeld in a 2002 press briefing about US intelligence on Iraq's possible possession of weapons of mass destruction: "There are known knowns; there are things we know that we know. There are known unknowns; that is to say, there are things that we now know we don't know. But there are also unknown unknowns—*there are things we do not know we don't know.*"

The emphasis here is ours. We make it to drive home the point that students who don't quiz themselves (and most do not) tend to overestimate how well they have mastered class material. Why? When they hear a lecture or read a text that is a paragon of clarity, the ease with which they follow the argument gives them the feeling that they already know it and don't need to study it. In other words, they tend not to know what they don't know; when put to the test, they find they cannot recall the critical ideas or apply them in a new context. Likewise, when they've reread their lecture notes and texts to the point of fluency, their fluency gives them the false sense that they're in possession of the underlying content, principles, and implications that constitute real learning, confident that they can recall them at a moment's notice. The upshot is that even the most diligent students are often hobbled by two liabilities: a failure to know the areas where their learning is weak—that is, where they need to do more work to bring up their knowledge—and a preference for study methods that create a false sense of mastery.[11]

Knowledge: Not Sufficient, but Necessary

Albert Einstein declared "creativity is more important than knowledge," and the sentiment appears to be widely shared by college students, if their choice in t-shirt proclamations is any indication. And why wouldn't they seize on the sentiment? It embodies an obvious and profound truth, for without creativity where would our scientific, social, or economic breakthroughs come from? Besides which, accumulating knowledge can feel like a grind, while creativity sounds like a lot more fun. But of course the dichotomy is false. You wouldn't want to see that t-shirt on your neurosurgeon or on the captain who's flying your plane across the Pacific. But the sentiment has gained some currency as a reaction to standardized testing, fearing that this kind of testing leads to an emphasis on memorization at the expense of high-level skills. Notwithstanding the pitfalls of standardized testing, what we really ought to ask is how to do better at building knowledge *and* creativity, for without knowledge you don't have the foundation for the higher-level skills of analysis, synthesis, and creative problem solving. As the psychologist Robert Sternberg and two colleagues put it, "one cannot apply what one knows in a practical manner if one does not know anything to apply."[12]

Mastery in any field, from cooking to chess to brain surgery, is a gradual accretion of knowledge, conceptual understanding, judgment, and skill. These are the fruits of variety in the practice of new skills, and of striving, reflection, and mental rehearsal. Memorizing facts is like stocking a construction site with the supplies to put up a house. Building the house requires not only knowledge of countless different fittings and materials but conceptual understanding, too, of aspects like the load-bearing properties of a header or roof truss system, or the principles of energy transfer and conservation that will keep the house warm but the roof deck cold so the owner doesn't call six months later with ice dam problems. Mastery requires both the possession of ready knowledge and the conceptual understanding of how to use it.

When Matt Brown had to decide whether or not to kill his right engine he was problem solving, and he needed to know from memory the procedures for flying with a dead engine and the tolerances of his plane in order to predict whether he would fall out of the air or be unable to straighten up for landing. The would-be neurosurgeon in her first year of med school has to memorize the whole nervous system, the whole skeletal system, the whole muscular system, the humeral system. If she can't, she's not going to be a neurosurgeon. Her success will depend on diligence, of course, but also on finding study strategies that will enable her to learn the sheer volume of material required in the limited hours available.

Testing: Dipstick versus Learning Tool

There are few surer ways to raise the hackles of many students and educators than talking about testing. The growing focus over recent years on standardized assessment, in particular, has turned testing into a lightning rod for frustration over how to achieve the country's education goals. Online forums and news articles are besieged by readers who charge that emphasis on testing favors memorization at the expense of a larger grasp of context or creative ability; that testing creates extra stress for students and gives a false measure of ability; and so on. But if we stop thinking of testing as a dipstick to measure learning—if we think of it as practicing retrieval of learning from memory rather than "testing," we open ourselves to another possibility: *the use of testing as a tool for learning.*

One of the most striking research findings is the power of active retrieval—testing—to strengthen memory, and that the more effortful the retrieval, the stronger the benefit. Think flight simulator versus PowerPoint lecture. Think quiz versus rereading. The act of retrieving learning from memory has two profound benefits. One, it tells you what you know and don't know, and therefore where to focus further study to improve the areas where you're weak. Two, recalling what you have learned causes your brain to reconsolidate the memory, which strengthens its connections to what you already know and makes it easier for you to recall in the future. In effect, retrieval—testing—interrupts forgetting. Consider an eighth grade science class. For the class in question, at a middle school in Columbia, Illinois, researchers arranged for part of the material covered during the course to be the subject of low-stakes quizzing (with feedback) at three points in the semester. Another part of the material was never quizzed but was studied three times in review. In a test a month later, which material was better recalled? The students averaged A- on the material that was quizzed and C+ on the material that was not quizzed but reviewed.[13]

In Matt Brown's case, even after ten years piloting the same business jet, his employer reinforces his mastery every six months in a battery of tests and flight simulations that require him to retrieve the information and maneuvers that are essential to stay in control of his plane. As Matt points out, you hardly ever have an emergency, so if you don't practice what to do, there's no way to keep it fresh.

Both of these cases—the research in the classroom and the experience of Matt Brown in updating his knowledge—point to the critical role of retrieval practice in keeping our knowledge accessible to us when we need it. The power of active retrieval is the topic of Chapter 2.[14]

The Takeaway

For the most part, we are going about learning in the wrong ways, and we are giving poor advice to those who are coming up behind us. A great deal of what we think we know about how to learn is taken on faith and based on intuition but does not hold up under empirical research. Persistent illusions of knowing lead us to labor at unproductive strategies; as recounted in Chapter 3, this is true even of people who have participated in empirical studies and seen the evidence for themselves, firsthand. Illusions are potent persuaders. One of the best habits a learner can instill in herself is regular self-quizzing to recalibrate her understanding of what she does and does not know. Second Lieutenant Kiley Hunkler, a 2013 graduate of West Point and winner of a Rhodes Scholarship, whom we write about in Chapter 8, uses the phrase "shooting an azimuth" to describe how she takes practice tests to help refocus her studying. In overland navigation, shooting an azimuth means climbing to a height, sighting an object on the horizon in the direction you're traveling, and adjusting your compass heading to make sure you're still gaining on your objective as you beat through the forest below.

The good news is that we now know of simple and practical strategies that anybody can use, at any point in life, to learn better and remember longer: various forms of retrieval practice, such as low-stakes quizzing and self-testing, spacing out practice, interleaving the practice of different but related topics or skills, trying to solve a problem before being taught the solution, distilling the underlying principles or rules that differentiate types of problems, and so on. In the chapters that follow we describe these in depth. And because learning is an iterative process that requires that you revisit what you have learned earlier and continually update it and connect it with new knowledge, we circle through these topics several times along the way. At the end, in Chapter 8, we pull it all together with specific tips and examples for putting these tools to work.

2

To Learn, Retrieve

MIKE EBERSOLD GOT CALLED into a hospital emergency room one afternoon late in 2011 to examine a Wisconsin deer hunter who'd been found lying unconscious in a cornfield. The man had blood at the back of his head, and the men who'd found and brought him in supposed he'd maybe stumbled and cracked his skull on something.

Ebersold is a neurosurgeon. The injury had brain protruding, and he recognized it as a gunshot wound. The hunter regained consciousness in the ER, but when asked how he'd hurt himself, he had no idea.

Recounting the incident later, Ebersold said, "Somebody from some distance away must have fired what appeared to be a 12-gauge shotgun, which arced over God only knows what distance, hit this guy in the back of his head, fractured his skull, and lodged into the brain about an inch. It must have been pretty much spent, or it would have gone deeper."[1]

Ebersold is tall, slender, and counts among his forebears the Dakota chiefs named Wapasha and the French fur traders named Rocque who populated this part of the Mississippi River Valley where the Mayo brothers would later found their famous clinic. Ebersold's formal training included four years of college, four years of medical school, and seven years of neurosurgery training—building a foundation of knowledge and skills that has been broadened and deepened through continuing medical education classes, consultations with his colleagues, and his practice at the Mayo Clinic and elsewhere. He carries himself with a midwestern modesty that belies a career that counts a long list of high-profile patients who have sought out his services. When President Ronald Reagan needed treatment for injuries after a fall from his horse, Ebersold participated in the surgery and postsurgical care. When Sheikh Zayed bin Sultan Al Nahyan, president of the United Arab Emirates, needed delicate spinal repair, he and what seemed like half the nation's ministry and security forces settled in Rochester while Mike Ebersold made the repair and oversaw Zayed's recovery. Following a long career at Mayo, Mike had returned to help out at the clinic in Wisconsin, feeling indebted to it for his early medical training. The hunter whose bad luck put him in the way of an errant 12-gauge slug was luckier than he likely knows that Mike was on the job that day.

The bullet had entered an area of the skull beneath which there is a large venous sinus, a soft-tissue channel that drains the brain cavity. As he examined the hunter, Ebersold knew from experience that when he opened up the wound, there was a high probability he would find this vein was torn. As he described it,

You say to yourself, "This patient is going to need surgery. There's brain coming out of the wound. We have to clean this up and repair this as best we can, but in so doing we may get into this big vein and that could be very, very serious." So you go through the checklist. You say, "I might need a blood transfusion for this patient," so you set up some blood. You review the steps, A, B, C, and D. You set up the operating room, telling them ahead of time what you might be encountering. All of this is sort of protocol, pretty much like a cop getting ready to pull over a car, you know what the book says, you've gone through all these steps.

Then you get to the operating room, and now you're still in this mode where you have time to think through it. You say, "Gee, I don't want to just go and pull that bullet out if there might be major bleeding. What I'll try to do is I'll work around the edges and get things freed up so I'm ready for what could go wrong, and then I'll pull it out."

It turned out that the bullet and bone were lodged in the vein, serving as plugs, another lucky turn for the hunter. If the wound hadn't corked itself in the field, he would not have lived for more than two or three minutes. When Ebersold removed the bullet, the fractured bone chips fell away, and the vein let loose in a torrent. "Within five minutes, you've lost two or so units of blood and now you sort of transfer out of the mode where you're thinking through this, going through the options. Now it becomes reflex, mechanical. You know it's going to bleed very, very much, so you have a very short time. You're just thinking, 'I have to get a suture around this structure, and I know from previous experience I have to do it in this particular way.'"

The vein in question, which is about the size of an adult's small finger, was torn in several places over a distance of about an inch and a half. It needed to be tied off above and below the rupture, but it's a flat structure that he knows well: you can't just put a stitch around it, because when you tighten it, the tissue tears, and the ligature leaks. Working urgently and mechanically, he fell back on a technique he'd developed out of necessity in past surgeries involving this vein. He cut two little pieces of muscle, from where the patient's skin had been opened up in surgery, and imported them to the site and stitched the ends of the torn vein to them. These plugs of muscle served to close the vein without deflecting its natural shape or tearing its tissue. It's a solution Mike has taught himself—one he says you won't find written anywhere, but handy in the moment, to say the least. In the sixty or so seconds it took to do, the patient lost another two hundred cubic centimeters of blood, but once the plugs were in place, the bleeding stopped. "Some people can't tolerate this sinus vein being closed off. They get increased brain pressure because the blood doesn't drain properly. But this patient was one of the fortunate who can." The hunter left the hospital a week later. He was minus some peripheral vision but otherwise remarkably unscathed from a very close brush with mortality.

Reflection Is a Form of Practice

What inferences can we draw from this story about how we learn and remember? In neurosurgery (and, arguably, in all aspects of life from the moment you leave the womb), there's an essential kind of learning that comes from reflection on personal experience. Ebersold described it this way:

> A lot of times something would come up in surgery that I had difficulty with, and then I'd go home that night thinking about what happened and what could I do, for example, to improve the way a suturing went. How can I take a bigger bite with my needle, or a smaller bite, or should the stitches be closer together? What if I modified it this way or that way? Then the

next day back, I'd try that and see if it worked better. Or even if it wasn't the next day, at least I've thought through this, and in so doing I've not only revisited things that I learned from lectures or from watching others performing surgery but also I've complemented that by adding something of my own to it that I missed during the teaching process.

Reflection can involve several cognitive activities that lead to stronger learning: retrieving knowledge and earlier training from memory, connecting these to new experiences, and visualizing and mentally rehearsing what you might do differently next time.

It was this kind of reflection that originally had led Ebersold to try a new technique for repairing the sinus vein at the back of the head, a technique he practiced in his mind and in the operating room until it became the kind of reflexive maneuver you can depend on when your patient is spouting blood at two hundred cubic centimeters a minute.

To make sure the new learning is available when it's needed, Ebersold points out, "you memorize the list of things that you need to worry about in a given situation: steps A, B, C, and D," and you drill on them. Then there comes a time when you get into a tight situation and it's no longer a matter of thinking through the steps, it's a matter of reflexively taking the correct action. "Unless you keep recalling this maneuver, it will not become a reflex. Like a race car driver in a tight situation or a quarterback dodging a tackle, you've got to act out of reflex before you've even had time to think. Recalling it over and over, practicing it over and over. That's just so important."

The Testing Effect

A child stringing cranberries on a thread goes to hang them on the tree, only to find they've slipped off the other end. Without the knot, there's no making a string. Without the knot there's no necklace, there's no beaded purse, no magnificent tapestry. Retrieval ties the knot for memory. Repeated retrieval snugs it up and adds a loop to make it fast.

Since as far back as 1885, psychologists have been plotting "forgetting curves" that illustrate just how fast our cranberries slip off the string. In very short order we lose something like 70 percent of what we've just heard or read. After that, forgetting begins to slow, and the last 30 percent or so falls away more slowly, but the lesson is clear: a central challenge to improving the way we learn is finding a way to interrupt the process of forgetting.[2]

The power of retrieval as a learning tool is known among psychologists as the testing effect. In its most common form, testing is used to measure learning and assign grades in school, but we've long known that the act of retrieving knowledge from memory has the effect of making that knowledge easier to call up again in the future. In his essay on memory, Aristotle wrote: "exercise in repeatedly recalling a thing strengthens the memory." Francis Bacon wrote about this phenomenon, as did the psychologist William James. Today, we know from empirical research that practicing retrieval makes learning stick far better than reexposure to the original material does. This is the testing effect, also known as the retrieval-practice effect.[3]

To be most effective, retrieval must be repeated again and again, in spaced out sessions so that the recall, rather than becoming a mindless recitation, requires some cognitive effort. Repeated recall appears to help memory consolidate into a cohesive representation in the brain and to strengthen and multiply the neural routes by which the knowledge can later be retrieved. In recent decades, studies have confirmed what Mike Ebersold and every seasoned quarterback, jet pilot, and teenaged texter knows from experience—that repeated retrieval can so embed knowledge and skills that they become reflexive: the brain acts before the mind has time to think.

Yet despite what research and personal experience tell us about the power of testing as a learning tool, teachers and students in traditional educational settings rarely use it as such, and the technique remains little understood or utilized by teachers or students as a learning tool in traditional educational settings. Far from it.

In 2010 the *New York Times* reported on a scientific study that showed that students who read a passage of text and then took a test asking them to recall what they had read retained an astonishing 50 percent more of the information a week later than students who had not been tested. This would seem like good news, but here's how it was greeted in many online comments:

"Once again, another author confuses learning with recalling information."

"I personally would like to avoid as many tests as possible, especially with my grade on the line. Trying to learn in a stressful environment is no way to help retain information."

"Nobody should care whether memorization is enhanced by practice testing or not. Our children cannot *do* much of anything anymore."[4]

Forget memorization, many commenters argued; education should be about high-order skills. Hmmm. If memorization is irrelevant to complex problem solving, don't tell your neurosurgeon. The frustration many people feel toward standardized, "dipstick" tests given for the sole purpose of measuring learning is understandable, but it steers us away from appreciating one of the most potent learning tools available to us. Pitting the learning of basic knowledge against the development of creative thinking is a false choice. Both need to be cultivated. The stronger one's knowledge about the subject at hand, the more nuanced one's creativity can be in addressing a new problem. Just as knowledge amounts to little without the exercise of ingenuity and imagination, creativity absent a sturdy foundation of knowledge builds a shaky house.

Studying the Testing Effect in the Lab

The testing effect has a solid pedigree in empirical research. The first large-scale investigation was published in 1917. Children in grades 3, 5, 6, and 8 studied brief biographies from *Who's Who in America*. Some of them were directed to spend varying lengths of the study time looking up from the material and silently reciting to themselves what it contained. Those who did not do so simply continued to reread the material. At the end of the period, all the children were asked to write down what they could remember. The recall test was repeated three to four hours later. All the groups who had engaged in the recitation showed better retention than those who had not done so but had merely continued to review the material. The best results were from those spending about 60 percent of the study time in recitation.

A second landmark study, published in 1939, tested over three thousand sixth graders across Iowa. The kids studied six-hundred-word articles and then took tests at various times before a final test two months later. The experiment showed a couple of interesting results: the longer the first test was delayed, the greater the forgetting, and second, once a student had taken a test, the forgetting nearly stopped, and the student's score on subsequent tests dropped very little.[5]

Around 1940, interest turned to the study of forgetting, and investigating the potential of testing as a form of retrieval practice and as a learning tool fell out of favor. So did the use of testing as a research tool: since testing interrupts forgetting, you can't use it to measure forgetting because that "contaminates" the subject.

Interest in the testing effect resurfaced in 1967 with the publication of a study showing that research subjects who were presented with lists of thirty-six words learned as much from repeated testing after initial exposure to the words as they did from repeated studying. These results—that testing led to as much learning as studying did—challenged the received wisdom, turned researchers' attention back to the potential of testing as a learning tool, and stimulated a boomlet in testing research.

In 1978, researchers found that massed studying (cramming) leads to higher scores on an immediate test but results in faster forgetting compared to practicing retrieval. In a second test two days after an initial test, the crammers had forgotten 50 percent of what they had been able to recall on the initial test, while those who had spent the same period practicing retrieval instead of studying had forgotten only 13 percent of the information recalled initially.

A subsequent study was aimed at understanding what effect taking multiple tests would have on subjects' long-term retention. Students heard a story that named sixty concrete objects. Those students who were tested immediately after exposure recalled 53 percent of the objects on this initial test but only 39 percent a week later. On the other hand, a group of students who learned the same material but were not tested at all until a week later recalled 28 percent. Thus, taking a single test boosted performance by 11 percent after a week.

But what effect would three immediate tests have relative to one? Another group of students were tested three times after initial exposure and a week later they were able to recall 53 percent of the objects—the same as on the initial test for the group receiving one test. In effect, the group that received three tests had been "immunized" against forgetting, compared to the one-test group, and the one-test group remembered more than those who had received no test immediately following exposure. Thus, and in agreement with later research, multiple sessions of retrieval practice are generally better than one, especially if the test sessions are spaced out.[6]

In another study, researchers showed that simply asking a subject to fill in a word's missing letters resulted in better memory of the word. Consider a list of word pairs. For a pair like *foot-shoe,* those who studied the pair intact had lower subsequent recall than those who studied the pair from a clue as obvious as *foot-s_ _e.* This experiment was a demonstration of what researchers call the "generation effect." The modest effort required to generate the cued answer while studying the pairs strengthened memory of the target word tested later (shoe). Interestingly, this study found that the ability to recall the word pair on later tests was greater if the practice retrieval was delayed by twenty intervening word pairs than when it came immediately after first studying the pair.[7] Why would that be? One argument suggested that the greater effort required by the delayed recall solidified the memory better. Researchers began to ask whether the schedule of testing mattered.

The answer is yes. When retrieval practice is spaced, allowing some forgetting to occur between tests, it leads to stronger long-term retention than when it is massed.

Researchers began looking for opportunities to take their inquiries out of the lab and into the classroom, using the kinds of materials students are required to learn in school.

Studying the Testing Effect "In the Wild"

In 2005, we and our colleagues approached Roger Chamberlain, the principal of a middle school in nearby Columbia, Illinois, with a proposition. The positive effects of retrieval practice had been demonstrated many times in controlled laboratory settings but rarely in a regular classroom setting. Would the principal, teachers, kids, and parents of Columbia Middle School be willing subjects in a study to see how the testing effect would work "in the wild"?

Chamberlain had concerns. If this was just about memorization, he wasn't especially interested. His aim is to raise the school's students to higher forms of learning—analysis, synthesis, and application, as he put it. And he was concerned about his teachers, an energetic faculty with curricula and varied instructional methods he was loath to disrupt. On the other hand, the study's results could be instructive, and participation would bring enticements in the form of smart boards and "clickers"—automated response systems—for the classrooms of participating teachers. Money for new technology is famously tight.

A sixth grade social studies teacher, Patrice Bain, was eager to give it a try. For the researchers, a chance to work in the classroom was compelling, and the school's terms were accepted: the study would be minimally intrusive by fitting within existing curricula, lesson plans, test formats, and teaching methods. The same textbooks would be used. The only difference in the class would be the introduction of occasional short quizzes. The study would run for three semesters (a year and a half), through several chapters of the social studies textbook, covering topics such as ancient Egypt, Mesopotamia, India, and China. The project was launched in 2006. It would prove to be a good decision.

For the six social studies classes a research assistant, Pooja Agarwal, designed a series of quizzes that would test students on roughly one-third of the material covered by the teacher. These quizzes were for "no stakes," meaning that scores were not counted toward a grade. The teacher excused herself from the classroom for each quiz so as to remain unaware of which material was being tested. One quiz was given at the start of class, on material from assigned reading that hadn't yet been discussed. A second was given at the end of class after the teacher had covered the material for the day's lesson. And a review quiz was given twenty-four hours before each unit exam.

There was concern that if students tested better in the final exam on material that had been quizzed than on material not quizzed, it could be argued that the simple act of reexposing them to the material in the quizzes was responsible for the superior learning, not the retrieval practice. To counter this possibility, some of the nonquizzed material was interspersed with the quiz material, provided as simple review statements, like "The Nile River has two major tributaries: the White Nile and the Blue Nile," with no retrieval required. The facts were quizzed for some classes but just restudied for others.

The quizzes took only a few minutes of classroom time. After the teacher stepped out of the room, Agarwal projected a series of slides onto the board at the front of the room and read them to the students. Each slide presented either a multiple choice question or a statement of fact. When the slide contained a question, students used clickers (handheld, cell-phone-like remotes) to indicate their answer choice: A, B, C, or D. When all had responded, the correct answer was revealed, so as to provide feedback and correct errors. (Although teachers were not present for these quizzes, under normal circumstances, with teachers administering quizzes, they would see immediately how well students are tracking the study material and use the results to guide further discussion or study.)

Unit exams were the normal pencil-and-paper tests given by the teacher. Exams were also given at the end of the semester and at the end of the year. Students had been exposed to all of the material tested in these exams through the teacher's normal classroom lessons, homework, worksheets, and so on, but they had also been quizzed three times on one-third of the material, and they had seen another third presented for additional study three times. The balance of the material was neither quizzed nor additionally reviewed in class beyond the initial lesson and whatever reading a student may have done.

The results were compelling: The kids scored a full grade level higher on the material that had been quizzed than on the material that had not been quizzed. Moreover, test results for the material that had been reviewed as statements of fact but not quizzed were no better than those for the nonreviewed material. Again, mere rereading does not much help.

In 2007, the research was extended to eighth grade science classes, covering genetics, evolution, and anatomy. The regimen was the same, and the results equally impressive. At the end of three semesters, the eighth graders averaged 79 percent (C+) on the science material that had not been quizzed, compared to 92 percent (A–) on the material that had been quizzed.

The testing effect persisted eight months later at the end-of-year exams, confirming what many laboratory studies have shown about the long-term benefits of retrieval practice. The effect doubtless would have been greater if the retrieval practice had continued and occurred once a month, say, in the intervening months.[8]

The lesson from these studies has been taken to heart by many of the teachers at Columbia Middle School. Long after concluding their participation in the research studies, Patrice Bain's sixth grade social studies classes continue today to follow a schedule of quizzes before lessons, quizzes after lessons, and then a review quiz prior to the chapter test. Jon Wehrenberg, an eighth grade history teacher who was not part of the research, has knitted retrieval practice into his classroom in many different forms, including quizzing, and he provides additional online tools at his website, like flashcards and games. After reading passages on the history of slavery, for example, his students are asked to write down ten facts about slavery they hadn't known before reading the passages. You don't need electronic gadgetry to practice retrieval.

Seven sixth and seventh graders needing to improve their reading and comprehension skills sat in Michelle Spivey's English classroom one period recently with their reading books open to an amusing story. Each student was invited to read a paragraph aloud. Where a student stumbled, Miss Spivey had him try again. When he'd gotten it right, she probed the class to explain the meaning of the passage and what might have been going on in the characters' minds. Retrieval and elaboration; again, no technology required.

Quizzes at Columbia Middle School are not onerous events. Following completion of the research studies, students' views were surveyed on this question. Sixty-four percent said the quizzing reduced their anxiety over unit exams, and 89 percent felt it increased learning. The kids expressed disappointment on days when clickers were not used, because the activity broke up the teacher's lecture and proved enjoyable.

Principal Chamberlain, when asked what he thought the study results indicated, replied simply: "Retrieval practice has a significant impact on kids' learning. This is telling us that it's valuable, and that teachers are well advised to incorporate it into their instructional technique."[9]

Are similar effects found at a later age?

Andrew Sobel teaches a class in international political economics at Washington University in St. Louis, a lecture course populated by 160–170 students, mostly freshmen and sophomores. Over a period of several years he noticed a growing problem with attendance. On any given day by midsemester, 25–35 percent of the class would be absent, compared to earlier in the semester when maybe 10 percent would be absent. The problem wasn't unique to his class, he says. A lot of professors give students their PowerPoint slides, so the students just stop coming to class. Sobel fought back by withholding his slides, but by the end of the semester, many students stopped showing up anyway. The class syllabus included two big tests, a midterm and a final. Looking for some way to leverage attendance, Sobel replaced the big tests with nine pop quizzes. Because the quizzes would determine the course grade and would be unannounced, students would be well advised to show up for class.

The results were distressing. Over the semester, a third or more of the students bailed out. "I really got hammered in the teaching reviews," Sobel told us. "The kids hated it. If they didn't do well on a quiz they dropped the course rather than get a bad grade in it. Of those who stayed, I got this bifurcation between those who actually showed up and did the work, and those who didn't. I found myself handing out A-plusses, which I'd never given before, and more Cs than I'd ever given."[10]

With so much pushback, he had little choice but to drop the experiment and reinstate the old format, lectures with a midterm and final. A couple of years later, however, after hearing a presentation about the learning benefits of testing, he added a third major test during the semester to see what effect it might have on his students' learning. They did better, but not by as much as he'd hoped, and the attendance problems persisted.

He scratched his head and changed the syllabus once again. This time he announced that there would be nine quizzes during the semester, and he was explicit about when they would be. No surprises, and no midterm or final exams, because he didn't want to give up that much of his lecture time.

Despite fears that enrollments would plummet again, they actually increased by a handful. "Unlike the pop quizzes, which kids hate, these were all on the syllabus. If they missed one it was their own fault. It wasn't because I surprised them or was being pernicious. They were comfortable with that." Sobel took satisfaction in seeing attendance improve as well. "They would skip some classes on the days they didn't have a quiz, particularly the spring semester, but they showed up for the quizzes."

Like the course, the quizzes were cumulative, and the questions were similar to those on the exams he used to give, but the quality of the answers he was getting by midsemester was much better than he was accustomed to seeing on the midterms. Five years into this new format, he's sold on it. "The quality of discussions in class has gone way up. I see that big a difference in their written work, just by going from three exams to nine quizzes." By the end of the semester he has them writing paragraphs on the concepts covered in class, sometimes a full-page essay, and the quality is comparable to what he's seeing in his upper division classes.

"Anybody can design this structure. But I also realize that, Oh, god, if I'd done this years ago I would have taught them that much more stuff. The interesting thing about adopting this strategy is I now recognize that as good a teacher as I might think I am, my teaching is only a component of their learning, and how I structure it has a lot to do with it, maybe even more." Meanwhile, the course enrollment has grown to 185 and counting.

Exploring Nuances

Andy Sobel's example is anecdotal and likely reflects a variety of beneficial influences, not least being the cumulative learning effects that accrue like compounded interest when course material is carried forward in a regime of quizzes across an entire semester. Nonetheless, his experience squares with empirical research designed to tease apart the effects and nuances of testing.

For example, in one experiment college students studied prose passages on various scientific topics like those taught in college and then either took an immediate recall test after the initial exposure or restudied the material. After a delay of two days, the students who took the initial test recalled more of the material than those who simply restudied it (68 v. 54 percent), and this advantage was sustained a week later (56 v. 42 percent). Another experiment found that after one week a study-only group showed the most forgetting of what they initially had been able to recall, forgetting 52 percent, compared to a repeated-testing group, who forgot only 10 percent.[11]

How does giving feedback on wrong answers to test questions affect learning? Studies show that giving feedback strengthens retention more than testing alone does, and, interestingly, some evidence shows that delaying the feedback briefly produces better long-term learning than immediate feedback. This finding is counterintuitive but is consistent with researchers' discoveries about how we learn motor tasks, like making lay-ups or driving a golf ball toward a distant green. In motor learning, trial and error with delayed feedback is a more awk-ward but effective way of acquiring a skill than trial and cor-rection through immediate feedback; immediate feedback is like the training wheels on a bicycle: the learner quickly comes to depend on the continued presence of the correction.

In the case of learning motor skills, one theory holds that when there's immediate feedback it comes to be part of the task, so that later, in a real-world setting, its absence becomes a gap in the established pattern that disrupts performance. Another idea holds that frequent interruptions for feedback make the learning sessions too variable, preventing establish-ment of a stabilized pattern of performance.[12]

In the classroom, delayed feedback also yields better long-term learning than immediate feedback does. In the case of the students studying prose passages on science topics, some were shown the passage again even while they were asked to answer questions about it, in effect providing them with con-tinuous feedback during the test, analogous to an open-book exam. The other group took the test without the study mate-rial at hand and only afterward were given the passage and instructed to look over their responses. Of course, the open-book group performed best on the immediate test, but those who got corrective feedback after completing the test retained the learning better on a later test. Delayed feedback on writ-ten tests may help because it gives the student practice that's spaced out in time; as discussed in the next chapter, spacing practice improves retention.[13]

Are some kinds of retrieval practice more effective for long-term learning than others? Tests that require the learner to supply the answer, like an essay or short-answer test, or simply practice with flashcards, appear to be more effective than simple recognition tests like multiple choice or true/false tests. However, even multiple choice tests like those used at Columbia Middle School can yield strong benefits. While any kind of retrieval practice generally benefits learning, the implication seems to be that where more cognitive effort is required for retrieval, greater retention results. Retrieval practice has been studied extensively in recent years, and an analysis of these studies shows that even a single test in a class can produce a large improvement in final exam scores, and gains in learning continue to increase as the number of tests increases.[14]

Whichever theories science eventually tells us are correct about *how* repeated retrieval strengthens memory, empirical research shows us that the testing effect is real—that the act of retrieving a memory changes the memory, making it easier to retrieve again later.

How widely is retrieval practice used as a study technique? In one survey, college students were largely unaware of its effectiveness. In another survey, only 11 percent of college students said they use this study strategy. Even when they did report testing themselves, they mostly said they did it to discover what they didn't know, so they could study that material more. That's a perfectly valid use of testing, but few students realize that retrieval itself creates greater retention.[15]

Is repeated testing simply a way to expedite rote learning? In fact, research indicates that testing, compared to rereading, can facilitate better transfer of knowledge to new contexts and problems, and that it improves one's ability to retain and retrieve material that is related but not tested. Further research is needed on this point, but it seems that retrieval practice can make information more accessible when it is needed in various contexts.

Do students resist testing as a tool for learning? Students do generally dislike the idea of tests, and it's not hard to see why, in particular in the case of high-stakes tests like midterms and finals, where the score comes with significant consequences. Yet in all studies of testing that reported students' attitudes, the students who were tested frequently rated their classes more favorably at the end of the semester than those tested less frequently. Those who were frequently tested reached the end of the semester on top of the material and did not need to cram for exams.

How does taking a test affect subsequent studying? After a test, students spend more time restudying the material they missed, and they learn more from it than do their peers who restudy the material without having been tested. Students whose study strategies emphasize rereading but not self-testing show overconfidence in their mastery. Students who have been quizzed have a double advantage over those who have not: a more accurate sense of what they know and don't know, and the strengthening of learning that accrues from retrieval practice.[16]

Are there any further, indirect benefits of regular, low-stakes classroom testing? Besides strengthening learning and retention, a regime of this kind of testing improves student attendance. It increases studying before class (because students know they'll be quizzed), increases attentiveness during class if students are tested at the end of class, and enables students to better calibrate what they know and where they need to bone up. It's an antidote to mistaking fluency with the text, resulting from repeated readings, for mastery of the subject. Frequent low-stakes testing helps dial down test anxiety among students by diversifying the consequences over a much larger sample: no single test is a make-or-break event. And this kind of testing enables instructors to identify gaps in students' understanding and adapt their instruction to fill them. These benefits of low-stakes testing accrue whether instruction is delivered online or in the classroom.[17]

The Takeaway

Practice at retrieving new knowledge or skill from memory is a potent tool for learning and durable retention. This is true for anything the brain is asked to remember and call up again in the future—facts, complex concepts, problem-solving techniques, motor skills.

Effortful retrieval makes for stronger learning and retention. We're easily seduced into believing that learning is better when it's easier, but the research shows the opposite: when the mind has to work, learning sticks better. The greater the effort to retrieve learning, provided that you succeed, the more that learning is strengthened by retrieval. After an initial test, *delaying subsequent retrieval practice* is more potent for reinforcing retention than immediate practice, because delayed retrieval requires more effort.

Repeated retrieval not only makes memories more durable but produces knowledge that can be retrieved more readily, in more varied settings, and applied to a wider variety of problems.

While cramming can produce better scores on an immediate exam, the advantage quickly fades because there is much greater forgetting after rereading than after retrieval practice. The benefits of retrieval practice are *long-term*.

Simply including one test (retrieval practice) in a class yields a large improvement in final exam scores, and gains continue to increase as the frequency of classroom testing increases.

Testing doesn't need to be initiated by the instructor. Students can practice retrieval anywhere; no quizzes in the classroom are necessary. Think flashcards—the way second graders learn the multiplication tables can work just as well for learners at any age to quiz themselves on anatomy, mathematics, or law. Self-testing may be unappealing because it takes more effort than rereading, but as noted already, the greater the effort at retrieval, the more will be retained.

Students who take practice tests have *a better grasp of their progress* than those who simply reread the material. Similarly, such testing enables an instructor to *spot gaps and misconceptions* and adapt instruction to correct them.

Giving students *corrective feedback* after tests keeps them from incorrectly retaining material they have misunderstood and produces better learning of the correct answers.

Students in classes that incorporate low-stakes quizzing come to embrace the practice. Students who are tested frequently rate their classes more favorably.

What about Principal Roger Chamberlain's initial concerns about practice quizzing at Columbia Middle School—that it might be nothing more than a glorified path to rote learning?

When we asked him this question after the study was completed, he paused for a moment to gather his thoughts. "What

I've really gained a comfort level with is this: for kids to be able to evaluate, synthesize, and apply a concept in different settings, they're going to be much more efficient at getting there when they have the base of knowledge and the retention, so they're not wasting time trying to go back and figure out what that word might mean or what that concept was about. It allows them to go to a higher level."

3

Mix Up Your Practice

IT MAY NOT BE INTUITIVE that retrieval practice is a more powerful learning strategy than repeated review and rereading, yet most of us take for granted the importance of testing in sports. It's what we call "practice-practice-practice." Well, here's a study that may surprise you.

A group of eight-year-olds practiced tossing beanbags into buckets in gym class. Half of the kids tossed into a bucket three feet away. The other half mixed it up by tossing into buckets two feet and four feet away. After twelve weeks of this they were all tested on tossing into a three-foot bucket. The kids who did the best by far were those who'd practiced on two- and four-foot buckets but *never on three-foot buckets.*[1]

Why is this? We will come back to the beanbags, but first a little insight into a widely held myth about how we learn.

The Myth of Massed Practice

Most of us believe that learning is better when you go at something with single-minded purpose: the practice-practice-practice that's supposed to burn a skill into memory. Faith in focused, repetitive practice of one thing at a time until we've got it nailed is pervasive among classroom teachers, athletes, corporate trainers, and students. Researchers call this kind of practice "massed," and our faith rests in large part on the simple fact that when we do it, we can see it making a difference. Nevertheless, despite what our eyes tell us, this faith is misplaced.

If learning can be defined as picking up new knowledge or skills and being able to apply them later, then how *quickly* you pick something up is only part of the story. Is it *still there* when you need to use it out in the everyday world? While practicing is vital to learning and memory, studies have shown that practice is far more effective when it's broken into separate periods of training that are spaced out. The rapid gains produced by massed practice are often evident, but the rapid forgetting that follows is not. Practice that's spaced out, interleaved with other learning, and varied produces better mastery, longer retention, and more versatility. But these benefits come at a price: when practice is spaced, interleaved, and varied, it requires more effort. You feel the increased effort, but not the benefits the effort produces. Learning feels slower from this kind of practice, and you don't get the rapid improvements and affirmations you're accustomed to seeing from massed practice. Even in studies where the participants have shown superior results from spaced learning, they don't perceive the improvement; they *believe* they learned better on the material where practice was massed.

Almost everywhere you look, you find examples of massed practice: summer language boot camps, colleges that offer concentration in a single subject with the promise of fast learning, continuing education seminars for professionals where training is condensed into a single weekend. Cramming for exams is a form of massed practice. It feels like a productive strategy, and it may get you through the next day's midterm, but most of the material will be long forgotten by the time you sit down for the final. Spacing out your practice feels less productive for the very reason that some forgetting has set in and you've got to work harder to recall the concepts. It doesn't feel like you're on top of it. What you don't sense in the moment is that this added effort is making the learning stronger.[2]

Spaced Practice

The benefits of spacing out practice sessions are long established, but for a vivid example consider this study of thirty-eight surgical residents. They took a series of four short lessons in microsurgery: how to reattach tiny vessels. Each lesson included some instruction followed by some practice. Half the docs completed all four lessons in a single day, which is the normal in-service schedule. The others completed the same four lessons but with a week's interval between them.[3]

In a test given a month after their last session, those whose lessons had been spaced a week apart outperformed their colleagues in all areas—elapsed time to complete a surgery, number of hand movements, and success at reattaching the severed, pulsating aortas of live rats. The difference in performance between the two groups was impressive. The residents who had taken all four sessions in a single day not only scored lower on all measures, but 16 percent of them damaged the rats' vessels beyond repair and were unable to complete their surgeries.

Why is spaced practice more effective than massed practice? It appears that embedding new learning in long-term memory requires a process of consolidation, in which memory traces (the brain's representations of the new learning) are strengthened, given meaning, and connected to prior knowledge—a process that unfolds over hours and may take several days. Rapid-fire practice leans on short-term memory. Durable learning, however, requires time for mental rehearsal and the other processes of consolidation. Hence, spaced practice works better. The increased effort required to retrieve the learning after a little forgetting has the effect of retriggering consolidation, further strengthening memory. We explore some of the theories about this process in the next chapter.

Interleaved Practice

Interleaving the practice of two or more subjects or skills is also a more potent alternative to massed practice, and here's a quick example of that. Two groups of college students were taught how to find the volumes of four obscure geometric solids (wedge, spheroid, spherical cone, and half cone). One group then worked a set of practice problems that were clustered by problem type (practice four problems for computing the volume of a wedge, then four problems for a spheroid, etc.). The other group worked the same practice problems, but the sequence was mixed (interleaved) rather than clustered by type of problem. Given what we've already presented, the results may not surprise you. During practice, the students who worked the problems in clusters (that is, massed) averaged 89 percent correct, compared to only 60 percent for those who worked the problems in a mixed sequence. But in the final test a week later, the students who had practiced solving problems clustered by type averaged only 20 percent correct, while the students whose practice was interleaved averaged 63 percent. The mixing of problem types, which boosted final test performance by a remarkable 215 percent, actually *impeded* performance during initial learning.[4]

Now, suppose you're a trainer in a company trying to teach employees a complicated new process that involves ten procedures. The typical way of doing this is to train up in procedure 1, repeating it many times until the trainees really seem to have it down cold. Then you go to procedure 2, you do many repetitions of 2, you get that down, and so on. That appears to produce fast learning. What would interleaved practice look like? You practice procedure 1 just a few times, then switch to procedure 4, then switch to 3, then to 7, and so on. (Chapter 8 tells how Farmers Insurance trains new agents in a spiraling series of exercises that cycle back to key skillsets in a seemingly random sequence that adds layers of context and meaning at each turn.)

The learning from interleaved practice feels slower than learning from massed practice. Teachers and students sense the difference. They can see that their grasp of each element is coming more slowly, and the compensating long-term advantage is not apparent to them. As a result, interleaving is unpopular and seldom used. Teachers dislike it because it feels sluggish. Students find it confusing: they're just starting to get a handle on new material and don't feel on top of it yet when they are forced to switch. But the research shows unequivocally that mastery and long-term retention are much better if you interleave practice than if you mass it.

Varied Practice

Okay, what about the beanbag study where the kids who did best had *never* practiced the three-foot toss that the other kids had *only* practiced?

The beanbag study focused on mastery of motor skills, but much evidence has shown that the underlying principle applies to cognitive learning as well. The basic idea is that *varied* practice—like tossing your beanbags into baskets at mixed distances—improves your ability to transfer learning from one situation and apply it successfully to another. You develop a broader understanding of the relationships between different conditions and the movements required to succeed in them; you discern context better and develop a more flexible "movement vocabulary"—different movements for different situations. Whether the scope of variable training (e.g., the two- and four-foot tosses) must encompass the particular task (the three-foot toss) is subject for further study.

The evidence favoring variable training has been supported by recent neuroimaging studies that suggest that different kinds of practice engage different parts of the brain. The learning of motor skills from varied practice, which is more cognitively challenging than massed practice, appears to be consolidated in an area of the brain associated with the more difficult process of learning higher-order motor skills. The learning of motor skills from massed practice, on the other hand, appears to be consolidated in a different area of the brain that is used for learning more cognitively simple and less challenging motor skills. The inference is that learning gained through the less challenging, massed form of practice is encoded in a simpler or comparatively impoverished representation than the learning gained from the varied and more challenging practice which demands more brain power and encodes the learning in a more flexible representation that can be applied more broadly.[5]

Among athletes, massed practice has long been the rule: take your hook shot, knock the twenty-foot putt, work your backhand return, throw the pass while rolling out: again and again and again—to get it right and train your "muscle memory." Or so the notion holds. The benefits of variable training for motor learning have been gaining broader acceptance, albeit slowly. Consider the one-touch pass in hockey. That's where you receive the puck and immediately pass it to a team-mate who's moving down the ice, keeping the opposition off balance and unable to put pressure on the puck carrier. Jamie Kompon, when he was assistant coach of the Los Angeles Kings, was in the habit of running team practice on one-touch passes from the same position on the rink. Even if this move is interleaved with a sequence of other moves in practice, if you only do it at the same place on the rink or in the same sequence of moves, you are only, as it were, throwing your beanbags into the three-foot bucket. Kompon is onto the difference now and has changed up his drills. Since we talked, he's gone over to the Chicago Blackhawks. We would have said "Keep an eye on those Blackhawks" here, but as we revise to go into produc-tion, Kompon and team have already won the Stanley Cup. Perhaps no coincidence?

The benefits of variable practice for cognitive as opposed to motor skills learning were shown in a recent experiment that adapted the beanbag test to verbal learning: in this case, the students solved anagrams–that is, they rearranged letters to form words (*tmoce* becomes *comet*). Some subjects practiced the same anagram over and over, whereas others practiced mul-tiple anagrams for the word. When they were all tested on the same anagram that the former group had practiced on, the latter group performed better on it! The same benefits will apply whether you are practicing to identify tree species, differentiate the principles of case law, or master a new computer program.[6]

Developing Discrimination Skills

Compared to massed practice, a significant advantage of interleaving and variation is that they help us learn better how to assess context and discriminate between problems, selecting and applying the correct solution from a range of possibilities. In math education, massing is embedded in the textbook: each chapter is dedicated to a particular kind of problem, which you study in class and then practice by working, say, twenty examples for homework before you move on. The next chapter has a different type of problem, and you dive into the same kind of concentrated learning and practice of that solution. On you march, chapter by chapter, through the semester. But then, on the final exam, lo and behold, the problems are all mixed up: you're staring at each one in turn, asking yourself *Which algorithm do I use?* Was it in chapter 5, 6, or 7? When you have learned under conditions of massed or blocked repetition, you have had no practice on that critical sorting process. But this is the way life usually unfolds: problems and opportunities come at us unpredictably, out of sequence. For our learning to have practical value, we must be adept at discerning "What kind of problem is this?" so we can select and apply an appropriate solution.

Several studies have demonstrated the improved powers of discrimination to be gained through interleaved and varied practice. One study involved learning to attribute paintings to the artists who created them, and another focused on learning to identify and classify birds.

Researchers initially predicted that massed practice in identifying painters' works (that is, studying many examples of one painter's works before moving on to study many examples of another's works) would best help students learn the defining characteristics of each artist's style. Massed practice of each artist's works, one artist at a time, would better enable students to match artworks to artists later, compared to interleaved exposure to the works of different artists. The idea was that interleaving would be too hard and confusing; students would never be able to sort out the relevant dimensions. The researchers were wrong. The *commonalities* among one painter's works that the students learned through massed practice proved less useful than the *differences* between the works of multiple painters that the students learned through interleaving. Interleaving enabled better discrimination and produced better scores on a later test that required matching the works with their painters. The interleaving group was also better able to match painters' names correctly to new examples of their work that the group had never viewed during the learning phase. Despite these results, the students who participated in these experiments persisted in preferring massed practice, convinced that it served them better. Even after they took the test and could have realized from their own performance that interleaving was the better strategy for learning, they clung to their belief that the concentrated viewing of paintings by one artist was better. The myths of massed practice are hard to exorcise, even when you're experiencing the evidence yourself.[7]

The power of interleaving practice to improve discriminability has been reaffirmed in studies of people learning bird classification. The challenge here is more complex than it might seem. One study addressed twenty different bird families (thrashers, swallows, wrens, finches, and so on). Within each family, students were presented with a dozen species (brown thrasher, curve-billed thrasher, Bendire's thrasher, etc.). To identify a bird's family, you consider a wide range of traits like size, plumage, behavior, location, beak shape, iris color, and so on. A problem in bird identification is that members of a family share many traits in common but not all. For instance, many but not all thrashers have a long, slightly hooked beak. There are traits that are *typical* of a family but none that occur in *all* members of that family and can serve as unique identifiers. Because rules for classification can only rely on these characteristic traits rather than on defining traits (ones that hold for every member), bird classification is a matter of learning concepts and making judgments, not simply memorizing features. Interleaved and variable practice proved more helpful than massed practice for learning the underlying concepts that unite and differentiate the species and families.

To paraphrase a conclusion from one of these studies, recall and recognition require "factual knowledge," considered to be a lower level of learning than "conceptual knowledge." Conceptual knowledge requires an understanding of the interrelationships of the basic elements within a larger structure that enable them to function together. Conceptual knowledge is required for classification. Following this logic, some people argue that practicing retrieval of facts and exemplars would fall short as a strategy for comprehending general characteristics that are required for higher levels of intellectual behavior. The bird classification studies suggest the opposite: strategies of learning that help students identify and discern complex prototypes (family resemblances) can help them grasp the kinds of contextual and functional differences that go beyond the acquisition of simple forms of knowledge and reach into the higher sphere of comprehension.[8]

Improving Complex Mastery for Medical Students

The distinction between straightforward knowledge of facts and deeper learning that permits flexible use of the knowledge may be a little fuzzy, but it resonates with Douglas Larsen at Washington University Medical School in St. Louis, who says that the skills required for bird classification are similar to those required of a doctor diagnosing what's wrong with a patient. "The reason variety is important is it helps us see more nuances in the things that we can compare against," he says. "That comes up a lot in medicine, in the sense that every patient visit is a test. There are many layers of explicit and implicit memory involved in the ability to discriminate between symptoms and their interrelationships." Implicit memory is your automatic retrieval of past experience in interpreting a new one. For example, the patient comes in and gives you a story. As you listen, you're consciously thinking through your mental library to see what fits, while also unconsciously polling your past experiences to help interpret what the patient is telling you. "Then you're left with making a judgment call," Larsen says.[9]

Larsen is a pediatric neurologist seeing patients in the university clinic and hospital. He's a busy guy: in addition to practicing medicine, he supervises the work of physicians in training, he teaches, and as time permits, he conducts research into medical education, working in collaboration with cognitive psychologists. He's drawing on all of these roles to redesign and strengthen the school's training curriculum in pediatric neurology.

As you'd expect, the medical school employs a wide spectrum of instructional techniques. Besides classroom lectures and labs, students practice resuscitations and other procedures on high-tech mannequins in three simulation centers the school maintains. Each "patient" is hooked up to monitors, has a heartbeat, blood pressure, pupils that dilate and constrict, and the ability to listen and speak, thanks to a controller who observes and operates the mannequin from a back room. The school also makes use of "standardized patients," actors who follow scripts and exhibit symptoms the students are required to diagnose. The center is set up like a regular medical clinic, and students must show proficiency in all aspects of a patient encounter, from bedside manner, physical exam skills, and remembering to ask the full spectrum of pertinent questions to arriving at a diagnosis and treatment plan.

From studies of these teaching methods, Larsen has drawn some interesting conclusions. First—and this may seem self-evident: you do better on a test to demonstrate your competency at seeing patients in a clinic if your learning experience has involved seeing patients in a clinic. Simply reading about patients is not enough. However, on written final exams, medical students who have examined patients and those who have learned via written tests do equally well. The reason is that in a written test the student is being given considerable structure and being asked for specific information. When examining the patient, you have to come up on your own with the right mental model and the steps to follow. Having practiced these steps on patients or simulated patients improves performance relative to just reading about how to do it. In other words, the kind of retrieval practice that proves most effective is one that reflects what you'll be doing with the knowledge later. It's not just what you know, but how you practice what you know that determines how well the learning serves you later. As the sports adage goes, "practice like you play and you will play like you practice." This conclusion lines up with other research into learning, and with some of the more sophisticated training practices in science and industry, including the increasingly broad use of simulators—not just for jet pilots and medical students but for cops, towboat pilots, and people in almost any field you can name that requires mastery of complex knowledge and skills and where the stakes for getting it right are high. Book learning is not enough in these cases; actual hands-on practice is needed.

Second, while it is important for a medical student to build breadth by seeing a wide variety of patients manifesting different diseases, placing too much emphasis on variety runs the risk of underemphasizing repeated retrieval practice on the basics—on the typical way the disease presents itself in most patients.

"There's a certain set of diseases that we want you to know very well," Larsen says. "So we're going to have you see these standardized patients again and again, and assess your performance until you really have that down and can show us, 'I really do that well.' It's not either/or, variety versus repetition. We need to make sure we're appropriately balanced, and also recognize that we sometimes fall into the trap of familiarity. 'I've already seen a bunch of patients with this problem, I don't need to keep seeing them.' But really, repeated retrieval practice is crucial to long-term retention, and it's a critical aspect of training."

A third critical aspect is practical experience. For a doctor, seeing patients provides a natural cycle of spaced retrieval practice, interleaving, and variety. "So much of medicine is based on learning by experience, which is why, after the first two years, we take students out of the classroom and start putting them into clinical settings. A huge question is, what is it about learning and experience that come together? We have lots of experiences we don't learn from. What differentiates those that teach us something?"

One form of practice that helps us learn from experience, as the neurosurgeon Mike Ebersold recounted in Chapter 2, is reflection. Some people are more given to the act of reflection than others, so Doug Larsen has broadened his research to study how you might structure reflection as an integral part of the training, helping students cultivate it as a habit. He is experimenting with requiring students to write daily or weekly summaries of what they did, how it worked, and what they might do differently next time to get better results. He speculates that daily reflection, as a form of spaced retrieval practice, is probably just as critical in the real-world application of medicine as quizzing and testing are in building competencies in medical school.

What about the classroom lecture, or the typical in-service training conference that's compressed over a couple of days? Larsen figures his school's interns spend 10 percent of their time sitting in conferences listening to lectures. It may be a talk on metabolic diseases, on different infectious diseases, or on different drugs. The speaker puts the PowerPoint slideshow up and starts going through it. Usually there's lunch, and the docs eat, listen, and leave.

"In my mind, considering how much forgetting occurs, it's very discouraging that we're putting so many resources into an activity that, the way it is currently done, learning research tells us is so ineffective. Medical students and residents go to these conferences and they have no repeated exposure whatsoever to it. It's just a matter of happenstance whether they end up finally seeing a patient in the future whose problem relates back to the conference topic. Otherwise, they don't study the material, they are certainly not tested on the material, they just listen then they walk out."

At a minimum, Larsen would like to see something done to interrupt the forgetting: give a quiz at the end of a conference and follow it with spaced retrieval practice. "Make quizzing a standard part of the culture and the curriculum. You just know every week you're going to get in your email your ten questions that you need to work through."

He asks, "How are we designing education and training systems that prevent or at least intervene in the amount of forgetting that goes on, and making sure they're systematic throughout the school in support of what we're trying to accomplish? As it stands now, medical resident programs are simply dictating: you have to have the curriculum, you have to have the conferences, and it ends there. They present these big conferences, they have all the faculty come through and give their talks. And in the end, what we actually accomplish is really kind of minimal."[10]

These Principles Are Broadly Applicable

College football might seem an incongruous place to look for a learning model, but a conversation with Coach Vince Dooley about the University of Georgia's practice regime provides an intriguing case.

Dooley is authoritative on the subject. As head coach of Bulldogs football from 1964–1988, he piled up an astonishing 201 wins with only 77 losses and 10 tied games, winning six conference titles and a national championship. He went on to serve as the university's athletic director, where he built one of the most impressive athletics programs in the country.

We asked Coach Dooley how players go about mastering all the complexities of the game. His theories of coaching and training revolve around the weekly cycle of one Saturday game to the next. In that short period there's a lot to learn: studying the opposition's type of game in the classroom, discussing offensive and defensive strategies for opposing it, taking the discussion onto the playing field, breaking the strategies down to the movements of individual positions and trying them out, knitting the parts into a whole, and then repeating the moves until they run like clockwork.

While all this is going on, the players must also keep their fundamental skills in top form: blocking, tackling, catching the ball, bringing the ball in, carrying the ball. Dooley believes that (1) you have to keep practicing the fundamentals from time to time, forever, so you keep them sharp, otherwise you're cooked, but (2) you need to change it up in practice because too much repetition is boring. The position coaches work with players individually on specific skills and then on how they're playing their positions during team practice.

What else? There's practicing the kicking game. There's the matter of each player's mastery of the playbook. And there are the special plays from the team's repertoire that often make the difference between winning and losing. In Dooley's narrative, the special plays stand as exemplars of spaced learning: they're practiced only on Thursdays, so there's always a week between sessions, and the plays are run in a varied sequence.

With all this to be done, it's not surprising that a critical aspect of the team's success is a very specific daily and weekly schedule that interleaves the elements of individual and team practice. The start of every day's practice is strictly focused on the fundamentals of each player's position. Next, players practice in small groups, working on maneuvers involving several positions. These parts are gradually brought together and run as a team. Play is speeded up and slowed down, rehearsed mentally as well as physically. By midweek the team is running the plays in real time, full speed.

"You're coming at it fast, and you've got to react fast," Dooley said. "But as you get closer to game time, you slow it down again. Now it's a kind of rehearsal without physical contact. The play basically starts out the same each time, but then what the opponent does changes it. So you've got to be able to adjust to that. You start into the motion and say, 'If they react like this, then this is what you would do.' You practice adjustments. If you do it enough times in different situations, then you're able to do it pretty well in whatever comes up on the field."[11]

How does a player get on top of his playbook? He takes it home and goes over the plays in his mind. He may walk through them. Everything in practice can't be physically strenuous, Dooley said, or you'd wear yourself out, "so if the play calls for you to step this way and then go the other way, you can rehearse that in your mind, maybe just lean your body as if to go that way. And then if something happens where you have to adjust, you can do that mentally. By reading the playbook, rehearsing it in your mind, maybe taking a step or two to walk through it, you simulate something happening. So that kind of rehearsal is added to what you get in the classroom and on the field."

The final quarterback meetings are held on Saturday morning, reviewing the game plan and running through it mentally. The offensive coaches can make all the plans they want to about the hypothetical game, but once play gets under way, the execution rests in the hands of the quarterback.

For Coach Dooley's team, it's all there: retrieval, spacing, interleaving, variation, reflection, and elaboration. The seasoned quarterback going into Saturday's game—mentally running through the plays, the reactions, the adjustments—is doing the same thing as the seasoned neurosurgeon who's rehearsing what's about to unfold in the operating room.

The Takeaway

Here's a quick rundown of what we know today about massed practice and its alternatives. Scientists will continue to deepen our understanding.

We harbor deep convictions that we learn better through single-minded focus and dogged repetition, and these beliefs are validated time and again by the visible improvement that comes during "practice-practice-practice." But scientists call this heightened performance during the acquisition phase of a skill "momentary strength" and distinguish it from "underlying habit strength." The very techniques that build habit strength, like spacing, interleaving, and variation, slow visible acquisition and fail to deliver the improvement during practice that helps to motivate and reinforce our efforts.[12]

Cramming, a form of massed practice, has been likened to binge-and-purge eating. A lot goes in, but most of it comes right back out in short order. The simple act of spacing out study and practice in installments and allowing time to elapse between them makes both the learning and the memory stronger, in effect building habit strength.

How big an interval, you ask? The simple answer: enough so that practice doesn't become a mindless repetition. At a minimum, enough time so that a little forgetting has set in. A little forgetting between practice sessions can be a good thing, if it leads to more effort in practice, but you do not want so much forgetting that retrieval essentially involves relearning the material. The time periods between sessions of practice let memories consolidate. Sleep seems to play a large role in memory consolidation, so practice with at least a day in between sessions is good.

Something as simple as a deck of flashcards can provide an example of *spacing*. Between repetitions of any individual card, you work through many others. The German scientist Sebastian Leitner developed his own system for spaced practice of flashcards, known as the Leitner box. Think of it as a series of four file-card boxes. In the first are the study materials (be they musical scores, hockey moves, or Spanish vocabulary flashcards) that must be practiced frequently because you often make mistakes in them. In the second box are the cards you're pretty good at, and that box gets practiced less often than the first, perhaps by a half. The cards in the third box are practiced less often than those in the second, and so on. If you miss a question, make mistakes in the music, flub the one-touch pass, you move it up a box so you will practice it more often. The underlying idea is simply that *the better your mastery, the less frequent the practice,* but if it's important to retain, it will *never disappear completely* from your set of practice boxes.

Beware of the familiarity trap: the feeling that you know something and no longer need to practice it. This familiarity can hurt you during self-quizzing if you take shortcuts. Doug Larsen says, "You have to be disciplined to say, 'All right, I'm going to make myself recall all of this and if I don't, what did I miss, how did I not know that?' Whereas if you have an instructor-generated test or quiz, suddenly you *have* to do it, there's an expectation, you can't cheat, you can't take mental shortcuts around it, you simply have to do that."

The nine quizzes Andy Sobel administers over the twenty-six meetings of his political economics course are a simple example of spaced retrieval practice, and of interleaving—because he rolls forward into each successive quiz questions pertaining to work from the beginning of the semester.

Interleaving two or more subjects during practice also provides a form of spacing. Interleaving can also help you develop your ability to *discriminate* later between different kinds of problems and select the right tool from your growing toolkit of solutions.

In interleaving, you don't move from a complete practice set of one topic to go to another. You *switch before each practice is complete.* A friend of ours describes his own experience with this: "I go to a hockey class and we're learning skating skills, puck handling, shooting, and I notice that I get frustrated because we do a little bit of skating and just when I think I'm getting it, we go to stick handling, and I go home frustrated, saying, 'Why doesn't this guy keep letting us do these things until we get it?'" This is actually the rare coach who understands that it's more effective to distribute practice across these different skills than polish each one in turn. The athlete gets frustrated because the learning's not proceeding quickly, but the next week he will be better at all aspects, the skating, the stick handling, and so on, than if he'd dedicated each session to polishing one skill.

Like interleaving, *varied practice* helps learners build a broad schema, an ability to assess changing conditions and adjust responses to fit. Arguably, interleaving and variation help learners reach beyond memorization to higher levels of conceptual learning and application, building more rounded, deep, and durable learning, what in motor skills shows up as underlying habit strength.

Something the researchers call *"blocked practice" is easily mistaken for varied practice.* It's like the old LP records that could only play their songs in the same sequence. In blocked practice, which is commonly (but not only) found in sports, a drill is run over and over. The player moves from one station to the next, performing a different maneuver at each station. That's how the LA Kings were practicing their one-touch pass before they got religion and started changing it up. It would be like always practicing flashcards in the same order. You need to shuffle your flashcards. If you always practice the same skill in the same way, from the same place on the ice or field, in the same set of math problems, or during the same sequence in a flight simulator, you're starving your learning on short rations of variety.

Spacing, interleaving, and variability are *natural features* of how we conduct our lives. Every patient visit or football game is a test and an exercise in retrieval practice. Every routine traffic stop is a test for a cop. And every traffic stop is different, adding to a cop's explicit and implicit memory and, if she pays attention, making her more effective in the future. The common term is "learning from experience." Some people never seem to learn. One difference, perhaps, between those who do and don't is whether they have cultivated the habit of reflection. *Reflection is a form of retrieval practice* (What happened? What did I do? How did it work out?), enhanced with elaboration (What would I do differently next time?).

As Doug Larsen reminds us, the connections between the neurons in the brain are very plastic. "Making the brain work is actually what seems to make a difference—bringing in more complex networks, then using those circuits repeatedly, which makes them more robust."

4

Embrace Difficulties

WHEN MIA BLUNDETTO, age twenty-three, first lieutenant, U.S. Marine Corps, was billeted to logistics in Okinawa, she had to get her ticket punched at jump school. Describing that moment two years later, she said, "I hate falling, that feeling in your chest. There's not a day in my life I wanted to jump out of an airplane. I wouldn't even go down a water slide until I was in middle school. But I was in charge of a platoon of Marines who rigged parachutes and jumped out of airplanes and dropped cargo. It's one of the most sought-out billets as a logistics officer, very hard to get. My commanding officer said, you know, 'You will be air delivery platoon commander. If you don't want to do that, I'll put you somewhere else and we'll let the next guy have that job.' There's no way I could let somebody else have this job that everybody wanted. So I looked him straight in the face and said, 'Yes, sir, I'll jump out of planes.' "[1]

Mia is five feet seven inches of blonde ambition. Her father, Frank, ex-marine, is in awe. "She'll do more pull-ups than most of the guys in her class. She has the Maryland state record in the bench press, she was sixth in the NCAA for powerlifting. Very soft-spoken; you just don't see it coming." When we had Mia to ourselves, we asked her if Frank was blowing smoke. She laughed. "He likes to exaggerate." But when pressed, she admitted to the facts. Until recently, women in the Marines were required to do flex arm hangs instead of pull-ups (where the chin crosses the plane of the pull-up bar), but the newly toughened rules effective in 2014 require a minimum of three pull-ups, the same as the minimum for men. Targets are eight pull-ups for women, twenty for men. Mia does thirteen and is shooting for twenty. As a student at the Naval Academy, she qualified two years in a row for nationals in powerlifting— three sets each of bench press, squats, and dead lifts—setting Maryland state records.

So we know she's tough. An aversion to falling is an instinctual reflex for self-preservation, but her decision to take the assignment was a foregone conclusion, the kind of grit the Marines and the Blundettos are known for. Mia has a sister and two brothers. They're *all* active duty Marines.

As it turned out, the third time Mia threw herself out the jump door of a C130 troop transport at 1,250 feet, she plummeted right onto another soldier's inflated parachute. But we're getting ahead of the story.

We're interested in her jump school training because it's a great example of how some difficulties that elicit more effort and that slow down learning—spacing, interleaving, mixing up practice, and others—will more than compensate for their inconvenience by making the learning stronger, more precise, and more enduring. Short-term impediments that make for stronger learning have come to be called *desirable difficulties,* a term coined by the psychologists Elizabeth and Robert Bjork.[2]

The army's jump school at Fort Benning, Georgia, is designed to make sure you get it right and get it done, and it's a model of learning through desirable difficulty. You are not allowed to carry a notebook and write notes. You listen, watch, rehearse, and execute. Jump school is a place where testing is the principal instructional medium, and the test is in the doing. And, like all things military, jump school adheres to a strict protocol. Get it right or get the boot.

The parachute landing fall, or PLF in military parlance, is a technique of hitting the ground and rolling in a way that distributes the impact over the balls of your feet, the side of your calf, the side of your thigh, the side of your hip, and the side of your back. There are six possible directions in which to execute the fall along the length of your body, determined by conditions in the moment such as the direction of your drift, the terrain, wind, and whether you're oscillating as you approach the ground. In your first exposure to this essential skill of parachuting, you stand in a gravel pit where the PLF is explained and demonstrated. Then you try it: you practice falling along different planes of the body, you get corrective feedback, and you practice it again.

Over the ensuing week the difficulty is notched up. You stand on a platform two feet off the ground. On the command "Ready," you rock up on the balls of your feet, feet and knees together, arms skyward. On the command "land," you jump off the wall and execute your PLF.

The test becomes more difficult. You clip yourself onto a zip line a dozen feet off the ground, grab onto an overhead T-bar, and drift down to a landing site, where, on command, you release and execute the PLF. You practice falling to the right and left, forward and backward, mixing it up.

The difficulty is increased again. You climb to a platform twelve feet off the ground, where you practice strapping on your harness, checking gear using the buddy system, and jumping through a mockup of an airplane jump door. The harness has risers like those from a parachute, hooked to a zip line but allowing for the same long arc of suspension, and when you jump, you have the momentary downward sensation of free fall, followed by the broad oscillations of suspension as you move along the cable, getting familiar with the motions of a real jump. But at the bottom it's the instructor, not you, who pulls the release and drops you the last two or three feet to earth, so now you're executing your fall randomly, from all directions, simulating what's to come.

Next, you climb a thirty-four-foot tower to practice all the elements of a jump and the choreography of a mass exit from the aircraft, learning how it feels to fall from a height, how to deal with equipment malfunctions, how to jump with a load of heavy combat equipment.

Through demonstration and simulation, in escalating levels of difficulty that must be mastered in order to progress from one to the next, you learn how to board the aircraft as a part of a jump crew and participate in the command sequence of thirty troops positioning for a mass exit over a drop zone. How to get out the jump door correctly, how to count one-thousand, two-thousand, three-thousand, four-thousand and feel your chute deploy, or if you get to six-thousand, to pull the cord on your reserve chute; how to deal with twisted suspension lines, avoid collisions, hold into the wind, sort out a tangled control line; how to avoid stealing air from another jumper; the contingencies for landing in trees, water, or power lines; how to jump by day or night, in different wind and weather.

The knowledge and skills to be acquired are many, and practice is spaced and interleaved, both by default, as you wait your turn at each of the staging areas, airplane mock-ups, jump platforms, and harness mechanisms, and by necessity, in order to cover all that must be mastered and integrate the disparate components. Finally, if you make it to week 3 without washing out, you jump for real, making five exits from a military transport. With successful completion of the training and five successful jumps, you earn your jump wings and Airborne certificate.

On Mia's third jump, she was first in line at the port jump door with fourteen jumpers queued behind her and another fourteen queued behind the guy standing at the opposite door. "So what the first person does, in this case me, you hand off your static line to the Sergeant Airborne, and there's a light and it's red or green, and you get the one-minute warning, then the thirty-second warning. I'm standing at this door for a few minutes and it's beautiful. It's probably one of the prettiest things I've ever seen, but I was terrified. There was nothing to get in my way, nothing I had to think about except just waiting, waiting for the 'Go!' The guy at the other door went, then I jumped, and I'm counting one-thousand, two-thousand—and suddenly, at four thousand, I had a green parachute wrapped all around me! I'm thinking, There's no way this can be my parachute! I'd felt my chute open, I'd felt that lift. I realized that I was on top of the first jumper, so I just sort of swam out of his parachute and steered away from him."

Jumpers are staggered, but in the four turbulent seconds until your chute opens you have neither awareness nor control over your proximity to other jumpers. The incident, which amounted to nothing, thanks to her training, is telling none-theless. Had it frightened her? Not at all, she said. Mia was prepared to handle it, and her confidence gave her the cool to "just sort of swim out."

It's one thing to *feel* confident of your knowledge; it's some-thing else to *demonstrate* mastery. Testing is not only a power-ful learning strategy, it is a potent reality check on the accuracy of your own judgment of what you know how to do. When confidence is based on repeated performance, demonstrated through testing that simulates real-world conditions, you can lean into it. Facing the jump door may always reawaken feel-ings of terror, but the moment she's out, Mia says, the fear evaporates.

How Learning Occurs

To help you understand how difficulty can be desirable, we'll briefly describe here how learning occurs.

Encoding

Let's imagine you're Mia, standing in a gravel pit watching a jump instructor explain and demonstrate the parachute land-ing fall. The brain converts your perceptions into chemical and electrical changes that form a mental representation of the patterns you've observed. This process of converting sen-sory perceptions into meaningful representations in the brain is still not perfectly understood. We call the process encoding, and we call the new representations within the brain *memory traces*. Think of notes jotted or sketched on a scratchpad, our short-term memory.

Much of how we run our day-to-day lives is guided by the ephemera that clutter our short-term memory and are, fortu-nately, soon forgotten—how to jigger the broken latch on the locker you used when you suited up at the gym today; re-membering to stop for an oil change after your workout. But the experiences and learning that we want to salt away for the future must be made stronger and more durable—in Mia's case, the distinctive moves that will enable her to hit the ground without breaking an ankle, or worse.[3]

Consolidation

The process of strengthening these mental representations for long-term memory is called consolidation. New learning is labile: its meaning is not fully formed and therefore is easily altered. In consolidation, the brain reorganizes and stabilizes the memory traces. This may occur over several hours or lon-ger and involves deep processing of the new material, during which scientists believe that the brain replays or rehearses the learning, giving it meaning, filling in blank spots, and making connections to past experiences and to other knowledge al-ready stored in long-term memory. Prior knowledge is a pre-requisite for making sense of new learning, and forming those connections is an important task of consolidation. Mia's con-siderable athletic skills, physical self-awareness, and prior ex-perience represent a large body of knowledge to which the elements of a successful PLF would find many connections. As we've noted, sleep seems to help memory consolidation, but in any case, consolidation and transition of learning to long-term storage occurs over a period of time.

An apt analogy for how the brain consolidates new learn-ing may be the experience of composing an essay. The first draft is rangy, imprecise. You discover what you want to say by trying to write it. After a couple of revisions you have sharp-ened the piece and cut away some of the extraneous points. You put it aside to let it ferment. When you pick it up again a day or two later, what you want to say has become clearer in your mind. Perhaps you now perceive that there are three main points you are making. You connect them to examples and supporting information familiar to your audience. You rearrange and draw together the elements of your argument to make it more effective and elegant.

Similarly, the process of learning something often starts out feeling disorganized and unwieldy; the most important aspects are not always salient. Consolidation helps organize and solidify learning, and, notably, so does retrieval after a lapse of some time, because the act of retrieving a memory from long-term storage can both strengthen the memory traces and at the same time make them modifiable again, enabling them, for example, to connect to more recent learning. This process is called *recon-*solidation. This is how retrieval practice modifies and strengthens learning.

Suppose that on day 2 of jump school, you're put on the spot to execute your parachute landing fall and you struggle to recall the correct posture and compose yourself—feet and knees together, knees slightly bent, eyes on the horizon—but in the reflex to break your fall you throw your arm out, forgetting to pull your elbows tight to your sides. You could have broken the arm or dislocated your shoulder if this were the real deal. This effort to reconstruct what you learned the day before is ragged, but in making it, critical elements of the maneuver come clearer and are reconsolidated for stronger memory. If you're practicing something over and over in rapid-fire fashion, whether it's your parachute landing fall or the conjugation of foreign verbs, you're leaning on short-term memory, and very little mental effort is required. You show gratifying improvement rather quickly, but you haven't done much to strengthen the underlying representation of those skills. Your performance in the moment is not an indication of durable learning. On the other hand, when you let the memory recede a little, for example by spacing or interleaving the practice, retrieval is harder, your performance is less accomplished, and you feel let down, but your learning is deeper and you will retrieve it more easily in the future.[4]

Retrieval

Learning, remembering, and forgetting work together in interesting ways. Durable, robust learning requires that we do two things. First, as we recode and consolidate new material from short-term memory into long-term memory, we must anchor it there securely. Second, we must associate the material with a diverse set of cues that will make us adept at recalling the knowledge later. Having effective retrieval cues is an aspect of learning that often goes overlooked. The task is more than committing knowledge to memory. Being able to retrieve it when we need it is just as important.

The reason we don't remember how to tie knots even after we've been taught is because we don't practice and apply what we've learned. Say you're in the city park one day and come across an Eagle Scout teaching knots. On a whim you take an hour's lesson. He demonstrates eight or ten specimens, explains what each is useful for, has you practice tying them, and sends you away with a short length of rope and a cheat sheet. You head home committed to learning these knots, but life is full, and you fail to practice them. They are soon forgotten, and this story could end there, with no learning. But then, as it happens, the following spring you buy a small fishing boat, and you want to attach an anchor on a line. With rope in hand and feeling mildly stumped, you recall from your lesson that there was a knot for putting a loop in the end of a line. You are now practicing retrieval. You find your cheat sheet and relearn how to tie a bowline. You put a small loop in the rope and then take the short end and draw it through, silently reciting the little memory device you were given: the rabbit comes up from his hole, goes around the tree, and goes back down. Retrieval again. A little snugging-up, and there you have your knot, a dandy piece of scoutcraft of the kind you'd always fancied knowing. Later, you put a piece of rope beside the chair where you watch TV and practice the bowline during commercials. You are doing spaced practice. Over the coming weeks you're surprised at how many little jobs are easier if you have a piece of rope with a loop in the end. More spaced practice. By August you have discovered every possible use and purpose in your life for the bowline knot.

Knowledge, skills, and experiences that are vivid and hold significance, and those that are periodically practiced, stay with us. If you know you're soon to throw yourself out of a troop transport, you listen up good when they're telling you when and how to pull the rip cord on your reserve chute, or what can go wrong at twelve hundred feet and how to "just sort of swim out of it." The mental rehearsal you conduct while lying in your bunk too tired to sleep and wishing the next day was already over and well-jumped is a form of spaced practice, and that helps you, too.

Extending Learning: Updating Retrieval Cues

There's virtually no limit to how much learning we can remember as long as we relate it to what we already know. In fact, because new learning depends on prior learning, the more we learn, the more possible connections we create for further learning. Our retrieval capacity, though, is severely limited. Most of what we've learned is not accessible to us at any given moment. This limitation on retrieval is helpful to us: if every memory were always readily to hand, you would have a hard time sorting through the sheer volume of material to put your finger on the knowledge you need at the moment: where did I put my hat, how do I sync my electronic devices, what goes into a perfect brandy Manhattan?

Knowledge is more durable if it's deeply entrenched, meaning that you have firmly and thoroughly comprehended a concept, it has practical importance or keen emotional weight in your life, and it is connected with other knowledge that you hold in memory. How readily you can recall knowledge from your internal archives is determined by context, by recent use, and by the number and vividness of cues that you have linked to the knowledge and can call on to help bring it forth.[5]

Here's the tricky part. As you go through life, you often need to forget cues associated with older, competing memories so as to associate them successfully with new ones. To learn Italian in middle age, you may have to forget your high school French, because every time you think "to be" and hope to come up with the Italian *essere,* up pops *etre,* despite your most earnest intentions. Traveling in England, you have to suppress your cues to drive on the right side of the road so you can establish reliable cues to stay on the left. Knowledge that is well entrenched, like real fluency in French or years of experience driving on the right side of the road, is easily relearned later, after a period of disuse or after being interrupted by competition for retrieval cues. It's not the knowledge itself that has been forgotten, but the cues that enable you to find and retrieve it. The cues for the new learning, driving on the left, displace those for the old, driving on the right (if we are lucky).

The paradox is that some forgetting is often essential for new learning.[6] When you change from a PC to a Mac, or from one Windows platform to another, you have to do enormous forgetting in order to learn the architecture of the new system and become adept at manipulating it so readily that your attention can focus on doing your work and not on working the machine. Jump school training provides another example: After their military service, many paratroopers take an interest in smoke jumping. Smokejumpers use different airplanes, different equipment, and different jump protocols. Having trained at the army's jump school is cited as a distinct *disadvantage* for smoke jumping, because you have to unlearn one set of procedures that you have practiced to the point of reflex and replace them with another. Even in cases where both bodies of learning seem so similar to the uninitiated—jumping out of an airplane with a parachute on your back—you may have to forget the cues to a complex body of learning that you possess if you are to acquire a new one.

We know this problem of reassigning cues to memory from our own lives, even on the simplest levels. When our friend Jack first takes up with Joan, we sometimes call the couple "Jack and Jill," as the cue "Jack and" pulls up the old nursery rhyme that's so thoroughly embedded in memory. About the time we have "Jack and" reliably cuing "Joan," alas, Joan throws him over, and he takes up with Jenny. Good grief! Half of the time that we mean to say Jack and Jenny we catch ourselves saying Jack and Joan. It would have been easier had Jack picked up with Katie, so that the trailing *K* sound in his name handed us off to the initiating *K* in hers, but no such luck. Alliteration can be a handy cue, or a subversive one. In all of this turmoil you don't forget Jill, Joan, or Jenny, but you "repurpose" your cues so that you can keep pace with the changing opera of Jack's life.[7]

It is a critical point that as you learn new things, you don't lose from long-term memory most of what you have learned well in life; rather, through disuse or the reassignment of cues, you forget it in the sense that you're unable to call it up easily. For example, if you've moved several times, you may not be able to recall a previous address from twenty years ago. But if you are given a multiple choice test for the address, you can probably pick it out easily, for it still abides, as it were, in the uncleaned closet of your mind. If you have ever immersed yourself in writing stories of your past, picturing the people and places of earlier days, you may have been surprised by the memories that started flooding back, things long forgotten now coming to mind. Context can unleash memories, as when the right key works to open an old lock. In Marcel Proust's *Remembrance of Things Past,* the narrator grieves over his inability to recall the days of his adolescence in the French village of his aunt and uncle, until one day the taste of a cake dipped in lime blossom tea brings it all rushing back, all the people and events he thought had long since been lost to time. Most people have experiences like Proust's when a sight or sound or smell brings back a memory in full force, even some episode you have not thought about in years.[8]

Easier Isn't Better

Psychologists have uncovered a curious inverse relationship between the ease of retrieval practice and the power of that practice to entrench learning: the easier knowledge or a skill is for you to retrieve, the less your retrieval practice will benefit your retention of it. Conversely, the more effort you have to expend to retrieve knowledge or skill, the more the practice of retrieval will entrench it.

Not long ago the California Polytechnic State University baseball team, in San Luis Obispo, became involved in an interesting experiment in improving their batting skills. They were all highly experienced players, adept at making solid contact with the ball, but they agreed to take extra batting practice twice a week, following two different practice regimens, to see which type of practice produced better results.

Hitting a baseball is one of the hardest skills in sports. It takes less than half a second for a ball to reach home plate. In this instant, the batter must execute a complex combination of perceptual, cognitive, and motor skills: determining the type of pitch, anticipating how the ball will move, and aiming and timing the swing to arrive at the same place and moment as the ball. This chain of perceptions and responses must be so deeply entrenched as to become automatic, because the ball is in the catcher's mitt long before you can even begin to think your way through how to connect with it.

Part of the Cal Poly team practiced in the standard way. They practiced hitting forty-five pitches, evenly divided into three sets. Each set consisted of one type of pitch thrown fifteen times. For example, the first set would be fifteen fastballs, the second set fifteen curveballs, and the third set fifteen changeups. This was a form of massed practice. For each set of 15 pitches, as the batter saw more of that type, he got gratifyingly better at anticipating the balls, timing his swings, and connecting. Learning seemed easy.

The rest of the team were given a more difficult practice regimen: the three types of pitches were randomly interspersed across the block of forty-five throws. For each pitch, the batter had no idea which type to expect. At the end of the forty-five swings, he was still struggling somewhat to connect with the ball. These players didn't seem to be developing the proficiency their teammates were showing. The interleaving and spacing of different pitches made learning more arduous and feel slower.

The extra practice sessions continued twice weekly for six weeks. At the end, when the players' hitting was assessed, the two groups had clearly benefited differently from the extra practice, and not in the way the players expected. Those who had practiced on the randomly interspersed pitches now displayed markedly better hitting relative to those who had practiced on one type of pitch thrown over and over. These results are all the more interesting when you consider that these players were already skilled hitters prior to the extra training. Bringing their performance to an even higher level is good evidence of a training regimen's effectiveness.

Here again we see the two familiar lessons. First, that some difficulties that require more effort and slow down apparent gains—like spacing, interleaving, and mixing up practice—will feel less productive at the time but will more than compensate for that by making the learning stronger, precise, and enduring. Second, that our judgments of what learning strategies work best for us are often mistaken, colored by illusions of mastery.

When the baseball players at Cal Poly practiced curveball after curveball over fifteen pitches, it became easier for them to remember the perceptions and responses they needed for that type of pitch: the look of the ball's spin, how the ball changed direction, how fast its direction changed, and how long to wait for it to curve. Performance improved, but the growing ease of recalling these perceptions and responses led to little durable learning. It is one skill to hit a curveball when you know a curveball will be thrown; it is a different skill to hit a curveball when you don't know it's coming. Baseball players need to build the latter skill, but they often practice the former, which, being a form of massed practice, builds performance gains on short-term memory. It was more challenging for the Cal Poly batters to retrieve the necessary skills when practice involved random pitches. Meeting that challenge made the performance gains painfully slow but also long lasting.

This paradox is at the heart of the concept of desirable difficulties in learning: the more effort required to retrieve (or, in effect, relearn) something, the better you learn it. In other words, the more you've forgotten about a topic, the more effective relearning will be in shaping your permanent knowledge.[9]

How Effort Helps

Reconsolidating Memory

Effortful recall of learning, as happens in spaced practice, requires that you "reload" or reconstruct the components of the skill or material anew from long-term memory rather than mindlessly repeating them from short-term memory.[10] During this focused, effortful recall, the learning is made pliable again: the most salient aspects of it become clearer, and the consequent reconsolidation helps to reinforce meaning, strengthen connections to prior knowledge, bolster the cues and retrieval routes for recalling it later, and weaken competing routes. Spaced practice, which allows some forgetting to occur between sessions, strengthens both the learning and the cues and routes for fast retrieval when that learning is needed again, as when the pitcher tries to surprise the batter with a curveball after pitching several fastballs. The more effort that is required to recall a memory or to execute a skill, provided that the effort succeeds, the more the act of recalling or executing benefits the learning.[11]

Massed practice gives us the warm sensation of mastery because we're looping information through short-term memory without having to reconstruct the learning from long-term memory. But just as with rereading as a study strategy, the fluency gained through massed practice is transitory, and our sense of mastery is illusory. It's the effortful process of reconstructing the knowledge that triggers reconsolidation and deeper learning.

Creating Mental Models

With enough effortful practice, a complex set of interrelated ideas or a sequence of motor skills fuse into a meaningful whole, forming a mental model somewhat akin to a "brain app". Learning to drive a car involves a host of simultaneous actions that require all of our powers of concentration and dexterity while we are learning them. But over time, these combinations of cognition and motor skills—for example, the perceptions and maneuvers required to parallel park or manipulate a stick shift—become ingrained as sets of mental models associated with driving. Mental models are forms of deeply entrenched and highly efficient skills (seeing and unloading on a curveball) or knowledge structures (a memorized sequence of chess moves) that, like habits, can be adapted and applied in varied circumstances. Expert performance is built through thousands of hours of practice in your area of expertise, in varying conditions, through which you accumulate a vast library of such mental models that enables you to correctly discern a given situation and instantaneously select and execute the correct response.

Broadening Mastery

Retrieval practice that you perform at different times and in different contexts and that interleaves different learning material has the benefit of linking new associations to the material. This process builds interconnected networks of knowledge that bolster and support mastery of your field. It also multiplies the cues for retrieving the knowledge, increasing the versatility with which you can later apply it.

Think of an experienced chef who has internalized the complex knowledge of how flavors and textures interact; how ingredients change form under heat; the differing effects to be achieved with a saucepan versus a wok, with copper versus cast iron. Think of the fly fisher who can sense the presence of trout and accurately judge the likely species, make the right choice of dry fly, nymph, or streamer, judge the wind, and know how and where to drop that fly to make the trout rise. Think of the kid on the BMX bike who can perform bunny-hops, tail whips, 180s, and wall taps off the features of an unfamiliar streetscape. Interleaving and variation mix up the contexts of practice and the other skills and knowledge with which the new material is associated. This makes our mental models more versatile, enabling us to apply our learning to a broader range of situations.

Fostering Conceptual Learning

How do humans learn concepts, for example the difference between dogs and cats? By randomly coming across dissimilar examples—Chihuahuas, tabby cats, Great Danes, picture book lions, calico cats, Welsh terriers. Spaced and interleaved exposure characterizes most of humans' normal experience. It's a good way to learn, because this type of exposure strengthens the skills of discrimination—the process of noticing particulars (a turtle comes up for air but a fish doesn't)—and of induction: surmising the general rule (fish can breathe in water). Recall the interleaved study of birds in one case, and of paintings in another, that helped learners distinguish between bird types or the works of different painters while at the same time learning to identify underlying commonalities of the examples within a species or an artist's body of work. When asked about their preferences and beliefs, the learners thought that the experience of studying multiple examples of one species of bird before studying examples of another species resulted in better learning. But the interleaved strategy, which was more difficult and felt clunky, produced superior discrimination of differences between types, without hindering the ability to learn commonalities within a type. As was true for the baseball players' batting practice, interleaving produced difficulty in retrieving past examples of a particular species, which further solidified the learning of which birds are representative of a particular species.

The difficulty produced by interleaving provides a second type of boost to learning. Interleaved practice of related but dissimilar geometric solids requires that you notice similarities and differences in order to select the correct formula for computing the volume. It's thought that this heightened sensitivity to similarities and differences during interleaved practice leads to the encoding of more complex and nuanced representations of the study material—a better understanding of how specimens or types of problems are distinctive and why they call for a different interpretation or solution. Why a northern pike will strike a spoon or a crankbait, say, but a bass will happily powder his nose until you see fit to throw him a grub or a popper.[12]

Improving Versatility

The retrieval difficulties posed by spacing, interleaving, and variation are overcome by invoking the same mental processes that will be needed later in applying the learning in everyday settings. By mimicking the challenges of practical experience, these learning strategies conform to the admonition to "practice like you play, and you'll play like you practice," improving what scientists call transfer of learning, which is the ability to apply what you've learned in new settings. In the Cal Poly batting practice experiment, the act of overcoming the difficulties posed by random types of pitches built a broader "vocabulary" of mental processes for discerning the nature of the challenge (e.g., what the pitcher is throwing) and selecting among possible responses than did the narrower mental processes sufficient for excelling during massed, non-varied experience. Recall the grade school students who proved more adept at tossing beanbags into three-foot baskets after having practiced tossing into two- and four-foot baskets, compared to the students who only practiced tossing into three-foot basket. Recall the increasing difficulty and complexity of the simulation training in jump school, or the cockpit simulator of Matt Brown's business jet.

Priming the Mind for Learning

When you're asked to struggle with solving a problem before being shown how to solve it, the subsequent solution is better learned and more durably remembered. When you've bought your fishing boat and are attempting to attach an anchor line, you're far more likely to learn and remember the bowline knot than when you're standing in a city park being shown the bowline by a Boy Scout who thinks you would lead a richer life if you had a handful of knots in your repertoire.

Other Learning Strategies That Incorporate Desirable Difficulties

We usually think of interference as a detriment to learning, but certain kinds of interference can produce learning benefits, and the positive effects are sometimes surprising. Would you rather read an article that has normal type or type that's somewhat out of focus? Almost surely you would opt for the former. Yet when text on a page is slightly out of focus or presented in a font that is a little difficult to decipher, people recall the content better. Should the outline of a lecture follow the precise flow of a chapter in a textbook, or is it better if the lecture mismatches the text in some ways? It turns out that when the outline of a lecture proceeds in a different order from the textbook passage, the effort to discern the main ideas and reconcile the discrepancy produces better recall of the content. In another surprise, when letters are omitted from words in a text, requiring the reader to supply them, reading is slowed, and retention improves. In all of these examples, the change from normal presentation introduces a difficulty—disruption of fluency—that makes the learner work harder to construct an interpretation that makes sense. The added effort increases comprehension and learning. (Of course, learning will not improve if the difficulty completely obscures the meaning or cannot be overcome.)[13]

The act of trying to answer a question or attempting to solve a problem rather than being presented with the information or the solution is known as *generation*. Even if you're being quizzed on material you're familiar with, the simple act of filling in a blank has the effect of strengthening your memory of the material and your ability to recall it later. In testing, being required to supply an answer rather than select from multiple choice options often provides stronger learning benefits. Having to write a short essay makes them stronger still. Overcoming these mild difficulties is a form of active learning, where students engage in higher-order thinking tasks rather than passively receiving knowledge conferred by others.

When you're asked to supply an answer or a solution to something that's new to you, the power of generation to aid learning is even more evident. One explanation for this effect is the idea that as you cast about for a solution, retrieving related knowledge from memory, you strengthen the route to a gap in your learning even before the answer is provided to fill it and, when you do fill it, connections are made to the related material that is fresh in your mind from the effort. For example, if you're from Vermont and are asked to name the capital of Texas you might start ruminating on possibilities: Dallas? San Antonio? El Paso? Houston? Even if you're unsure, thinking about alternatives before you hit on (or are given) the correct answer will help you. (Austin, of course.) Wrestling with the question, you rack your brain for something that might give you an idea. You may get curious, even stumped or frustrated and acutely aware of the hole in your knowledge that needs filling. When you're then shown the solution, a light goes on. Unsuccessful attempts to solve a problem encourage deep processing of the answer when it is later supplied, creating fertile ground for its encoding, in a way that simply reading the answer cannot. It's better to solve a problem than to memorize a solution. It's better to attempt a solution and supply the incorrect answer than not to make the attempt.[14]

The act of taking a few minutes to review what has been learned from an experience (or in a recent class) and asking yourself questions is known as *reflection*. After a lecture or reading assignment, for example, you might ask yourself: What are the key ideas? What are some examples? How do these relate to what I already know? Following an experience where you are practicing new knowledge or skills, you might ask: What went well? What could have gone better? What might I need to learn for better mastery, or what strategies might I use the next time to get better results?

Reflection can involve several cognitive activities we have discussed that lead to stronger learning. These include retrieval (recalling recently learned knowledge to mind), elaboration (for example, connecting new knowledge to what you already know), and generation (for example, rephrasing key ideas in your own words or visualizing and mentally rehearsing what you might do differently next time).

One form of reflection that is gaining currency in classroom settings is called "write to learn." In essence, students reflect on a recent class topic in a brief writing assignment, where they may express the main ideas in their own words and relate them to other concepts covered in class, or perhaps outside class. (For an example, read in Chapter 8 about the "learning paragraphs" Mary Pat Wenderoth assigns her students in her human physiology course.) The learning benefits from the various cognitive activities that are engaged during reflection (retrieval, elaboration, generation) have been well established through empirical studies.

An interesting recent study specifically examined "write to learn" as a learning tool. Over eight hundred college students in several introductory psychology classes listened to lectures throughout the semester. Following the presentation of a key concept within a given lecture, the instructor asked students to write to learn. Students generated their own written summaries of the key ideas, for example restating concepts in their own words and elaborating on the concepts by generating examples of them. For other key concepts presented during the lecture, students were shown a set of slides summarizing the concepts and spent a few minutes copying down key ideas and examples verbatim from the slide.

What was the result? On exams administered during the semester, the students were asked questions that assessed their understanding of the key concepts that they had worked on learning. They scored significantly (approximately half a letter grade) better on the ones they had written about in their own words than on those they had copied, showing that it was not simply exposure to the concepts that produced the learning benefit. In follow-up tests approximately two months later to measure retention, the benefits of writing to learn as a form of reflection had dropped but remained robust.[15]

Failure and the Myth of Errorless Learning

In the 1950s and 1960s, the psychologist B. F. Skinner advocated the adoption of "errorless learning" methods in education in the belief that errors by learners are counterproductive and result from faulty instruction. The theory of errorless learning gave rise to instructional techniques in which learners were spoonfed new material in small bites and immediately quizzed on them while they still remained on the tongue, so to speak, fresh in short-term memory and easily spit out onto the test form. There was virtually no chance of making an error. Since those days we've come to understand that retrieval from short-term memory is an ineffective learning strategy and that errors are an integral part of striving to increase one's mastery over new material. Yet in our Western culture, where achievement is seen as an indicator of ability, many learners view errors as failure and do what they can to avoid committing them. The aversion to failure may be reinforced by instructors who labor under the belief that when learners are allowed to make errors it's the errors that they will learn.[16]

This is a misguided impulse. When learners commit errors and are given corrective feedback, the errors are not learned.

Even strategies that are highly likely to result in errors, like asking someone to try to solve a problem before being shown how to do it, produce stronger learning and retention of the correct information than more passive learning strategies, provided there is corrective feedback. Moreover, people who are taught that learning is a struggle that often involves making errors will go on to exhibit a greater propensity to tackle tough challenges and will tend to see mistakes not as failures but as lessons and turning points along the path to mastery. To see the truth of this, look no further than the kid down the hall who is deeply absorbed in working his avatar up through the levels of an action game on his Xbox video console.

A fear of failure can poison learning by creating aversions to the kinds of experimentation and risk taking that characterize striving, or by diminishing performance under pressure, as in a test setting. In the latter instance, students who have a high fear of making errors when taking tests may actually do worse on the test because of their anxiety. Why? It seems that a significant portion of their working memory capacity is expended to monitor their performance (How am I doing? Am I making mistakes?), leaving less working memory capacity available to solve the problems posed by the test. "Working memory" refers to the amount of information you can hold in mind while working through a problem, especially in the face of distraction. Everyone's working memory is severely limited, some more than others, and larger working memory capacities correlate with higher IQs.

To explore this theory about how fear of failure reduces test performance, sixth graders in France were given very difficult anagram problems that none of them could solve. After struggling unsuccessfully with the problems, half of the kids received a ten-minute lesson in which they were taught that difficulty is a crucial part of learning, errors are natural and to be expected, and practice helps, just as in learning to ride a bicycle. The other kids were simply asked how they had gone about trying to solve the anagrams. Then both groups were given a difficult test whose results provided a measure of working memory. The kids who had been taught that errors are a natural part of learning showed significantly better use of working memory than did the others. These children did not expend their working memory capacity in agonizing over the difficulty of the task. The theory was further tested in variations of the original study. The results support the finding that difficulty can create feelings of incompetence that engender anxiety, which in turn disrupts learning, and that "students do better when given room to struggle with difficulty."[17]

These studies point out that not all difficulties in learning are desirable ones. Anxiety while taking a test seems to represent an undesirable difficulty. These studies also underscore the importance of learners understanding that difficulty in learning new things is not only to be expected but can be beneficial. To this point, the French study stands on the shoulders of many others, among the foremost being the works of Carol Dweck and of Anders Ericsson, both of whom we discuss in Chapter 7 in relation to the topic of increasing intellectual abilities. Dweck's work shows that people who believe that their intellectual ability is fixed from birth, wired in their genes, tend to avoid challenges at which they may not succeed, because failure would appear to be an indication of lesser native ability. By contrast, people who are helped to understand that effort and learning change the brain, and that their intellectual abilities lie to a large degree within their own control, are more likely to tackle difficult challenges and persist at them. They view failure as a sign of effort and as a *turn* in the road rather than as a measure of inability and the *end* of the road. Anders Ericsson's work investigating the nature of expert performance shows that to achieve expertise requires thousands of hours of dedicated practice in which one strives to surpass one's current level of ability, a process in which failure becomes an essential experience on the path to mastery.

The study of the French sixth graders received wide publicity and inspired the staging of a "Festival of Errors" by an elite graduate school in Paris, aimed at teaching French schoolchildren that making mistakes is a constructive part of learning: not a sign of failure but of effort. Festival organizers argued that modern society's focus on showing results has led to a culture of intellectual timorousness, starving the kind of intellectual ferment and risk-taking that produced the great discoveries that mark French history.

It doesn't require a great conceptual leap to get from Paris's "Festival of Errors" to San Francisco's "FailCon," where technology entrepreneurs and venture capitalists meet once a year to study failures that gave them critical insights they needed in order to pivot in their business strategies so as to succeed. Thomas Edison called failure the source of inspiration, and is said to have remarked, "I've not failed. I've just found 10,000 ways that don't work." He argued that perseverance in the face of failure is the key to success.

Failure underlies the scientific method, which has advanced our understanding of the world we inhabit. The qualities of persistence and resiliency, where failure is seen as useful information, underlie successful innovation in every sphere and lie at the core of nearly all successful learning. Failure points to the need for redoubled effort, or liberates us to try different approaches. Steve Jobs, in his remarks to the Stanford University graduating class of 2005, spoke of being fired at age thirty in 1985 from Apple Computer, which he had cofounded. "I didn't see it then, but it turned out that getting fired from Apple was the best thing that could have ever happened to me. The heaviness of being successful was replaced by the lightness of being a beginner again, less sure about everything. It freed me to enter one of the most creative periods of my life."

It's not the failure that's desirable, it's the dauntless effort despite the risks, the discovery of what works and what doesn't that sometimes only failure can reveal. It's trusting that trying to solve a puzzle serves us better than being spoon-fed the solution, even if we fall short in our first attempts at an answer.

An Example of Generative Learning

As we said earlier, the process of trying to solve a problem without the benefit of having been taught how is called *generative learning*, meaning that the learner is generating the answer rather than recalling it. Generation is another name for old-fashioned trial and error. We're all familiar with the stories of skinny kids in Silicon Valley garages messing around with computers and coming out billionaires. We would like to serve up a different kind of example here: Minnesota's Bonnie Blodgett.

Bonnie is a writer and a self-taught ornamental gardener in a constant argument with a voice in her head that keeps nattering about all the ways her latest whim is sure to go haywire and embarrass her. While she is a woman of strong aesthetic sensibilities, she is also one of epic doubts. Her "learning style" might be called leap-before-you-look-because-if-you-look-first-you-probably-won't-like-what-you-see. Her garden writing appears under the name "The Blundering Gardener." This moniker is a way of telling her voices of doubt to take a hike, because whatever the consequences of the next whim, she's already rolling up her sleeves. "Blundering means that you get going on your project before you have figured out how to do it in the proper way, before you know what you're getting into. For me, the risk of knowing what you're getting into is that it becomes an overwhelming obstacle to getting started."[18]

Bonnie's success shows how struggling with a problem makes for strong learning, and how a sustained commitment to advancing in a particular field of endeavor through trial-and-error effort leads to complex mastery and greater knowledge of the interrelationships of things. When we spoke, she had just traveled to southern Minnesota to meet with a group of farmers who wanted her gardening insights on a gamut of issues ranging from layout and design to pest control and irrigation. In the years since she first sank her spade, Bonnie's garden writing has won national recognition and found a devoted following far and wide through many outlets, and her garden has become a destination for other gardeners.

She came to ornamental gardening about the time she found herself eyeballing middle age. She had no training, just a burning desire to get her hands dirty making beautiful spaces on the corner lot of the home she shares with her husband in a historic neighborhood of St. Paul.

"The experience of creating beauty calms me down," she says, but it's strictly a discovery process. She has always been a writer, and some years after having launched herself into the garden, she began publishing the *Garden Letter,* a quarterly for northern gardeners in which she chronicles her exploits, mishaps, lessons, and successes. She writes the same way that she gardens, with boldness and self-effacing humor, passing along the entertaining snafus and unexpected insights that are the fruits of experience. In calling herself the Blundering Gardener, she is giving herself and us, her readers, permission to make mistakes and get on with it.

Note that in *writing* about her experiences, Bonnie is engaging two potent learning processes beyond the act of gardening itself. She is retrieving the details and the story of what she has discovered—say, about an experiment in grafting two species of fruit trees—and then she is elaborating by explaining the experience to her readers, connecting the outcome to what she already knows about the subject or has learned as a result.

Her leap-taking impulses have taken her through vast swaths of the plant kingdom, of course, and deeply into the Latin nomenclature and the classic horticultural literature. These impulses have also drawn her into the aesthetics of space and structure and the mechanics thereof: building stone walls; digging and wiring water features; putting a cupola on the garage; building paths, stairs, and gates; ripping out a Gothic picket fence and reusing the wood to create something more open and with stronger horizontal lines to pull down the soaring verticality of her three-story Victorian house and connect it with the gardens that surround it; making the outdoor spaces airier and more easily seen from the street, while still circumscribed, so as to impart that essential sense of privacy that makes a garden a room of its own. Her spaces are idiosyncratic and asymmetrical, giving the illusion of having evolved naturally, yet they cohere, through the repetition of textures, lines, and geometry.

A simple example of how she has backed into more and more complex mastery is the manner in which she came to embrace plant classification and the Latin terminology. "When I started, the world of plants was a completely foreign language to me. I would read gardening books and be completely lost. I didn't know what plant names were, common or Latin. I wasn't thinking about learning this stuff, ever. I'm like, Why would you want to do that? Why wouldn't you just get outside and dig a hole and put something in it?" What she relished were pictures that gave her ideas and passages of text where the designers used phrases like "my process" in describing

how they had achieved the desired effect. It was the posses-
sive pronoun, *my* process, that affirmed Bonnie in her head-
long rush to learn by doing. The notion is that every gardener's
process is uniquely his or her own. Bonnie's process did not
involve taking direction from experts, much less mastering
the Linnaean taxonomy or the Latin names of what she stuck
in holes and dragged her water hose to. But as she thrashed
around, working to achieve in dirt the magical spaces that
danced in her mind, she came to Latin and Linnaeus despite
herself.

"You begin to discover that the Latin names are helpful.
They can give you a shortcut to understanding the nature of
the plants, and they can help you remember. Tardiva, which
is a species name, comes after hydrangea, which is a genus."
Bonnie had taken Latin in high school, along with French,
and of course English, and the cues to those memories began
to reawaken. "I can easily see that tardiva means late, like
tardy. The same word comes after many plant varieties, so
you see the genus and then the species is tardiva, and now
you know that particular plant is a late bloomer. So you begin to realize that the Latin names are a way of helping you
remember, and you find yourself using them more and more.
Also you remember plants better, because it's second nature
to you that procumbus means prostrate, crawling on the
ground. It makes sense. So now it's not so hard to remember
that particular species name when it's attached to a genus.
It's also important to know the Latin names because then
you can be absolutely specific about a plant. Plants have
common names, and common names are regional. Actaea
racemosa has a common name of black cohosh, but it's also
known as snakeroot, and those names are often given to
other plants. There's only one Actaea racemosa." Gradually,
and despite her inclination to resist, she came to grasp the

classical taxonomy of ornamental plants and to appreciate how Linnaeus's schema frames family connections and communicates attributes.

Bonnie said that the farmers she had recently met were particularly interested in what she has learned about the advantages of composting and earthworms over chemical fertilizers for building nutrients and soil aeration, and how to get strong root growth on low rations of water through a homemade system of drip irrigation. She paused in recounting her meeting with them, reflecting on how all of this knowledge has sneaked up on her. It was never something she set out to conquer. "Look, blundering's really not a bad thing. It's a good thing in that you get stuff done. A lot of people, when they contemplate the enormity of the task and they see all that's entailed, they're stopped in their tracks."

Of course, in some settings—like learning to jump out of airplanes and walk away with your life—blundering is not the optimal learning strategy.

Undesirable Difficulties

Elizabeth and Robert Bjork, who coined the phrase "desirable difficulties," write that difficulties are desirable because "they trigger encoding and retrieval processes that support learning, comprehension, and remembering. If, however, the learner does not have the background knowledge or skills to respond to them successfully, they become undesirable difficulties."[19] Cognitive scientists know from empirical studies that testing, spacing, interleaving, variation, generation, and certain kinds of contextual interference lead to stronger learning and retention. Beyond that, we have an intuitive sense of what kinds of difficulties are *undesirable* but, for lack of the needed research, we cannot yet be definitive.

Clearly, impediments that you cannot overcome are not desirable. Outlining a lesson in a sequence different from the one in the textbook is not a desirable difficulty for learners who lack the reading skills or language fluency required to hold a train of thought long enough to reconcile the discrepancy. If your textbook is written in Lithuanian and you don't know the language, this hardly represents a desirable difficulty. To be desirable, a difficulty must be something learners can overcome through increased effort.

Intuitively it makes sense that difficulties that don't strengthen the skills you will need, or the kinds of challenges you are likely to encounter in the real-world application of your learning, are not desirable. Having somebody whisper in your ear while you read the news may be essential training for a TV anchor. Being heckled by role-playing protestors while honing your campaign speech may help train up a politician. But neither of these difficulties is likely to be helpful for Rotary Club presidents or aspiring YouTube bloggers who want to improve their stage presence. A cub towboat pilot on the Mississippi might be required in training to push a string of high-riding empty barges into a lock against a strong side wind. A baseball player might practice hitting with a weight on his bat to strengthen his swing. You might teach a football player some of the principles of ballet for learning balance and movement, but you probably would not teach him the techniques for an effective golf drive or backhand tennis serve.

Is there an overarching rule that determines the kinds of impediments that make learning stronger? Time and further research may yield an answer. But the kinds of difficulties we've just described, whose desirability is well documented, offer a large and diverse toolkit already at hand.

The Takeaway

Learning is at least a three-step process: initial *encoding* of information is held in short-term working memory before being consolidated into a cohesive representation of knowledge in long-term memory. *Consolidation* reorganizes and stabilizes memory traces, gives them meaning, and makes connections to past experiences and to other knowledge already stored in long-term memory. *Retrieval* updates learning and enables you to apply it when you need it.

Learning always builds on a store of prior knowledge. We interpret and remember events by building connections to what we already know.

Long-term memory capacity is virtually limitless: the more you know, the more possible connections you have for adding new knowledge.

Because of the vast capacity of long-term memory, having the ability to locate and recall what you know when you need it is key; your facility for calling up what you know depends on the *repeated use* of the information (to keep retrieval routes strong) and on your establishing powerful *retrieval cues* that can reactivate the memories.

Periodic retrieval of learning helps strengthen connections to the memory and the cues for recalling it, while also weakening routes to competing memories. Retrieval practice that's easy does little to strengthen learning; the more difficult the practice, the greater the benefit.

When you recall learning from short-term memory, as in rapid-fire practice, little mental effort is required, and little long-term benefit accrues. But when you recall it after some time has elapsed and your grasp of it has become a little rusty, you have to make an effort to reconstruct it. This effortful retrieval both strengthens the memory but also makes the learning *pliable* again, leading to its *reconsolidation.* Reconsolidation helps update your memories with new information and connect them to more recent learning.

Repeated effortful recall or practice helps integrate learning into *mental models,* in which a set of interrelated ideas or a sequence of motor skills are fused into a meaningful whole that can be adapted and applied in later settings. Examples are the perceptions and manipulations involved in driving a car or in knocking a curveball out of the ballpark.

When practice conditions are varied or retrieval is interleaved with the practice of other material, we increase our abilities of *discrimination* and *induction* and the versatility with which we can apply the learning in new settings at a later date. Interleaving and variation build new connections, expanding and more firmly entrenching knowledge in memory and increasing the number of cues for retrieval.

Trying to come up with an answer rather than having it presented to you, or trying to solve a problem before being shown the solution, leads to better learning and longer retention of the correct answer or solution, even when your attempted response is wrong, so long as corrective feedback is provided.

5

Avoid Illusions of Knowing

AT THE ROOT of our effectiveness is our ability to grasp the world around us and to take the measure of our own performance. We're constantly making judgments about what we know and don't know and whether we're capable of handling a task or solving a problem. As we work at something, we keep an eye on ourselves, adjusting our thinking or actions as we progress.

Monitoring your own thinking is what psychologists call metacognition (*meta* is Greek for "about"). Learning to be accurate self-observers helps us to stay out of blind alleys, make good decisions, and reflect on how we might do better next time. An important part of this skill is being sensitive to the ways we can delude ourselves. One problem with poor judgment is that we usually don't know when we've got it. Another problem is the sheer scope of the ways our judgment can be led astray.[1]

In this chapter we discuss perceptual illusions, cognitive biases, and distortions of memory that commonly mislead people. Then we suggest techniques for keeping your judgment squared with reality.

The consequences of poor judgment fill the daily papers. During the summer of 2008, three stickup artists in Minneapolis had a system going of phoning in large fast-food orders and then relieving the delivery man of all the goods and cash he carried. As a livelihood it was a model of simplicity. They kept at it, failing to consider the wisdom of always placing their orders from the same two cell phones and taking delivery at the same two addresses.

David Garman, a Minneapolis cop, was working undercover that summer. "It was getting more aggressive. At the beginning, it was 'maybe they had a gun,' then all of a sudden there were a couple of guns, and then they were hurting the people when they were robbing them."

It was a night in August when Garman got a call about a large order phoned in to a Chinese restaurant. He organized a small team on short notice and prepared to pose as the delivery guy. He pulled on a bulletproof vest, covered it with a casual shirt, and shoved his .45 automatic into his pants. While his colleagues staked out positions near the delivery address, Garman picked up the food, drove there, and parked with his brights shining on the front door. He'd cut a slit in the bottom of the food bag and tucked a .38 inside to rest in his hand as he carried the package. "The .38 has a covered hammer on it, so I can shoot it in a bag. If I were to put the automatic in there, it'd jam and I'd be screwed."

So I walk up with the package and I say, "Hey, sir, did you order some food?" He says, "Yup," and I'm thinking this guy's really just going to pay me and I'm going to be out of here, and this is going to be the dumbest thing we've ever done. I'm thinking if he hands me $40, I don't even know how much this food is. But he turns his head to look halfway back and two other guys start to come up, and as they're walking towards me they flip hoods over their heads. That's when I know it's game time. The first guy whips a gun out of his pocket and racks it and puts it to my head all in one motion, saying, "Give me everything you've got motherfucker or I'll kill you." I ended up shooting him through the bag. It was four rounds.[2]

Not such a great livelihood after all. The guy was hit low and survived, although he is a lesser man as a result. Garman would have aimed higher if the food package hadn't been so heavy, and he took a lesson from the experience: he's better prepared for the next time, though he'd rather we didn't describe just how.

We like to think we're smarter than the average doodle, and even if we're not, we feel affirmed in this delusion each year when the newest crop of Darwin Awards circulates by email, that short list of self-inflicted fatalities caused by spectacularly poor judgment, as in the case of the attorney in Toronto who was demonstrating the strength of the windows in his twenty-two-story office tower by throwing his shoulder against the glass when he broke it and fell through. The truth is that we're all hardwired to make errors in judgment. Good judgment is a skill one must acquire, becoming an astute observer of one's own thinking and performance. We start at a disadvantage for several reasons. One is that when we're incompetent, we tend to overestimate our competence and see little reason to change. Another is that, as humans, we are readily misled by illusions, cognitive biases, and the stories we construct to explain the world around us and our place within it. To become more competent, or even expert, we must learn to recognize competence when we see it in others, become more accurate judges of what we ourselves know and don't know, adopt learning strategies that get results, and find objective ways to track our progress.

Two Systems of Knowing

In his book *Thinking, Fast and Slow,* Daniel Kahneman describes our two analytic systems. What he calls System 1 (or the automatic system) is unconscious, intuitive, and immediate. It draws on our senses and memories to size up a situation in the blink of an eye. It's the running back dodging tackles in his dash for the end zone. It's the Minneapolis cop, walking up to a driver he's pulled over on a chilly day, taking evasive action even before he's fully aware that his eye has seen a bead of sweat run down the driver's temple.

System 2 (the controlled system) is our slower process of conscious analysis and reasoning. It's the part of thinking that considers choices, makes decisions, and exerts self-control. We also use it to train System 1 to recognize and respond to particular situations that demand reflexive action. The running back is using System 2 when he walks through the moves in his playbook. The cop is using it when he practices taking a gun from a shooter. The neurosurgeon is using it when he rehearses his repair of the torn sinus.

System 1 is automatic and deeply influential, but it is susceptible to illusion, and you depend on System 2 to help you manage yourself: by checking your impulses, planning ahead, identifying choices, thinking through their implications, and staying in charge of your actions. When a guy in a restaurant walks past a mother with an infant and the infant cries out "Dada!" that's System 1. When the blushing mother says,

"No, dear, that's not Dada, that's a *man*," she is acting as a surrogate System 2, helping the infant refine her System 1.

System 1 is powerful because it draws on our accumulated years of experience and our deep emotions. System 1 gives us the survival reflex in moments of danger, and the astonishing deftness earned through thousands of hours of deliberate practice in a chosen field of expertise. In the interplay between Systems 1 and 2—the topic of Malcolm Gladwell's book *Blink*—your instantaneous ability to size up a situation plays against your capacity for skepticism and thoughtful analysis. Of course, when System 1's conclusions arise out of misperception or illusion, they can steer you into trouble. Learning when to trust your intuition and when to question it is a big part of how you improve your competence in the world at large and in any field where you want to be expert. It's not just the dullards who fall victim. We all do, to varying degrees. Pilots, for example, are susceptible to a host of perceptual illusions. They are trained to beware of them and to use their instruments to know that they're getting things right.

A frightening example with a happy ending is China Airlines Flight 006 on a winter day in 1985. The Boeing 747 was 41,000 feet above the Pacific, almost ten hours into its eleven-hour flight from Taipei to LA, when engine number 4 lost power. The plane began to lose airspeed. Rather than taking manual control and descending below 30,000 feet to restart the engine, as prescribed in the flight book, the crew held at 41,000 with the autopilot engaged and attempted a restart. Meanwhile, loss of the outboard engine gave the plane asymmetrical thrust. The autopilot tried to correct for this and keep the plane level, but as the plane continued to slow it also began to roll to the right. The captain was aware of the deceleration, but not the extent to which the plane had entered a right bank; his System 1 clue would have been his vestibular reflex—how the inner ear senses balance and spatial orientation—but because of the plane's trajectory, he had the sensation of flying level. His System 2 clues would have been a glimpse at the horizon and his instruments. Correct procedure called for applying left rudder to help raise the right wing, but his System 2 focus was on the airspeed indicator and on the efforts of the first officer and engineer to restart the engine.

As its bank increased, the plane descended through 37,000 feet into high clouds, which obscured the horizon. The captain switched off the autopilot and pushed the nose down to get more speed, but the plane had already rolled beyond 45 degrees and now turned upside down and fell into an uncontrolled descent. The crew were confused by the situation. They understood the plane was behaving erratically but were unaware they had overturned and were in a dive. They could no longer discern thrust from engines 1–3 and concluded those engines had quit as well. The plane's dive was evident from their flight gauges, but the angle was so unlikely the crew decided the gauges had failed. At 11,000 feet they broke through the clouds, astonished to see that they were roaring toward earth. The captain and first officer both pulled back hard on the stick, exerting enormous forces on the plane but managing to level off. Landing gear hung from the plane's belly, and they'd lost one of their hydraulic systems, but all four engines came to life, and the captain was able to fly on, diverting successfully to San Francisco. An inspection revealed just how severe their maneuver had been. Strains five times the force of gravity had bent the plane's wings permanently upward, broken two landing gear struts, and torn away two landing gear doors and large parts of the rear horizontal stabilizers.

"Spatial disorientation" is the aeronautical term for a deadly combination of two elements: losing sight of the horizon and relying on human sensory perception that doesn't jibe with reality but is so convincing that pilots conclude their cockpit instruments have failed. As Kahneman says, System 1, the instinctual, reflexive system that detects danger and keeps us safe, can be very hard to overrule. Flight 006's initial incident, the loss of an engine cruising at altitude, is not considered an emergency, but it quickly became one as a result of the captain's actions. Rather than following prescribed procedure, and rather than fully engaging his System 2 analytic resources by monitoring all his instruments, he let himself become preoccupied with the engine restart and with a single flight indicator, airspeed. Then, when things spiraled out of control, he trusted his senses over his gauges, in effect trying to construct his own narrative of what was happening to the plane.

There's a long list of illusions to which pilots can fall prey (some with mordant names like "the leans," "graveyard spin," and "the black hole approach") and sites on the Internet where you can listen to the chilling last words of pilots struggling and failing to understand and correct what's gone wrong in the sky. Spatial disorientation was deemed the probable cause of the crash that killed Mel Carnahan, the governor of Missouri, while being flown through a thunderstorm one night in October 2000, and the probable cause of the crash that killed John F. Kennedy Jr. and his wife and her sister off the shore of Martha's Vineyard on a hazy night in July 1999. Fortunately, the China Airlines incident came to a good end, but the National Transportation Safety Board report of that incident reveals just how quickly training and professionalism can be hijacked by System 1 illusion, and therefore why we need to cultivate a disciplined System 2, conscious analysis and reasoning, that always keeps one eye on the flight instruments.[3]

Illusions and Memory Distortions

The filmmaker Errol Morris, in a series of articles on illusion in the *New York Times,* quotes the social psychologist David Dunning on humans' penchant for "motivated reasoning," or, as Dunning put it, the "sheer genius people have at convincing themselves of congenial conclusions while denying the truth of inconvenient ones."[4] (The British prime minister Benjamin Disraeli once said of a political opponent that his conscience was not his guide but his accomplice.) There are many ways that our System 1 and System 2 judgments can be led astray: perceptual illusions like those experienced by pilots, faulty narrative, distortions of memory, failure to recognize when a new kind of problem requires a new kind of solution, and a variety of cognitive biases to which we're prone. We describe a number of these hazards here, and then we offer measures you can take, akin to scanning the cockpit instruments, to help keep your thinking aligned with reality.

Our understanding of the world is shaped by a *hunger for narrative* that rises out of our discomfort with ambiguity and arbitrary events. When surprising things happen, we search for an explanation. The urge to resolve ambiguity can be surprisingly potent, even when the subject is inconsequential. In a study where participants thought they were being measured for reading comprehension and their ability to solve anagrams, they were exposed to the distraction of a background phone conversation. Some heard only one side of a conversation, and others heard both sides. The participants, not knowing that the distraction itself was the subject of the study, tried to ignore what they were hearing so as to stay focused on the reading and anagram solutions. The results showed that overhearing one side of a conversation proved more distracting than overhearing both sides, and the content of those partial conversations was better recalled later by the unintentional eavesdroppers. Why was this? Presumably, those overhearing half a conversation were strongly compelled to try to infer the missing half in a way that made for a complete narrative. As the authors point out, the study may help explain why we find one-sided cell phone conversations in public spaces so intrusive, but it also reveals the ineluctable way we are drawn to imbue the events around us with rational explanations.

The discomfort with ambiguity and arbitrariness is equally powerful, or more so, in our need for a rational understanding of our own lives. We strive to fit the events of our lives into a cohesive story that accounts for our circumstances, the things that befall us, and the choices we make. Each of us has a different narrative that has many threads woven into it from our shared culture and experience of being human, as well as many distinct threads that explain the singular events of one's personal past. All these experiences influence what comes to mind in a current situation and the narrative through which you make sense of it: Why nobody in my family attended college until me. Why my father never made a fortune in business. Why I'd never want to work in a corporation, or, maybe, Why I would never want to work for myself. We gravitate to the narratives that best explain our emotions. In this way, narrative and memory become one. The memories we organize meaningfully become those that are better remembered. Narrative provides not only meaning but also a mental framework for imbuing future experiences and information with meaning, in effect shaping new memories to fit our established constructs of the world and ourselves. No reader, when asked to account for the choices made under pressure by a novel's protagonist, can keep her own life experience from shading her explanation of what must have been going on in the character's interior world. The success of a magician or politician, like that of a novelist, relies on the seductive powers of narrative and on the audience's willing suspension of disbelief. Nowhere is this more evident than in the national political debate, where like-minded people gather online, at community meetings, and in the media to find common purpose and expand the story they feel best explains their sense of how the world works and how humans and politicians should behave.

You can see how quickly personal narrative is invoked to explain emotions when you read an article online whose author has argued a position on almost any subject—for example, an op-ed piece supporting the use of testing as a powerful tool for learning. Scan the comments posted by readers: some sing hallelujah while others can scarcely contain their umbrage, each invoking a personal story that supports or refutes the column's main argument. The psychologists Larry Jacoby, Bob Bjork, and Colleen Kelley, summing up studies on illusions of comprehension, competence, and remembering, write that it is nearly impossible to avoid basing one's judgments on subjective experience. Humans do not give greater credence to an objective record of a past event than to their subjective remembering of it, and we are surprisingly insensitive to the ways our particular construals of a situation are unique to ourselves. Thus the narrative of memory becomes central to our intuitions regarding the judgments we make and the actions we take.[5]

It is a confounding paradox, then, that the changeable nature of our memory not only can skew our perceptions but also is essential to our ability to learn. As will be familiar to you by now, every time we call up a memory, we make the mind's routes to that memory stronger, and this capacity to strengthen, expand, and modify memory is central to how we deepen our learning and broaden the connections to what we know and what we can do. Memory has some similarities to a Google search algorithm, in the sense that the more you connect what you learn to what you already know, and the more associations you make to a memory (for example, linking it with a visual image, a place, or a larger story), then the more mental cues you have through which to find and retrieve the memory again later. This capacity expands our agency: our ability to take action and be effective in the world. At the same time, because memory is a shape-shifter, reconciling the competing demands of emotion, suggestions, and narrative, it serves you well to stay open to the fallibility of your certainties: even your most cherished memories may not represent events in the exact way they occurred.

Memory can be distorted in many ways. People interpret a story in light of their world knowledge, imposing order where none had been present so as to make a more logical story. Memory is a reconstruction. We cannot remember every aspect of an event, so we remember those elements that have greatest emotional significance for us, and we fill in the gaps with details of our own that are consistent with our narrative but may be wrong.

People remember things that were implied but not specifically stated. The literature is full of examples. In one, many people who read a paragraph about a troubled girl named Helen Keller later mistakenly recalled the phrase "deaf, dumb, and blind" as being in the text. This mistake was rarely made by another group who read the same paragraph about a girl named Carol Harris.[6]

Imagination inflation refers to the tendency of people who, when asked to imagine an event vividly, will sometimes begin to believe, when asked about it later, that the event actually occurred. Adults who were asked "Did you ever break a window with your hand?" were more likely on a later life inventory to report that they believed this event occurred during their lifetimes. It seems that asking the question led them to imagine the event, and the act of having imagined it had the effect, later, of making them more likely to think it had occurred (relative to another group who answered the question without having previously imagined it occurring).

Hypothetical events that are imagined vividly can seat themselves in the mind as firmly as memories of actual events. For instance, when it is suspected that a child is being sexually abused and he is interviewed and questioned about it, he may imagine experiences that the interviewer describes and then later come to "remember" them as having occurred.[7] (Sadly, of course, many memories of childhood sexual abuse are absolutely true, usually ones reported soon after the occurrence.)

Another type of memory illusion is one caused by *suggestion*, which may arise simply in the way a question is asked. In one example, people watched a video of a car running a stop sign at an intersection and colliding with another car passing through. Those who were later asked to judge the speed of the vehicles when they "contacted" each other gave an average estimate of thirty-two miles per hour. Those who were asked to judge the speed when the two vehicles "smashed" into each other estimated on average forty-one miles per hour. If the speed limit was thirty miles per hour, asking the question the second way rather than the first could lead to the driver's being charged with speeding. Of course, the legal system knows the danger of witnesses being asked "leading questions" (ones that encourage a particular answer), but such questions are difficult to avoid completely, because suggestibility can be very subtle. After all, in the case just discussed, the two cars did "smash together."[8]

Some witnesses to crimes who are struggling to recall them are instructed to let their minds roam freely, to generate whatever comes to mind, even if it is a guess. However, the act of guessing about possible events causes people to provide their own misinformation, which, if left uncorrected, they may later come to retrieve as memories. That is one reason why people who have been interviewed after being hypnotized are barred from testifying in court in almost all states and Canadian provinces. The hypnotic interview typically encourages people to let their thoughts roam freely and produce everything that comes to mind, in hopes that they will retrieve information that would not otherwise be produced. However, this process causes them to produce much erroneous information, and studies have shown that when they are tested later, under instructions only to tell exactly what they remember of the actual events, their guesses made while under hypnosis cloud their memories about what truly happened. In particular, they remember events they produced under hypnosis as actual experiences, even under conditions (in the laboratory) when it is known that the events in question did not occur.[9]

Interference from other events can distort memory. Suppose the police interview a witness shortly after a crime, showing pictures of possible suspects. Time passes, but eventually the police nab a suspect, one whose picture had been viewed by the witness. If the witness is now asked to view a lineup, he may mistakenly remember one of the suspects whose photo he saw as having been present at the crime. A particularly vivid example of a related process happened to the Australian psychologist Donald M. Thomson. A woman in Sydney was watching television in midday when she heard a knock at the door. When she answered it, she was attacked, raped, and left unconscious. When she awoke and dialed the police, they came to her aid, got a description of her assailant, and launched a search. They spotted Donald Thomson walking down a Sydney street, and he matched the description. They arrested him on the spot. It turns out that Thomson had an airtight alibi—at the exact time of the rape, he was being interviewed on a live television show. The police did not believe him and sneered when he was being interrogated. However, the story was true. The woman had been watching the show when she heard the knock on the door. The description she gave the police was apparently of the man she saw on television, Donald Thomson, rather than the rapist. Her System 1 reaction— quick but sometimes mistaken—provided the wrong description, probably due to her extreme emotional state.[10]

What psychologists call the *curse of knowledge* is our tendency to underestimate how long it will take another person to learn something new or perform a task that we have already mastered. Teachers often suffer this illusion—the calculus instructor who finds calculus so easy that she can no longer place herself in the shoes of the student who is just starting out and struggling with the subject. The curse-of-knowledge effect is close kin to *hindsight bias,* or what is often called the *knew-it-all-along effect,* in which we view events after the fact as having been more predictable than they were before they occurred. Stock market pundits will confidently announce on the evening news why the stock market behaved as it did that day, even though they could not have predicted the movements that morning.[11]

Accounts that sound familiar can create *the feeling of knowing* and be mistaken for true. This is one reason that political or advertising claims that are not factual but are repeated can gain traction with the public, particularly if they have emotional resonance. Something you once heard that you hear again later carries a warmth of familiarity that can be mistaken for memory, a shred of something you once knew and cannot quite place but are inclined to believe. In the world of propaganda, this is called "the big lie" technique—even a big lie told repeatedly can come to be accepted as truth.

Fluency illusions result from our tendency to mistake fluency with a text for mastery of its content. For example, if you read a particularly lucid presentation of a difficult concept, you can get the idea that it is actually pretty simple and perhaps even that you knew it all along. As discussed earlier, students who study by rereading their texts can mistake their fluency with a text, gained from rereading, for possession of accessible knowledge of the subject and consequently overestimate how well they will do on a test.

Our memories are also subject to *social influence* and tend to align with the memories of the people around us. If you are in a group reminiscing about past experiences and someone adds a wrong detail about the story, you will tend to incorporate this detail into your own memory and later remember the experience with the erroneous detail. This process is called "memory conformity" or the "social contagion of memory": one person's error can "infect" another person's memory. Of course, social influences are not always bad. If someone recalls details of joint memory on which you are somewhat hazy, your subsequent memory will be updated and will hold a more accurate record of the past event.[12]

In the obverse of the social influence effect, humans are predisposed to assume that others share their beliefs, a process called the *false consensus effect*. We generally fail to recognize the idiosyncratic nature of our personal understanding of the world and interpretation of events and that ours differ from others'. Recall how surprised you were recently, on commiserating with a friend about the general state of affairs, to discover that she sees in an entirely different light matters on which you thought the correct view was fundamental and obvious: climate change, gun control, fracking of gas wells—or perhaps something very local, such as whether to pass a bond issue for a school building or to oppose construction of a big box store in the neighborhood.[13]

Confidence in a memory is not a reliable indication of its accuracy. We can have utmost faith in a vivid, nearly literal memory of an event and yet find that we actually have it all wrong. National tragedies, like the assassination of President John Kennedy or the events surrounding 9/11, create what psychologists call "flashbulb" memories, named for the vivid images that we retain: where we were when we got the news, how we learned it, how we felt, what we did. These memories are thought to be indelible, burned into our minds, and it is true that the broad outlines of such catastrophes, thoroughly reported in the media, are well remembered, but your memory of your personal circumstances surrounding the events may not necessarily be accurate. There have been numerous studies of this phenomenon, including surveys of fifteen hundred Americans' memories of the September 11 attacks. In this study, the respondents' memories were surveyed a week after the attacks, again a year later, and then again three years and ten years later. Respondents' most emotional memories of their personal details at the time they learned of the attacks are also those of which they are most confident and, paradoxically, the ones that have most changed over the years relative to other memories about 9/11.[14]

Mental Models

As we develop mastery in the various areas of our lives, we tend to bundle together the incremental steps that are required to solve different kinds of problems. To use an analogy from a previous chapter, you could think of them as something like smart-phone apps in the brain. We call them mental models. Two examples in police work are the choreography of the routine traffic stop and the moves to take a weapon from an assailant at close quarters. Each of these maneuvers involves a set of perceptions and actions that cops can adapt with little conscious thought in response to context and situation. For a barista, a mental model would be the steps and ingredients to produce a perfect sixteen-ounce decaf frappuccino. For the receptionist at urgent care, it's triage and registration.

The better you know something, the more difficult it becomes to teach it. So says physicist and educator Eric Mazur of Harvard. Why? As you get more expert in complex areas, your models in those areas grow more complex, and the component steps that compose them fade into the background of memory (the curse of knowledge). A physicist, for example, will create a mental library of the principles of physics she can use to solve the various kinds of problems she encounters in her work: Newton's laws of motion, for example, or the laws of conservation of momentum. She will tend to sort problems based on their underlying principles, whereas a novice will group them by similarity of surface features, like the apparatus being manipulated in the problem (pulley, inclined plane, etc.). One day, when she goes to teach an intro physics class, she explains how a particular problem calls for something from Newtonian mechanics, forgetting that her students have yet to master the underlying steps she has long ago bundled into one unified mental model. This presumption by the professor that her students will readily follow something complex that appears fundamental in her own mind is a metacognitive error, a misjudgment of the matchup between what she knows and what her students know. Mazur says that the person who knows best what a student is struggling with in assimilating new concepts is not the professor, it's another student.[15] This problem is illustrated through a very simple experiment in which one person plays a common tune inside her head and taps the rhythm with her knuckles and another person hearing the rhythmic taps must guess the tune. Each tune comes from a fixed set of twenty-five, so the statistical chance of guessing it is 4 percent. Tellingly, the participants who have the tune in mind estimate that the other person will guess correctly 50 percent of the time, but in fact the listeners guess correctly only 2.5 percent of the time, no better than chance.[16]

Like Coach Dooley's football players memorizing their playbooks, we all build mental libraries of myriad useful solutions that we can call on at will to help us work our way from one Saturday game to the next. But we can be tripped by these models, too, when we fail to recognize a new problem that appears to be a familiar one is actually something quite different and we pull out a solution to address it that doesn't work or makes things worse. The failure to recognize when your solution doesn't fit the problem is another form of faulty self-observation that can lead you into trouble.

Mike Ebersold, the neurosurgeon, was called into the operating room one day to help a surgical resident who, in the midst of removing a brain tumor, was losing the patient. The usual model for cutting out a tumor calls for taking your time, working carefully around the growth, getting a clean margin, saving the surrounding nerves. But when the growth is in the brain, and if you get bleeding behind it, pressure on the brain can turn fatal. Instead of slow-and-careful, you need just the opposite, cutting the growth out very quickly so the blood can drain, and then working to repair the bleeding. "Initially you might be a little timid to take the big step," Mike says. "It's not pretty, but the patient's survival depends on your knowing to switch gears and do it fast." Mike assisted, and the surgery was successful.

Like the infant who calls the stranger Dada, we must cultivate the ability to discern when our mental models aren't working: when a situation that seems familiar is actually different and requires that we reach for a different solution and do something new.

Unskilled and Unaware of It

Incompetent people lack the skills to improve because they are unable to distinguish between incompetence and competence. This phenomenon, of particular interest for metacognition, has been named the Dunning-Kruger effect after the psychologists David Dunning and Justin Kruger. Their research showed that incompetent people overestimate their own competence and, failing to sense a mismatch between their performance and what is desirable, see no need to try to improve. (The title of their initial paper on the topic was "Unskilled and Unaware of It.") Dunning and Kruger have also shown that incompetent people can be taught to raise their competence by learning the skills to judge their own performance more accurately, in short, to make their metacognition more accurate. In one series of studies that demonstrate this finding, they gave students a test of logic and asked them to rate their own performance. In the first experiment the results confirmed expectations that the least competent students were the most out of touch with their performance: students who scored at the twelfth percentile on average believed that their general logical reasoning ability fell at the sixty-eighth percentile.

In a second experiment, after taking an initial test and rating their own performance, the students were shown the other students' answers and then their own answers and asked to reestimate the number of test questions they had answered correctly. The students whose performance was in the bottom quartile failed to judge their own performance more accurately after seeing the more competent choices of their peers and in fact tended to raise their already inflated estimates of their own ability.

A third experiment explored whether poor performers could learn to improve their judgment. The students were given ten problems in logical reasoning and after the test were asked to rate their logical reasoning skills and test performance. Once again, the students in the bottom quartile grossly overestimated their performance. Next, half the students received ten minutes of training in logic (how to test the accuracy of a syllogism); the other half of the students were given an unrelated task. All the students were then asked to estimate again how well they had performed on the test. Now the students in the bottom quartile who had received the training were much more accurate estimators of the number of questions they got right and of how they performed compared to the other students. Those in the bottom quartile who didn't receive the training held to their mistaken conviction that they had performed well.

How is it that incompetent people fail to learn through experience that they are unskilled? Dunning and Kruger offer several theories. One is that people seldom receive negative feedback about their skills and abilities from others in everyday life, because people don't like to deliver the bad news. Even if people get negative feedback, they must come to an accurate understanding of why the failure occurred. For success everything must go right, but by contrast, failure can be attributed to any number of external causes: it's easy to blame the tool for what the hand cannot do. Finally, Dunning and Kruger suggest that some people are just not astute at reading how other people are performing and are therefore less able to spot competence when they see it, making them less able to make comparative judgments of their own performance.

These effects are more likely to occur in some contexts and with some skills than with others. In some domains, the revelation of one's incompetence can be brutally frank. The authors can all remember from their childhoods when a teacher would appoint two boys to pick other kids for softball teams.

The good players are picked first, the worst last. You learn your peers' judgments of your softball abilities in a very public manner, so it would be hard for the last-picked player to think "I must be really good at softball." However, most realms of life do not render such stark judgments of ability.[17]

To sum up, the means by which we navigate the world— Daniel Kahneman's Systems 1 and 2—rely on our perceptual systems, intuition, memory, and cognition, with all their tics, warts, biases, and flaws. Each of us is an astounding bundle of perceptual and cognitive abilities, coexisting with the seeds of our own undoing. When it comes to learning, what we choose to do is guided by our judgments of what works and what doesn't, and we are easily misled.

Our susceptibility to illusion and misjudgment should give us all pause, and especially so to the advocates of "student-directed learning," a theory now current among some parents and educators. This theory holds that students know best what they need to study to master a subject, and what pace and methods work best for them. For example, at Manhattan Free School in East Harlem, opened in 2008, students "do not receive grades, take tests or have to do anything they do not feel like doing." The Brooklyn Free School, which opened in 2004, along with a new crop of homeschooling families who call themselves "unschoolers," follows the precept that whatever intrigues the learner is what will result in the best learning. [18]

The intent is laudatory. We know that students need to take more control of their own learning by employing strategies like those we have discussed. For example, they need to test themselves, both to attain the direct benefits of increased retention and to determine what they know and don't know to more accurately judge their progress and focus on material that needs more work. But few students practice these strategies, and those who do will need more than encouragement if they are to practice them effectively: It turns out that even when students understand that retrieval practice is a superior strategy, they often fail to persist long enough to get the lasting benefit. For example, when students are presented with a body of material to master, say a stack of foreign vocabulary flashcards, and are free to decide when to drop a card out of the deck because they've learned it, most students drop the card when they've gotten it right once or twice, far sooner than they should. The paradox is that those students who employ the least effective study strategies overestimate their learning the most and, as a consequence of their misplaced confidence, they are not inclined to change their habits.

The football player preparing for next Saturday's game doesn't leave his performance to intuition, he runs through his plays and mixes it up to discover the rough edges and work them out on the field well before suiting up for the big game. If this kind of behavior were anywhere close to the norm for students in their academics today, then self-directed learning would be highly effective. But of course the football player is not self-directed, his practice is guided by a coach. Likewise, most students will learn academics better under an instructor who knows where improvement is needed and structures the practice required to achieve it.[19]

The answer to illusion and misjudgment is to replace subjective experience as the basis for decisions with a set of objective gauges outside ourselves, so that our judgment squares with the real world around us. When we have reliable reference points, like cockpit instruments, and make a habit of checking them, we can make good decisions about where to focus our efforts, recognize when we've lost our bearings, and find our way back again. Here are some examples.

Tools and Habits for Calibrating
Your Judgment

Most important is to make frequent use of *testing* and re-trieval practice to verify what you really do know versus what you think you know. Frequent low-stakes quizzes in class help the instructor verify that students are in fact learning as well as they appear to be and reveal the areas where extra atten-tion is needed. Doing cumulative quizzing, as Andy Sobel does in his political economics course, is especially powerful for consolidating learning and knitting the concepts from one stage of a course into new material encountered later. As a learner, you can use any number of practice techniques to self-test your mastery, from answering flashcards to explaining key concepts in your own words, and to peer instruction (see below).

Don't make the mistake of dropping material from your testing regime once you've gotten it correct a couple of times. If it's important, it needs to be practiced, and practiced again. And don't put stock in momentary gains that result from massed practice. Space your testing, vary your practice, keep the long view.

Peer instruction, a learning model developed by Eric Mazur, incorporates many of the foregoing principles. The material to be covered in class is assigned for reading beforehand. In class, the lecture is interspersed with quick tests that present students with a conceptual question and give them a minute or two to grapple with it; they then try, in small groups, to reach a consensus on the correct answer. In Mazur's experi-ence, this process engages the students in the underlying con-cepts of the lecture material; reveals students' problems in reaching understanding; and provides opportunities for them to explain their understanding, receive feedback, and assess their learning compared to other students. Likewise, the process serves as a gauge for the instructor of how well the students are assimilating the material and in what areas more or less work is needed. Mazur tries to pair students who initially had different answers to a question so that they can see another point of view and try to convince one another of who is right.

For two more examples of this technique, see the profiles of the professors Mary Pat Wenderoth and Michael D. Matthews in Chapter 8.[20]

Pay attention to the *cues* you're using to judge what you have learned. Whether something feels familiar or fluent is not always a reliable indicator of learning. Neither is your level of ease in retrieving a fact or a phrase on a quiz shortly after encountering it in a lecture or text. (Ease of retrieval after a delay, however, *is* a good indicator of learning.) Far better is to create a mental model of the material that integrates the various ideas across a text, connects them to what you already know, and enables you to draw inferences. How ably you can explain a text is an excellent cue for judging comprehension, because you must recall the salient points from memory, put them into your own words, and explain why they are significant—how they relate to the larger subject.

Instructors should give corrective *feedback*, and learners should seek it. In his interview with Errol Morris, the psychologist David Dunning argues that the path to self-insight leads through other people. "So it really depends on what sort of feedback you are getting. Is the world telling you good things? Is the world rewarding you in a way that you would expect a competent person to be rewarded? If you watch other people, you often find there are different ways to do things; there are better ways to do things. 'I'm not as good as I thought I was, but I have something to work on.'" Think of the kids lining up to join the softball team—would you be picked?[21]

In many fields, the practice of peer review serves as an external gauge, providing feedback on one's performance. Most medical practice groups have morbidity/mortality conferences, and if a doctor has a bad patient outcome, it will be presented there. The other doctors will pick it apart, or say "You did a good job, it was just a bad situation." Mike Ebersold argues that people in his field should practice as a part of a group. "If there are other neurosurgeons around you, it's a safeguard. If you're doing something that's not acceptable, they'll call you to task for it."

In many settings, your judgment and learning are calibrated by working alongside a more experienced partner: airline first officers with captains, rookies with seasoned cops, residents with experienced surgeons. The apprentice model is a very old one in human experience, as novices (whether cobblers or attorneys) have traditionally learned their craft from experienced practitioners.

In other settings, *teams* are formed of people with complementary areas of expertise. When doctors implant medical devices like pacemakers and neural stimulators of the type that treat incontinence or the symptoms of Parkinson's disease, the manufacturer has a product representative right in the operating room with the surgeon. The rep has seen many surgeries using the device, knows the kinds of patients that will benefit from it, knows the contraindications and adverse events, and has a hotline to the engineers and clinicians on the company's staff. The rep tracks the surgery to make sure the device is implanted in the correct position, the leads are inserted to the correct depth, and so on. Every part of the team benefits. The patient is assured of an appropriate and successful surgery. The doctor gets product and troubleshooting expertise at her fingertips. And the company makes sure its products are used correctly.

Training that simulates the kinds of demands and changeable conditions that can be expected in real-world settings helps learners and trainers assess mastery and focus on areas where understanding or competency need to be raised. Take police work, where many different forms of *simulation* are used in training. For firearms training it's often video-based scenarios, with a large screen set up at one end of a room where a number of props have been placed to imitate the situation confronting the officer, who enters the scene armed with a gun that has been modified to interact with the video.

Lieutenant Catherine Johnson of the Minneapolis Police Department describes a couple of such simulations in which she has trained:

> One was a traffic stop. The training room had the screen at one end and objects around the room—a big blue mailbox, a fire hydrant, a doorway—that you could use for cover in dealing with what was happening on the screen. I remember walking toward the screen, and the video simulating my coming up to the car as I did that, very realistic, and suddenly the trunk popped up and a guy with a shotgun rose out and shot me.

Which, to this day, every time I go up to a car on a traffic stop, I push down hard on the trunk to make sure it isn't open. And it's because of that one scenario in the training that I went through.

Another firearm simulation was a domestic call, and it starts where I am approaching the residence and there's a guy on his porch. The instant I show up I see that he has a gun in his hand. I order him to drop it, and the first thing he does is turn and start walking away. And my thinking at that point is that I can't shoot this guy in the back, and there's nobody over there that looks to be in danger, so what am I going to do? In the time it takes me to process whether or not I should shoot this guy, he's already turned around and shot me. Because my reaction was slower than his action. Action beats reaction every time. That's one mantra that's drilled into our minds.[22]

The firearms simulations can play out in a variety of ways both deadly and peaceful. There's not so much a right or wrong answer to the situation as there is a complex set of factors, some of which, like whether the individual on the porch has a criminal history, may be known to the officer when she enters the scene. At the conclusion, the officer debriefs with her trainer, getting feedback. The exercise isn't all about technique, it's about clear thinking and appropriate reflexes—visual and verbal clues to watch for, possible outcomes, being clear about the appropriate use of deadly force, and finding the words after the fact that will account for actions you have taken in the urgency of the moment.

Simulation is not perfect. Johnson recounts how officers are trained to take a gun from an assailant at close quarters, a maneuver they practice by role-playing with a fellow officer. It requires speed and deftness: striking an assailant's wrist with one hand to break his grip while simultaneously wresting the gun free with the other. It's a move that officers had been in the habit of honing through repetition, taking the gun, handing it back, taking it again. Until one of their officers, on a call in the field, took the gun from an assailant and handed it right back again. In their mutual astonishment, the officer managed to reseize the gun and hang onto it. The training regime had violated the cardinal rule that you should practice like you play, because you will play like you practice.

Sometimes the most powerful feedback for calibrating your sense of what you do and don't know are the mistakes you make in the field, assuming you survive them and are receptive to the lesson.[23]

6

Get Beyond Learning Styles

ALL LEARNERS ARE DIFFERENT, and all rising to a great place, as Francis Bacon tells us, is by a winding stair.[1]

Consider the story of Bruce Hendry, born in 1942, raised on the banks of the Mississippi north of Minneapolis by a machinist and a homemaker, just another American kid with skinned knees and fire in the belly to get rich. When we talk about self-made men, the story often sounds familiar. This is not that story. Bruce Hendry is self-made, but the story is in the winding stair, how he found his way, and what it helps us understand about differences in how people learn.

The idea that individuals have distinct learning styles has been around long enough to become part of the folklore of educational practice and an integral part of how many people perceive themselves. The underlying premise says that people receive and process new information differently: for example, some learn better from visual materials, and others learn better from written text or auditory materials. Moreover, the theory holds that people who receive instruction in a manner that is not matched to their learning style are at a disadvantage for learning.

In this chapter, we acknowledge that everyone has learning preferences, but we are not persuaded that you learn better when the manner of instruction fits those preferences. Yet there are other kinds of differences in how people learn that do matter. First, the story of Bruce, to help frame our argument.

Active Learning from the Get-Go

Part of the secret to Bruce is his sense, from the earliest age, of being the one in charge of Bruce. When he was two his mother, Doris, told him he couldn't cross the street because a car might hit him. Every day, Bruce crossed the street, and every day Doris gave him a spanking. "He was born aggressive," Doris told friends.

At eight he bought a ball of string at a garage sale for a dime, cut it up, and sold the pieces for a nickel each. At ten he got a paper route. At eleven he added caddying. At twelve he stuffed his pocket with $30 in savings, sneaked out of his bedroom window before dawn with an empty suitcase, and hitchhiked 255 miles to Aberdeen, South Dakota. He stocked up on Black Cats, cherry bombs, and roman candles, illegal in Minnesota, and hitched home before supper. Over the next week, Doris couldn't figure out why all the paperboys were dropping by the house for a few minutes and leaving. Bruce had struck gold, but the paper route supervisor found out and tipped off Bruce Senior. The father told the son if he ever did it again he'd get the licking of his life. Bruce repeated the buying trip the following summer and got the promised licking.

"It was worth it," he says.[2] He was thirteen, and he had learned a lesson about high demand and short supply.

The way Bruce figured, rich people were probably no smarter than he was, they just had knowledge he lacked. Looking at how he went after the knowledge he sought will illustrate some of the learning differences that matter. One, of course, is taking charge of your own education, a habit with Bruce from age two that he has exhibited through the years with remarkable persistence. There are other signal behaviors. As he throws himself into one scheme after another, he draws lessons that improve his focus and judgment. He knits what he learns into mental models of investing, which he then uses to size up more complex opportunities and find his way through the weeds, plucking the telling details from masses of irrelevant information to reach the payoff at the end. These behaviors are what psychologists call "rule learning" and "structure building." People who as a matter of habit extract underlying principles or rules from new experiences are more successful learners than those who take their experiences at face value, failing to infer lessons that can be applied later in similar situations. Likewise, people who single out salient concepts from the less important information they encounter in new material and who link these key ideas into a mental structure are more successful learners than those who cannot separate wheat from chaff and understand how the wheat is made into flour.

When he was barely a teenager, Bruce saw a flyer advertising wooded lots on a lake in central Minnesota. Advised that no one ever lost money on real estate, he bought one. Over four subsequent summers, with occasional help from his dad, he built a house on it, confronting each step in the process one at a time, figuring it out for himself or finding someone to show him how. To dig the basement, he borrowed a trailer and hooked it up to his '49 Hudson. He paid 50 cents for every load his friends excavated, shovel by shovel, and then charged the owner of a nearby lot that needed fill a dollar for it. He learned how to lay block from a friend whose father was in the cement business and then laid himself a foundation. He learned how to frame the walls from the salesman at the lumber yard. He plumbed the house and wired it the same way, a wide-eyed kid asking around how you do that sort of thing. "The electrical inspector disapproved it," Bruce recalls. "At the time, I figured it was because they wanted a union guy to do it, so I popped for a union guy to come up from the Cities and redo all my wiring. Looking back, I'm sure what I had done was totally dangerous."

He was nineteen and a university student the summer he traded the house for the down payment on a fourplex in Minneapolis. It was a simple premise: four apartments would generate four checks in the mail, month in and month out. Soon, besides his studies at university, he was managing the rental property, paying on the mortgage, answering midnight calls over broken plumbing, raising rents and losing tenants, trying to fill vacant units, and pouring in more money. He had learned how to parlay a vacant lot into a house, and a house into an apartment complex, but in the end the lesson proved a sour one, yielding more headache than reward. He sold the fourplex and swore off real estate for the next two decades.

Out of college, Bruce went to work for Kodak as a microfilm salesman. In his third year, he was one of five top salesmen in the country. That was the year he found out how much his branch manager was making: less than Bruce made as a salesman, if he factored in his company car and expense account. It pays better to be a rainmaker than a manager:

another lesson learned, another step up Bruce's winding stair. He quit to join a brokerage firm and sell stocks.

From this new vantage point, more lessons: "If I brought a dollar into the firm in trading commissions, half went to the firm and half of the remaining half went to the IRS. To make real money, I had to focus more on investing my own money and less on making sales commissions." Oops, another lesson: investing in stocks is risky. He lost as much investing his own money as he earned in commissions selling investments to his clients. "You have no control of the down side. If a stock drops 50 percent, it has to go up by 100 percent just to break even. A hundred percent is a lot harder to make than fifty is to lose!" More knowledge banked. He bided his time, casting his eyes about for the insight he was after.

Enter Sam Leppla.

As Bruce tells it, Leppla was just a guy who roamed the Minneapolis skyways in those days, from one investment firm to another, talking deals and giving advice. One day he told Bruce about some bonds in a distressed company that were selling for 22 cents on the dollar. "There were twenty-two points of unpaid back interest on these bonds," Bruce recalls, "so when the company came out of bankruptcy, you'd collect the back interest—in other words, 100 percent of your investment cost—and you'd still own a paying bond." It amounted to free money. "I didn't buy any," Bruce says. "But I watched it, and it worked out exactly like Sam predicted. So, I called him up and said, 'Can you come down and tell me what you're doing?'"

Leppla taught Bruce a more complex understanding of the relationships between price, supply, demand, and value than he'd learned from a suitcase full of fireworks. Leppla's modus operandi was drawn from the following precept. When a company runs into trouble, the first claim on its assets belongs not to its owners, the shareholders, but to its creditors: the suppliers and bondholders. There's a pecking order to bonds. Those bonds paid first are called senior bonds. Any residual assets after the senior bonds are paid go to pay off the junior bonds. Junior bonds in a troubled company get cheap if investors fear there won't be enough assets left over to cover their value, but investors' fear, laziness, and ignorance can depress bond prices far below the worth of the underlying assets. If you can ascertain that actual worth and you know the price of the bonds, you can invest with very little risk.

Here was the kind of knowledge Bruce had been seeking.

Florida real estate investment trusts were distressed at the time, so Sam and Bruce started looking into those, buying where they could see that the fire-sale prices significantly discounted the underlying values. "We'd buy these for 5 dollars and sell them for 50. Everything we bought made money." They had a good run, but market prices caught up with values, and soon they were in need of another idea.

At the time, eastern railroads were going bankrupt, and the federal government was buying their assets to form Conrail and Amtrak. As Bruce tells it, "One day Sam said, 'Railroads go bankrupt every fifty years and no one knows anything about them. They are real complicated and they take years to work out.' So we found a guy who knew about railroads. Barney Donahue. Barney was an ex–IRS agent and a railroad buff. If you've ever met a real railroad buff, they think it, they breathe it, they can tell you the weight of the track and they can tell you the numbers on the engines. He was one of those guys."

A central tenet of their investment model was to discover more than other investors knew about residual assets and the order in which the bonds were to be honored. Armed with the right knowledge, they could cherry-pick the underpriced junior bonds most likely to be paid off. Donahue checked out the different railroads and decided that the best one to invest in was the Erie Lackawanna, because it had the most modern equipment when it filed for bankruptcy. Hendry, Leppla, and Donahue dived in for a closer look. They traveled the entire length of the Erie's track to check its condition. They counted the equipment that remained, looked at its condition, and checked in Moody's transportation manuals to calculate values. "You just do the arithmetic: What's an engine worth? A boxcar? A mile of track?" The Erie had issued fifteen different bonds over its 150 years in operation, and the value of each bond was dependent in part on where it stood in seniority compared to the others. Bruce's research turned up a little document in which the financial institutions had agreed to the sequence in which bonds were to be paid off when the assets were liquidated. With a fix on the value of the company's assets, liabilities, and the bond structure, they knew what each class of bonds was worth. Bondholders who hadn't done this homework were in the dark. Junior bonds were selling at steeply discounted prices because they were so far down the food chain that investors doubted they would ever see their money. Bruce's calculations suggested otherwise, and he was buying.

It's a longer story than we have space to tell. A railroad bankruptcy is an astonishingly convoluted affair. Bruce committed himself to understanding the entirety of the process better than anybody else. Then he knocked on doors, challenged the good-old-boys' power structure that was managing the proceedings, and eventually succeeded in getting appointed by the courts to chair the committee that represented the bondholders' interests in the bankruptcy process. When the Erie came out of bankruptcy two years later, he was made chairman and CEO of the company. He hired Barney Donahue to run it. Hendry, Donahue, and the board guided the surviving corporation through the remaining lawsuits, and when the dust settled, Bruce's bonds paid twice face value, twenty times what he paid for some of the junior bonds he had purchased.

The Erie Lackawanna, with all its complexity and David versus Goliath qualities, was just the kind of mess that became Bruce Hendry's bread and butter: finding a company in trouble, burrowing into its assets and liabilities, reading the fine print on credit obligations, looking at its industry and where things are headed, understanding the litigation process, and wading into it armed with a pretty good idea of how things were going to play out.

There are stories of other remarkable conquests. He took control of Kaiser Steel, staved off its liquidation, guided it out of bankruptcy as CEO, and was awarded 2 percent ownership of the new corporation. He interceded in the failure of First RepublicBank of Texas and came out the other side with a 600 percent return on some of his first investments in the company. When manufacturers stopped making railroad boxcars because they were in oversupply, Bruce bought a thousand of the last ones built, collected 20 percent on his investment from lease contracts that the railroads were bound to honor, and then sold the cars a year later when they were in short supply and fetching a handsome price. The story of Hendry's rise is both familiar and particular; familiar in the nature of the quest and particular in the ways Bruce has "gone to school" on his ventures, building his own set of rules for what makes an investment opportunity attractive, stitching the rules into a template, and then finding new and different ways to apply it.

When he is asked how he accounts for his success, the lessons he cites are deceptively simple: go where the competition isn't, dig deep, ask the right questions, see the big picture, take risks, be honest. But these explanations aren't very satisfying. Behind them is a more interesting story, the one we infer from reading between the lines: how he figured out what knowledge he needed and how he then went after it; how early setbacks helped seed the skills of shrewder judgment; and how he developed a nose for value where others can only smell trouble. His gift for detecting value seems uncanny. His stories bring to mind the kid who, waking up on his fourth birthday to find a big pile of manure in the yard, dances around it crying, "I'm pretty sure there's a pony in there somewhere!"

All people are different, a truism we quickly discern as children, comparing ourselves to siblings. It's evident in grade school, on the sports field, in the boardroom. Even if we shared Bruce Hendry's desire and determination, even if we took his pointers to heart, how many of us would learn the art of knowing which pile had a pony in it? As the story of Bruce makes clear, some learning differences matter more than others. But which differences? That's what we'll explore in the rest of this chapter.

One difference that appears to matter a lot is how you see yourself and your abilities.

As the maxim goes, "Whether you think you can or you think you can't, you're right." The work of Carol Dweck, described in Chapter 7, goes a long way toward validating this sentiment. So does a *Fortune* article of a few years ago that tells of a seeming contradiction, the stories of people with dyslexia who have become high achievers in business and other fields despite their learning disabilities. Richard Branson, of Virgin Records and Virgin Atlantic Airways, quit school at sixteen to start and run businesses now worth billions; Diane Swonk is one of the top economic forecasters in the United States; Craig

McCaw is a pioneer of the cellular phone industry; Paul Orfa-lea founded Kinko's. These achievers and others, when asked, told their stories of overcoming adversity. All had trouble in school and with the accepted methods of learning, most were mislabeled low IQ, some were held back or shunted into classes for the mentally retarded, and nearly all were supported by parents, tutors, and mentors who believed in them. Branson recalled, "At some point, I think I decided that being dyslexic was better than being stupid." There, in a phrase, Branson's personal narrative of exceptionalism.[3]

The stories we create to understand ourselves become the narratives of our lives, explaining the accidents and choices that have brought us where we are: what I'm good at, what I care about most, and where I'm headed. If you're among the last kids standing on the sidelines as the softball teams are chosen up, the way you understand your place in the world likely changes a little, shaping your sense of ability and the subsequent paths you take.

What you tell yourself about your ability plays a part in shaping the ways you learn and perform–how hard you apply yourself, for example, or your tolerance for risk-taking and your willingness to persevere in the face of difficulty. But differences in skills, and your ability to convert new knowledge into building blocks for further learning, also shape your routes to success. Your finesse at softball, for example, depends on a constellation of different skills, like your ability to hit the ball, run the bases, and field and throw the ball. Moreover, skill on the playing field is not a prerequisite for becoming a star in the sport in a different capacity. Many of the best managers and coaches in pro sports were mediocre or poor players but happen to be exceptional students of their games. Although Tony LaRussa's career as a baseball player was short and un-distinguished, he went on to manage ball teams with remarkable success. When he retired, having chalked up six American and National League championships and three World Series titles, he was hailed as one of the greatest managers of all time.

Each of us has a large basket of resources in the form of aptitudes, prior knowledge, intelligence, interests, and sense of personal empowerment that shape how we learn and how we overcome our shortcomings. Some of these differences matter a lot—for example, our ability to abstract underlying principles from new experiences and to convert new knowledge into mental structures. Other differences we may think count for a lot, for example having a verbal or visual learning style, actually don't.

On any list of differences that matter most for learning, the level of *language fluency and reading ability* will be at or near the top. While some kinds of difficulties that require increased cognitive effort can strengthen learning, not all difficulties we face have that effect. If the additional effort required to overcome the deficit does not contribute to more robust learning, it's not desirable. An example is the poor reader who cannot hold onto the thread of a text while deciphering individual words in a sentence. This is the case with dyslexia, and while dyslexia is not the only cause of reading difficulties, it is one of the most common, estimated to affect some 15 percent of the population. It results from anomalous neural development during pregnancy that interferes with the ability to read by disrupting the brain's capacity to link letters to the sounds they make, which is essential for word recognition. People don't get over dyslexia, but with help they can learn to work with and around the problems it poses. The most successful programs emphasize practice at manipulating phonemes, building vocabulary, increasing comprehension, and improving fluency of reading. Neurologists and psychologists emphasize the importance of diagnosing dyslexia early and working with children before the third grade while the brain is still quite plastic and potentially more malleable, enabling the rerouting of neural circuits.

Dyslexia is far more common among prison inmates than the general population, as a result of a series of bad turns that often begin when children who can't read fall into a pattern of failure in school and develop low self-esteem. Some of them turn to bullying or other forms of antisocial behavior to compensate, and this strategy, if left unaddressed, can escalate into criminality.

While it is difficult for learners with dyslexia to gain essential reading skills and this disadvantage can create a constellation of other learning difficulties, the high achievers interviewed for the *Fortune* article argue that some people with dyslexia seem to possess, or to develop, a greater capacity for creativity and problem solving, whether as a result of their neural wiring or the necessity they face to find ways to compensate for their disability. To succeed, many of those interviewed reported that they had to learn at an early age how to grasp the big picture rather than struggling to decipher the component parts, how to think outside the box, how to act strategically, and how to manage risk taking—skills of necessity that, once learned, gave them a decided leg up later in their careers. Some of these skills may indeed have a neurological basis. Experiments by Gadi Geiger and Jerome Lettvin at Massachusetts Institute of Technology have found that individuals with dyslexia do poorly at interpreting information in their visual field of focus when compared to those without dyslexia. However, they significantly outperform others in their ability to interpret information from their peripheral vision, suggesting that a superior ability to grasp the big picture might have its origins in the brain's synaptic wiring.[4]

There's an enormous body of literature on dyslexia, which we won't delve into here beyond acknowledging that some neurological differences can count for a lot in how we learn, and for some subset of these individuals, a combination of high motivation, focused and sustained personal support, and compensating skills or "intelligences" have enabled them to thrive.

Belief in the *learning styles* credo is pervasive. Assessing students' learning styles has been recommended at all levels of education, and teachers are urged to offer classroom material in many different ways so that each student can take it in the way he or she is best equipped to learn it. Learning styles theory has taken root in management development, as well as in vocational and professional settings, including the training of military pilots, health care workers, municipal police, and beyond. A report on a 2004 survey conducted for Britain's Learning and Skills Research Centre compares more than seventy distinct learning styles theories currently being offered in the marketplace, each with its companion assessment instruments to diagnose a person's particular style. The report's authors characterize the purveyors of these instruments as an industry bedeviled by vested interests that tout "a bedlam of contradictory claims" and express concerns about the temptation to classify, label, and stereotype individuals. The authors relate an incident at a conference where a student who had completed an assessment instrument reported back: "I learned that I was a low auditory, kinesthetic learner. So there's no point in me reading a book or listening to anyone for more than a few minutes."[5] The wrongheadedness of this conclusion is manifold. It's not supported by science, and it instills a corrosive, misguided sense of diminished potential.

Notwithstanding the sheer number and variety of learning styles models, if you narrow the field to those that are most widely accepted you still fail to find a consistent theoretical pattern. An approach called VARK, advocated by Neil Fleming, differentiates people according to whether they prefer to learn through experiences that are primarily visual, auditory, reading, or kinesthetic (i.e., moving, touching, and active exploration). According to Fleming, VARK describes only one aspect of a person's learning style, which in its entirety consists of eighteen different dimensions, including preferences in temperature, light, food intake, biorhythms, and working with others versus working alone.

Other learning styles theories and materials are based on rather different dimensions. One commonly used inventory, based on the work of Kenneth Dunn and Rita Dunn, assesses six different aspects of an individual's learning style: environmental, emotional, sociological, perceptual, physiological, and psychological. Still other models assess styles along such dimensions as these:

- Concrete versus abstract styles of perceiving
- Active experimentation versus reflective observation modes of processing
- Random versus sequential styles of organizing

The Honey and Mumford Learning Styles Questionnaire, which is popular in managerial settings, helps employees determine whether their styles are predominantly "activist," "reflector," "theorist," or "pragmatist" and to improve in the areas where they score low so as to become more versatile learners.

The simple fact that different theories embrace such wildly discrepant dimensions gives cause for concern about their scientific underpinnings. While it's true that most all of us have a decided preference for how we like to learn new material, the premise behind learning styles is that we *learn better* when the mode of presentation matches the particular style in which an individual is best *able* to learn. That is the critical claim.

In 2008 the cognitive psychologists Harold Pashler, Mark McDaniel, Doug Rohrer, and Bob Bjork were commissioned to conduct a review to determine whether this critical claim is supported by scientific evidence. The team set out to answer two questions. First, what forms of evidence are needed for institutions to justify basing their instructional styles on assessments of students' or employees' learning styles? For the results to be credible, the team determined that a study would need to have several attributes. Initially, students must be divided into groups according to their learning styles. Then they must be randomly assigned to different classrooms teaching the same material but offering it through different instructional methods. Afterward, all the students must take the same test. The test must show that students with a particular learning style (e.g., visual learners) did the best when they received instruction in their own learning style (visual) relative to instruction in a different style (auditory); in addition, the other types of learners must be shown to profit more from their style of instruction than another style (auditory learners learning better from auditory than from visual presentation).

The second question the team asked was whether this kind of evidence existed. The answer was no. They found very few studies designed to be capable of testing the validity of learning styles theory in education, and of those, they found that virtually none validate it and several flatly contradict it. Moreover, their review showed that it is more important that the mode of instruction match the nature of the *subject* being taught: visual instruction for geometry and geography, verbal instruction for poetry, and so on. When instructional style matches the nature of the content, all learners learn better, regardless of their differing preferences for how the material is taught.

The fact that the evidence is not there to validate learning styles theory doesn't mean that all theories are wrong. Learning styles theories take many forms. Some may be valid. But if so, we can't know which: because the number of rigorous studies is extremely small, the research base does not exist to answer the question. On the basis of their findings, Pashler and his colleagues argued that the evidence currently available does not justify the huge investment of time and money that would be needed to assess students and restructure instruction around learning styles. Until such evidence is produced, it makes more sense to emphasize the instructional techniques, like those outlined in this book, that have been validated by research as benefiting learners regardless of their style preferences.[6]

Successful Intelligence

Intelligence is a learning difference that we do know matters, but what exactly is it? Every human society has a concept that corresponds to the idea of intelligence in our culture. The problem of how to define and measure intelligence in a way that accounts for people's intellectual horsepower and provides a fair indicator of their potential has been with us for over a hundred years, with psychologists trying to measure this construct since early in the twentieth century. Psychologists today generally accept that individuals possess at least two kinds of intelligence. *Fluid* intelligence is the ability to reason, see relationships, think abstractly, and hold information in mind while working on a problem; *crystallized* intelligence is one's accumulated knowledge of the world and the procedures or mental models one has developed from past learning and experience. Together, these two kinds of intelligence enable us to learn, reason, and solve problems.[7]

Traditionally, IQ tests have been used to measure individuals' logical and verbal potential. These tests assign an Intelligence Quotient, which denotes the ratio of mental age to physical age, times 100. That is, an eight-year-old who can solve problems on a test that most ten-year-olds can solve has an IQ of 125 (10 divided by 8, times 100). It used to be thought that IQ was fixed from birth, but traditional notions of intellectual capacity are being challenged.

One countervailing idea, put forward by the psychologist Howard Gardner to account for the broad variety in people's abilities, is the hypothesis that humans have as many as eight different kinds of intelligence:

Logical-mathematical intelligence: ability to think critically, work with numbers and abstractions, and the like;

Spatial intelligence: three-dimensional judgment and the ability to visualize with the mind's eye;

Linguistic intelligence: ability to work with words and languages;

Kinesthetic intelligence: physical dexterity and control of one's body;

Musical intelligence: sensitivity to sounds, rhythms, tones, and music;

Interpersonal intelligence: ability to "read" other people and work with them effectively;

Intrapersonal intelligence: ability to understand one's self and make accurate judgments of one's knowledge, abilities, and effectiveness;

Naturalistic intelligence: the ability to discriminate and relate to one's natural surroundings (for example, the kinds of
intelligence invoked by a gardener, hunter, or chef).

Gardner's ideas are attractive for many reasons, not the
least because they attempt to explain human differences that
we can observe but cannot account for with modern, Western
definitions of intelligence with their focus on language and
logic abilities. As with learning styles theory, the multiple intelligences model has helped educators to diversify the kinds
of learning experiences they offer. Unlike learning styles, which
can have the perverse effect of causing individuals to perceive
their learning abilities as limited, multiple intelligences theory
elevates the sheer variety of tools in our native toolkit. What
both theories lack is an underpinning of empirical validation,
a problem Gardner himself recognizes, acknowledging that
determining one's particular mix of intelligences is more an
art than a science.[8]

While Gardner helpfully expands our notion of intelligence,
the psychologist Robert J. Sternberg helpfully distills it again.
Rather than eight intelligences, Sternberg's model proposes
three: analytical, creative, and practical. Further, unlike Gardner's theory, Sternberg's is supported by empirical research.[9]

One of Sternberg's studies of particular interest to the question of how we measure intelligence was carried out in rural
Kenya, where he and his associates looked at children's informal knowledge of herbal medicines. Regular use of these
medicines is an important part of Kenyans' daily lives. This
knowledge is not taught in schools or assessed by tests, but
children who can identify the herbs and who know their appropriate uses and dosages are better adapted to succeed in
their environment than children without that knowledge. The
children who performed *best* on tests of this indigenous informal knowledge did *worst* relative to their peers on tests of the

formal academic subjects taught in school and, in Sternberg's words, appeared to be "stupid" by the metric of the formal tests. How to reconcile the discrepancy? Sternberg suggests that the children who excelled at indigenous knowledge came from families who valued such practical knowledge more highly than the families of the children who excelled at the academics taught in school. Children whose environments prized one kind of learning over another (practical over academic, in the case of the families who taught their children about herbs) were at a lower level of knowledge in the academic areas not emphasized by their environment. Other families placed more value on the analytic (school-based) information and less on the practical herbal knowledge.

There are two important ideas here. First, traditional measures of intelligence failed to account for environmental differences; there is no reason to suspect that kids who excelled at informal, indigenous knowledge can't catch up to or even surpass their peers in academic learning when given the appropriate opportunities. Second, for the kids whose environments emphasized indigenous knowledge, the mastery of academics is still developing. In Sternberg's view, we're all in a state of developing expertise, and any test that measures only what we know at any given moment is a static measure that tells us nothing about our *potential* in the realm the test measures.

Two other quick stories Sternberg cites are useful here. One is a series of studies of orphaned children in Brazil who must learn to start and run street businesses if they are to survive. Motivation is high; if they turn to theft as a means to sustain themselves, they risk running afoul of the death squads. These children, who are doing the math required in order to run successful businesses, cannot do the same math when the problems are presented in an abstract, paper-and-pencil format. Sternberg argues that this result makes sense when viewed from the standpoint of developing expertise: the children live in an environment that emphasizes practical skills, not academic, and it's the practical exigencies that determine the substance and form of the learning.[10]

The other story is about seasoned, expert handicappers at horse tracks who devise highly complex mental models for betting on horses but who measure only average on standard IQ tests. Their handicapping models were tested against those devised by less expert handicappers with equivalent IQs. Handicapping requires comparing horses against a long list of variables for each horse, such as its lifetime earnings, its lifetime speed, the races where it came in the money, the ability of its jockey in the current race, and a dozen characteristics of each of its prior races. Just to predict the speed with which a horse would run the final quarter mile, the experts relied on a complex mental model involving as many as seven variables. The study found that IQ is unrelated to handicapping ability, and "whatever it is that an IQ test measures, it is not the ability to engage in cognitively complex forms of multivariate reasoning."[11]

Into this void Robert Sternberg has introduced his three-part theory of successful intelligence. *Analytical* intelligence is our ability to complete problem-solving tasks such as those typically contained in tests; *creative* intelligence is our ability to synthesize and apply existing knowledge and skills to deal with new and unusual situations; *practical* intelligence is our ability to adapt to everyday life—to understand what needs to be done in a specific setting and then do it; what we call street smarts. Different cultures and learning situations draw on these intelligences differently, and much of what's required to succeed in a particular situation is not measured by standard IQ or aptitude tests, which can miss critical competencies.

Dynamic Testing

Robert Sternberg and Elena Grigorenko have proposed the idea of using testing to assess ability in a dynamic manner. Sternberg's concept of developing expertise holds that with continued experience in a field we are always moving from a lower state of competence to a higher one. His concept also holds that standardized tests can't accurately rate our potential because what they reveal is limited to a static report of where we are on the learning continuum at the time the test is given. In tandem with Sternberg's three-part model of intelligence, he and Grigorenko have proposed a shift away from static tests and replacing them with what they call dynamic testing: determining the state of one's expertise; refocusing learning on areas of low performance; follow-up testing to measure the improvement and to refocus learning so as to keep raising expertise. Thus, a test may assess a weakness, but rather than assuming that the weakness indicates a fixed inability, you interpret it as a lack of skill or knowledge that can be remedied. Dynamic testing has two advantages over standard testing. It focuses the learner and teacher on areas that need to be brought up rather than on areas of accomplishment, and the ability to measure a learner's progress from one test to the next provides a truer gauge of his or her learning potential.

Dynamic testing does not assume one must adapt to some kind of fixed learning limitation but offers an assessment of where one's knowledge or performance stands on some dimension and how one needs to move forward to succeed: what do I need to learn in order to improve? That is, where aptitude tests and much of learning styles theory tend to emphasize our strengths and encourage us to focus on them, dynamic testing helps us to discover our weaknesses and correct them.

In the school of life experience, setbacks show us where we need to do better. We can steer clear of similar challenges in the future, or we can redouble our efforts to master them, broadening our capacities and expertise. Bruce Hendry's experiences investing in rental property and in the stock market dealt him setbacks, and the lessons he took away were essential elements of his education: to be skeptical when somebody's trying to sell him something, to figure out the right questions, and to learn how to go dig out the answers. That's developing expertise.

Dynamic testing has three steps.

Step 1: a test of some kind—perhaps an experience or a paper exam—shows me where I come up short in knowledge or a skill.

Step 2: I dedicate myself to becoming more competent, using reflection, practice, spacing, and the other techniques of effective learning.

Step 3: I test myself again, paying attention to what works better now but also, and especially, to where I still need more work.

When we take our first steps as toddlers, we are engaging in dynamic testing. When you write your first short story, put it in front of your writers' group for feedback, and then revise and bring it back, you're engaging in dynamic testing, learning the writer's craft and getting a sense of your potential. The upper limits of your performance in any cognitive or manual skill may be set by factors beyond your control, such as your intelligence and the natural limits of your ability, but most of us can learn to perform nearer to our full potential in most areas by discovering our weaknesses and working to bring them up.[12]

Structure Building

There do appear to be cognitive differences in how we learn, though not the ones recommended by advocates of learning styles. One of these differences is the idea mentioned earlier that psychologists call structure building: the act, as we encounter new material, of extracting the salient ideas and constructing a coherent mental framework out of them. These frameworks are sometimes called mental models or mental maps. High structure-builders learn new material better than low structure-builders. The latter have difficulty setting aside irrelevant or competing information, and as a result they tend to hang on to too many concepts to be condensed into a workable model (or overall structure) that can serve as a foundation for further learning.

The theory of structure building bears some resemblance to a village built of Lego blocks. Suppose you're taking a survey course in a new subject. You start with a textbook full of ideas, and you set out to build a coherent mental model of the knowledge they contain. In our Lego analogy, you start with a box full of Lego pieces, and you set out to build the town that's pictured on the box cover. You dump out the pieces and sort them into a handful of piles. First you lay out the streets and sidewalks that define the perimeter of the city and the distinct places within it. Then you sort the remaining pieces according to the elements they compose: apartment complex, school, hospital, stadium, mall, fire station. Each of these elements is like a central idea in the textbook, and each takes more shape and nuance as added pieces snap into place. Together, these central ideas form the larger structure of the village.

Now suppose that your brother has used this Lego set before and dumped some pieces into the box from another set.

As you find pieces, some might not fit with your building blocks, and you can put them aside as extraneous. Or you may discover that some of the new pieces can be used to form a substructure of an existing building block, giving it more depth and definition (porches, patios, and back decks as substructures of apartments; streetlights, hydrants, and boulevard trees as substructures of streets). You happily add these pieces to your village, even though the original designers of the set had not planned on this sort of thing. High structure-builders develop the skill to identify foundational concepts and their key building blocks and to sort new information based on whether it adds to the larger structure and one's knowledge or is extraneous and can be put aside. By contrast, low structure-builders struggle in figuring out and sticking with an overarching structure and knowing what information needs to fit into it and what ought to be discarded. Structure building is a form of conscious and subconscious discipline: stuff fits or it doesn't; it adds nuance, capacity and meaning, or it obscures and overfreights.

A simpler analogy might be a friend who wants to tell you a rare story about this four-year-old boy she knows: she mentions who the mother is, how they became friends in their book club, finally mentioning that the mother, by coincidence, had a large load of manure delivered for her garden on the morning of the boy's birthday—the mother's an incredible gardener, her eggplants took a ribbon at the county fair and got her an interview on morning radio, and she gets her manure from that widowed guy in your church who raises the Clydesdale horses and whose son is married to—and so on and so on. Your friend cannot winnow the main ideas from the blizzard of irrelevant associations, and the story is lost on the listener. Story, too, is structure.

Our understanding of structure building as a cognitive difference in learning is still in the early stages: is low structure-building the result of a faulty cognitive mechanism, or is structure-building a skill that some pick up naturally and others must be taught? We know that when questions are embedded in texts to help focus readers on the main ideas, the learning performance of low structure-builders improves to a level commensurate with high structure-builders. The embedded questions promote a more coherent representation of the text than low-structure readers can build on their own, thus bringing them up toward the level achieved by the high structure-builders.

What's happening in this situation remains an open question for now, but the implication for learners seems to reinforce a notion offered earlier by the neurosurgeon Mike Ebersold and the pediatric neurologist Doug Larsen: that cultivating the habit of reflecting on one's experiences, of making them into a story, strengthens learning. The theory of structure building may provide a clue as to why: that reflecting on what went right, what went wrong, and how might I do it differently next time helps me isolate key ideas, organize them into mental models, and apply them again in the future with an eye to improving and building on what I've learned.[13]

Rule versus Example Learning

Another cognitive difference that appears to matter is whether you are a "rule learner" or "example learner," and the distinction is somewhat akin to the one we just discussed. When studying different kinds of problems in a chemistry class, or specimens in a course on birds and how to identify them, rule learners tend to abstract the underlying principles or "rules" that differentiate the examples being studied. Later, when they encounter a new chemistry problem or bird specimen, they apply the rules as a means to classify it and select the appropriate solution or specimen box. Example learners tend to memorize the examples rather than the underlying principles. When they encounter an unfamiliar case, they lack a grasp of the rules needed to classify or solve it, so they generalize from the nearest example they can remember, even if it is not particularly relevant to the new case. However, example learners may improve at extracting underlying rules when they are asked to compare two different examples rather than focus on studying one example at a time. Likewise, they are more likely to discover the common solution to disparate problems if they first have to compare the problems and try to figure out the underlying similarities.

By way of an illustration, consider two different hypothetical problems faced by a learner. These are taken from research into rule learning. In one problem, a general's forces are set to attack a castle that is protected by a moat. Spies have learned that the bridges over the moat have been mined by the castle's commander. The mines are set to allow small groups to cross the bridges, so that the occupants of the castle can retrieve food and fuel. How can the general get a large force over the bridges to attack the castle without tripping the mines?

The other problem involves an inoperable tumor, which can be destroyed by focused radiation. However, the radiation must also pass through healthy tissue. A beam of sufficient intensity to destroy the tumor will damage the healthy tissue through which it passes. How can the tumor be destroyed without damaging healthy tissue?

In the studies, students have difficulty finding the solution to either of these problems unless they are instructed to look for similarities between them. When seeking similarities, many students notice that (1) both problems require a large force to be directed at a target, (2) the full force cannot be massed and delivered through a single route without an adverse outcome, and (3) smaller forces can be delivered to the target, but a small force is insufficient to solve the problem. By identifying these similarities, students often arrive at a strategy of dividing the larger force into smaller forces and sending these in through different routes to converge on the target and destroy it without setting off mines or damaging healthy tissue. Here's the payoff: after figuring out this common, underlying solution, students are then able to go on to solve a variety of different convergence problems.[14]

As with high and low structure-builders, our understanding of rule versus example learners is very preliminary. However, we know that high structure-builders and rule learners are more successful in transferring their learning to unfamiliar situations than are low structure-builders and example learners. You might wonder if the tendency to be a high structure-builder is correlated with the tendency to be a rule learner. Unfortunately, research is not yet available to answer this question.

You can see the development of structure-building and rule-learning skills in a child's ability to tell a joke. A three-year-old probably cannot deliver a knock-knock joke, because he lacks an understanding of structure. You reply "Who's there?" and he jumps to the punch line: "Door is locked, I can't get in!" He doesn't understand the importance, after "Who's there?", of replying "Doris" to set up the joke. But by the time he's five, he has become a knock-knock virtuoso: he has memorized the structure. Nonetheless, at five he's not yet adept at other kinds of jokes because he hasn't yet learned the essential element that makes jokes work, which, of course, is the "rule" that a punch line of any kind needs a setup, explicit or implied.[15]

If you consider Bruce Hendry's early lesson in the high value of a suitcase full of scarce fireworks, you can see how, when he looks at boxcars many years later, he's working with the same supply-and-demand building block, but within a much more complex model that employs other blocks of knowledge that he has constructed over the years to address concepts of credit risk, business cycles, and the processes of bankruptcy. Why are boxcars in surplus? Because tax incentives to investors had encouraged too much money to flow into their production. What's a boxcar worth? They cost $42,000 each to build and were in like-new condition, as they had been some of the last ones built. He researched the lifespan of a boxcar and its scrap value and looked at the lease contracts. Even if all his cars stood idle, the lease payments would pay a pretty yield on his investment while the glut worked through the system and the market turned around.

Had we been there, we would have bought boxcars, too. Or so we'd like to think. But it's not like filling a satchel with fireworks, even if the underlying principle of supply and demand is the same. You had to buy the boxcars right, and understand the way to go about it. What in lay terms we call *knowhow*. Knowledge is not knowhow until you understand the underlying principles at work and can fit them together into a structure larger than the sum of its parts. Knowhow is learning that enables you to *go do*.

The Takeaway

Given what we know about learning differences, what's the takeaway?

Be the one in charge. There's an old truism from sales school that says you can't shoot a deer from the lodge. The same goes for learning: you have to suit up, get out the door, and find what you're after. Mastery, especially of complex ideas, skills, and processes, is a quest. It is not a grade on a test, something bestowed by a coach, or a quality that simply seeps into your being with old age and gray hair.

Embrace the notion of successful intelligence. Go wide: don't roost in a pigeonhole of your preferred learning style but take command of your resources and tap all of your "intelligences" to master the knowledge or skill you want to possess. Describe what you want to know, do, or accomplish. Then list the competencies required, what you need to learn, and where you can find the knowledge or skill. Then go get it.

Consider your expertise to be in a state of continuing development, practice dynamic testing as a learning strategy to discover your weaknesses, and focus on improving yourself in those areas. It's smart to build on your strengths, but you will become ever more competent and versatile if you also use testing and trial and error to continue to improve in the areas where your knowledge or performance are not pulling their weight.

Adopt active learning strategies like retrieval practice, spacing, and interleaving. Be aggressive. Like those with dyslexia who have become high achievers, develop workarounds or compensating skills for impediments or holes in your aptitudes.

Don't rely on what feels best: like a good pilot checking his instruments, use quizzing, peer review, and the other tools described in Chapter 5 to make sure your judgment of what you know and can do is accurate, and that your strategies are moving you toward your goals.

Don't assume that you're doing something wrong if the learning feels hard. Remember that difficulties you can overcome with greater cognitive effort will more than repay you in the depth and durability of your learning.

Distill the underlying principles; build the structure. If you're an example learner, study examples two at a time or more, rather than one by one, asking yourself in what ways they are alike and different. Are the differences such that they require different solutions, or are the similarities such that they respond to a common solution?

Break your idea or desired competency down into its component parts. If you think you are a low structure-builder or an example learner trying to learn new material, pause periodically and ask what the central ideas are, what the rules are. Describe each idea and recall the related points. Which are the big ideas, and which are supporting concepts or nuances? If you were to test yourself on the main ideas, how would you describe them?

What kind of scaffold or framework can you imagine that holds these central ideas together? If we borrowed the winding stair metaphor as a structure for Bruce Hendry's investment model, it might work something like this. Spiral stairs have three parts: a center post, treads, and risers. Let's say the center post is the thing that connects us from where we are (down here) to where we want to be (up there): it's the investment opportunity. Each tread is an element of the deal that protects us from losing money and dropping back, and each riser is an element that lifts us up a notch. Treads and risers must both be present for the stairs to function and for a deal to be attractive. Knowing the scrap value of boxcars is a tread—Bruce knows he won't get less than that for his investment. Another tread is the guaranteed lease income while his capital is tied up. What are some risers? Impending scarcity, which will raise values. The like-new condition of the cars, which is latent value. A deal that doesn't have treads and risers will not protect the downside or reliably deliver the upside.

Structure is all around us and available to us through the poet's medium of metaphor. A tree, with its roots, trunk, and branches. A river. A village, encompassing streets and blocks, houses and stores and offices. The structure of the village explains how these elements are interconnected so that the village has a life and a significance that would not exist if these elements were scattered randomly across an empty landscape.

By abstracting the underlying rules and piecing them into a structure, you go for more than knowledge. You go for know-how. And that kind of mastery will put you ahead.

7

Increase Your Abilities

IN A FAMOUS study from the 1970s, a researcher showed nursery school children one at a time into a room with no distractions except for a marshmallow resting on a tray on a desk. As the researcher left the room, the child was told he could eat the marshmallow now, or, if he waited for fifteen minutes, he would be rewarded with a second marshmallow.

Walter Mischel and his graduate students observed through a mirror as the children faced their dilemma. Some popped the marshmallow into their mouths the moment the researcher left, but others were able to wait. To help themselves hold back, these kids tried anything they could think of. They "covered their eyes with their hands, rested their heads on their arms, . . . talked to themselves, sang, invented games with their hands and feet, and even tried to fall asleep," to avert their eyes and divert themselves from the reward.

Of more than six hundred children who took part in the experiment, only one-third succeeded in resisting temptation long enough to get the second marshmallow.

A series of follow-up studies, the most recent in 2011, found that the nursery school children who had been more successful in delaying gratification in this exercise grew up to be more successful in school and in their careers.

The marshmallow study is sublime in its simplicity and as a metaphor for life. We are born with the gift of our genes, but to a surprising degree our success is also determined by focus and self-discipline, which are the offspring of motivation and one's sense of personal empowerment.[1]

Consider James Paterson, a spirited, thirty-something Welshman, and his unwitting seduction by the power of mnemonic devices and the world of memory competitions. The word "mnemonic" is from the Greek word for memory. Mnemonic devices are mental tools that can take many forms but generally are used to help hold a large volume of new material in memory, cued for ready recall.

James first learned of mnemonics when one of his university instructors fleetingly mentioned their utility during a lecture. He went straight home, searched the web, bought a book. If he could learn these techniques, he figured, he could memorize his classwork in short order and have a lot more time to hang out with friends. He started practicing memorizing things: names and dates for his psychology classes and the textbook page numbers where they were cited. He also practiced parlor tricks, like memorizing the sequence of playing cards in a shuffled deck or strings of random numbers read from lists made up by friends. He spent long hours honing his techniques, becoming adept and the life of the party among his social set. The year was 2006, and when he learned of a memory competition to be held in Cambridge, England, he decided on a lark to enter it. There he surprised himself by taking first place in the beginner category, a performance for which he pocketed a cool 1,000 euros. He was hooked. Figuring he had nothing to lose by taking a flyer, he went on to compete in his first World Memory Championships, in London, that same year.

With mnemonics James had figured to pocket some easy facts to ace his exams without spending the time and effort to fully master the material, but he discovered something entirely different, as we will recount shortly.

Memory athletes, as these competitors call themselves, all get their start in different ways. Nelson Dellis, the 2012 US Memory Champion, began after his grandmother died of Alzheimer's disease. Nelson watched her decline over time, with her ability to remember being the first cognitive faculty to go. Although only in his twenties, Nelson wondered if he were destined for the same fate and what he could do about it. He discovered mind sports, hoping that if he could develop his memory to great capacity, then he might have reserves if the disease did strike him later in life. Nelson is another memory athlete on his way up, and he has started a Foundation, Climb for Memory, to raise awareness about and funds for research for this terrible disease. Nelson also climbs mountains (twice reaching near the summit of Mt. Everest), hence the name. We meet others in this chapter who, like Paterson and Dellis, have sought successfully to raise their cognitive abilities in one way or another.

The brain is remarkably plastic, to use the term applied in neuroscience, even into old age for most people. In this chapter's discussion of raising intellectual abilities, we review some of the questions science is trying to answer about the brain's ability to change itself throughout life and people's ability to influence those changes and to raise their IQs. We then describe three known cognitive strategies for getting more out of the mental horsepower you've already got.

In a sense the infant brain is like the infant nation. When John Fremont arrived with his expeditionary force at Pueblo de Los Angeles in 1846 in the US campaign to take western territory from Mexico, he had no way to report his progress to President James Polk in Washington except to send his scout, Kit Carson, across the continent on his mule—a round-trip of nearly six thousand miles over mountains, deserts, wilderness and prairies. Fremont pressed Carson to whip himself into a lather, not even to stop to shoot game along the way but to sustain himself by eating the mules as they broke down and needed replacing. That such a journey would be required reveals the undeveloped state of the country. The five-foot-four-inch, 140-pound Carson was the best we had for getting word from one coast to the other. Despite the continent's boundless natural assets, the fledgling nation had little in the way of *capability*. To become mighty, it would need cities, universities, factories, farms and seaports, and the roads, trains, and telegraph lines to connect them.[2]

It's the same with a brain. We come into the world endowed with the raw material of our genes, but we become capable through the learning and development of mental models and neural pathways that enable us to reason, solve, and create. We have been raised to think that the brain is hardwired and our intellectual potential is more or less set from birth. We now know otherwise. Average IQs have risen over the past century with changes in living conditions. When people suffer brain damage from strokes or accidents, scientists have seen the brain somehow reassign duties so that adjacent networks of neurons take over the work of damaged areas, enabling people to regain lost capacities. Competitions between "memory athletes" like James Paterson and Nelson Dellis have emerged as an international sport among people who have trained themselves to perform astonishing acts of recall. Expert performance in medicine, science, music, chess, or sports has been shown to be the product not just of innate gifts, as had long been thought, but of skills laid down layer by layer, through thousands of hours of dedicated practice. In short, research and the modern record have shown that we and our brains are capable of much greater feats than scientists would have thought possible even a few decades ago.

Neuroplasticity

All knowledge and memory are physiological phenomena, held in our neurons and neural pathways. The idea that the brain is not hardwired but plastic, mutable, something that reorganizes itself with each new task, is a recent revelation, and we are just at the frontiers of understanding what it means and how it works.

In a helpful review of the neuroscience, John T. Bruer took on this question as it relates to the initial development and stabilization of the brain's circuitry and our ability to bolster the intellectual ability of our children through early stimulation. We're born with about 100 billion nerve cells, called neurons. A synapse is a connection between neurons, enabling them to pass signals. For a period shortly before and after birth, we undergo "an exuberant burst of synapse formation," in which the brain wires itself: the neurons sprout microscopic branches, called axons, that reach out in search of tiny nubs on other neurons, called dendrites. When axon meets dendrite, a synapse is formed. In order for some axons to find their target dendrites they must travel vast distances to complete the connections that make up our neural circuitry (a journey of such daunting scale and precision that Bruer likens it to finding one's way clear across the United States to a waiting partner on the opposite coast, not unlike Kit Carson's mission to President Polk for General Fremont). It's this circuitry that enables our senses, cognition, and motor skills, including learning and memory, and it is this circuitry that forms the possibilities and the limits of one's intellectual capacity.

The number of synapses peaks at the age of one or two, at about 50 percent higher than the average number we possess as adults. A plateau period follows that lasts until around puberty, whereupon this overabundance begins to decline as the brain goes through a period of synaptic pruning. We arrive at our adult complement at around age sixteen with a staggering number, thought to total about 150 trillion connections.

We don't know why the infant brain produces an overabundance of connections or how it subsequently determines which ones to prune. Some neuroscientists believe that the connections we don't use are the ones that fade and die away, a notion that would seem to manifest the "use it or lose it" principle and argue for the early stimulation of as many connections as possible in hopes of retaining them for life. Another theory suggests the burgeoning and winnowing is determined by genetics and we have little or no influence over which synapses survive and which do not.

"While children's brains acquire a tremendous amount of information during the early years," the neuroscientist Patricia Goldman-Rakic told the Education Commission of the States, most learning is acquired after synaptic formation stabilizes. "From the time a child enters first grade, through high school, college, and beyond, there is little change in the number of synapses. It is during the time when no, or little, synapse formation occurs that most learning takes place" and we develop adult-level skills in language, mathematics, and logic.[3] And it is likely during this period more than during infancy, in the view of the neuroscientist Harry T. Chugani, that experience and environmental stimulation fine-tune one's circuits and make one's neuronal architecture unique.[4] In a 2011 article, a team of British academics in the fields of psychology and sociology reviewed the evidence from neuroscience and concluded that the architecture and gross structure of the brain appear to be substantially determined by genes but that the fine structure of neural networks appears to be shaped by experience and to be capable of substantial modification.[5]

That the brain is mutable has become evident on many fronts. Norman Doidge, in his book *The Brain That Changes Itself*, looks at compelling cases of patients who have overcome severe impairments with the assistance of neurologists whose research and practice are advancing the frontiers of our understanding of neuroplasticity.

One of these was Paul Bach-y-Rita, who pioneered a device to help patients who have suffered damage to sensory organs. Bach-y-Rita's device enables them to regain lost skills by teaching the brain to respond to stimulation of other parts of their bodies, substituting one sensory system for another, much as a blind person can learn to navigate through echolocation, learning to "see" her surroundings by interpreting the differing sounds from the tap of a cane, or can learn to read through the sense of touch using Braille.[6]

One of Bach-y-Rita's patients had suffered damage to her vestibular system (how the inner ear senses balance and spatial orientation) that had left her so unbalanced that she was unable to stand, walk, or maintain her independence. Bach-y-Rita rigged a helmet with carpenters' levels attached to it and wired them to send impulses to a postage-stamp-sized strip of tape containing 144 microelectrodes placed on the woman's tongue. As she tilted her head, the electrodes sparkled on her tongue like effervescence, but in distinctive patterns reflecting the direction and angle of her head movements. Through practice wearing the device, the woman was gradually able to retrain her brain and vestibular system, recovering her sense of balance for longer and longer periods following the training sessions.

Another patient, a thirty-five-year-old man who had lost his sight at age thirteen, was outfitted with a small video camera mounted on a helmet and enabled to send pulses to the tongue. As Bach-y-Rita explained, the eyes are not what sees, the brain is. The eyes sense, and the brain interprets. The success of this device relies on the brain learning to interpret signals from the tongue as sight. The remarkable results were reported in the *New York Times*: The patient "found doorways, caught balls rolling toward him, and with his small daughter played a game of rock, paper and scissors for the first time in twenty years. [He] said that, with practice, the substituted sense gets better, 'as if the brain were rewiring itself.' "[7]

In yet another application, interesting in light of our earlier discussions of metacognition, stimulators are being attached to the chests of pilots to transmit cockpit instrument readings, helping the brain to sense changes in pitch and altitude that the pilot's vestibular system is unable to detect under certain flight conditions.

Neural cell bodies make up most of the part of our brains that scientists call the gray matter. What they call the white matter is made up of the wiring: the axons that connect to dendrites of other neural cell bodies, and the waxy myelin sheaths in which some axons are wrapped, like the plastic coating on a lamp cord. Both gray matter and white matter are the subject of intense scientific study, as we try to understand how the components that shape cognition and motor skills work and how they change through our lives, research that has been greatly advanced by recent leaps in brain imaging technology.

One ambitious effort is the Human Connectome Project, funded by the National Institutes of Health, to map the connections in the human brain. (The word "connectome" refers to the architecture of the human neurocircuitry in the same spirit that "genome" was coined for the map of the human genetic code.) The websites of participating research institutions show striking images of the fiber architecture of the brain, masses of wire-like human axons presented in neon colors to denote signal directions and bearing an uncanny resemblance to the massive wiring harnesses inside 1970s supercomputers. Early research findings are intriguing. One study, at the University of California, Los Angeles, compared the synaptic architecture of identical twins, whose genes are alike, and fraternal twins, who share only some genes. This study showed what others have suggested, that the speed of our mental abilities is determined by the robustness of our neural connections; that this robustness, at the initial stages, is largely determined by our genes, but that our neural circuitry does not mature as early as our physical development and instead continues to change and grow through our forties, fifties, and sixties. Part of the maturation of these connections is the gradual thickening of the myelin coating of the axons. Myelination generally starts at the backs of our brains and moves toward the front, reaching the frontal lobes as we grow into adulthood. The frontal lobes perform the executive functions of the brain and are the location of the processes of high-level reasoning and judgment, skills that are developed through experience.

The thickness of the myelin coating correlates with ability, and research strongly suggests that increased practice builds greater myelin along the related pathways, improving the strength and speed of the electrical signals and, as a result, performance. Increases in piano practice, for example, have shown correlated increases in the myelination of nerve fibers associated with finger movements and the cognitive processes that are involved in making music, changes that do not appear in nonmusicians.[8]

The study of habit formation provides an interesting view into neuroplasticity. The neural circuits we use when we take conscious action toward a goal are not the same ones we use when our actions have become automatic, the result of habit. The actions we take by habit are directed from a region located deeper in the brain, the basal ganglia. When we engage in extended training and repetition of some kinds of learning, notably motor skills and sequential tasks, our learning is thought to be recoded in this deeper region, the same area that controls subconscious actions such as eye movements. As a part of this process of recoding, the brain is thought to chunk motor and cognitive action sequences together so that they can be performed as a single unit, that is, without requiring a series of conscious decisions, which would substantially slow our responses. These sequences become reflexive. That is, they may start as actions we teach ourselves to take in pursuit of a goal, but they become automatic responses to stimuli. Some researchers have used the word "macro" (a simple computer app) to describe how this chunking functions as a form of highly efficient, consolidated learning. These theories about chunking as integral to the process of habit formation help explain the way in sports we develop the ability to respond to the rapid-fire unfolding of events faster than we're able to think them through, the way a musician's finger movements can outpace his conscious thoughts, or the way a chess player can learn to foresee the countless possible moves and implications presented by different configurations of the board. Most of us display the same talent when we type.

Another fundamental sign of the brain's enduring mutability is the discovery that the hippocampus, where we consolidate learning and memory, is able to generate new neurons throughout life. This phenomenon, called neurogenesis, is thought to play a central role in the brain's ability to recover from physical injury and in humans' lifelong ability to learn. The relationship of neurogenesis to learning and memory is a new field of inquiry, but already scientists have shown that the activity of associative learning (that is, of learning and remembering the relationship between unrelated items, such as names and faces) stimulates an increase in the creation of new neurons in the hippocampus. This rise in neurogenesis starts *before* the new learning activity is undertaken, suggesting the brain's intention to learn, and continues for a period *after* the learning activity, suggesting that neurogenesis plays a role in the consolidation of memory and the beneficial effects that spaced and effortful retrieval practice have on long-term retention.[9]

Of course, learning and memory are neural processes. The fact that retrieval practice, spacing, rehearsal, rule learning, and the construction of mental models improve learning and memory is evidence of neuroplasticity and is consistent with scientists' understanding of memory consolidation as an agent for increasing and strengthening the neural pathways by which one is later able to retrieve and apply learning. In the words of Ann and Richard Barnet, human intellectual development is "a lifelong dialogue between inherited tendencies and our life history."[10] The nature of that dialogue is the central question we explore in the rest of this chapter.

Is IQ Mutable?

IQ is a product of genes and environment. Compare it to height: it's mostly inherited, but over the decades as nutrition has improved, subsequent generations have grown taller. Likewise, IQs in every industrialized part of the world have shown a sustained rise since the start of standardized sampling in 1932, a phenomenon called the Flynn effect after the political scientist who first brought it to wide attention.[11] In the United States, the average IQ has risen eighteen points in the last sixty years. For any given age group, an IQ of 100 is the mean score of those taking the IQ tests, so the increase means that having an IQ of 100 today is the intelligence equivalent of those with an IQ 60 years ago of 118. It's the mean that has risen, and there are several theories why this is so, the principal one being that schools, culture (e.g., television), and nutrition have changed substantially in ways that affect people's verbal and math abilities as measured by the subtests that make up the IQ test.

Richard Nisbett, in his book *Intelligence and How to Get It,* discusses the pervasiveness of stimuli in modern society that didn't exist years ago, offering as one simple example a puzzle maze McDonald's included in its Happy Meals a few years ago that was more difficult than the mazes included in an IQ test for gifted children.[12] Nisbett also writes about "environmental multipliers," suggesting that a tall kid who goes out for basketball develops a proficiency in the sport that a shorter kid with the same aptitudes won't develop, just as a curious kid who goes for learning gets smarter than the equally bright but incurious kid who doesn't. The options for learning have expanded exponentially. It may be a very small genetic difference that makes one kid more curious than another, but the effect is multiplied in an environment where curiosity is easily piqued and readily satisfied.

Another environmental factor that shapes IQ is socioeconomic status and the increased stimulation and nurturing that are more generally available in families who have more resources and education. On average, children from affluent families test higher for IQ than children from impoverished families, and children from impoverished families who are adopted into affluent families score higher on IQ tests than those who are not, regardless of whether the birth parents were of high or low socioeconomic status.

The ability to raise IQ is fraught with controversy and the subject of countless studies reflecting wide disparities of scientific rigor. A comprehensive review published in 2013 of the extant research into raising intelligence in young children sheds helpful light on the issue, in part because of the strict criteria the authors established for determining which studies would qualify for consideration. The eligible studies had to draw from a general, nonclinical population; have a randomized, experimental design; consist of sustained interventions, not of one-shot treatments or simply of manipulations during the testing experience; and use a widely accepted, standardized measure of intelligence. The authors focused on experiments involving children from the prenatal period through age five, and the studies meeting their requirements involved over 37,000 participants.

What did they find? Nutrition affects IQ. Providing dietary supplements of fatty acids to pregnant women, breast-feeding women, and infants had the effect of increasing IQ by anywhere from 3.5 to 6.5 points. Certain fatty acids provide building blocks for nerve cell development that the body cannot produce by itself, and the theory behind the results is that these supplements support the creation of new synapses. Studies of other supplements, such as iron and B complex vitamins, strongly suggested benefits, but these need validation through further research before they can be considered definitive.

In the realm of environmental effects, the authors found that enrolling poor children in early education raises IQ by more than four points, and by more than seven if the intervention is based in a center instead of in the home, where stimulation is less consistently sustained. (Early education was defined as environmental enrichment and structured learning prior to enrollment in preschool.) More affluent children, who are presumed to have many of these benefits at home, might not show similar gains from enrolling in early education programs. In addition, no evidence supports the widely held notion that the younger children are when first enrolled in these programs the better the results. Rather, the evidence suggests, as John Bruer argues, that the earliest few years of life are not narrow windows for development that soon close.

Gains in IQ were found in several areas of cognitive training. When mothers in low-income homes were given the means to provide their children with educational tools, books, and puzzles and trained how to help their children learn to speak and identify objects in the home, the children showed IQ gains. When mothers of three-year-olds in low-income families were trained to talk to their children frequently and at length and to draw out the children with many open-ended questions, the children's IQs rose. Reading to a child age four or younger raises the child's IQ, especially if the child is an active participant in the reading, encouraged by the parent to elaborate. After age four, reading to the child does not raise

IQ but continues to accelerate the child's language development. Preschool boosts a child's IQ by more than four points, and if the school includes language training, by more than seven points. Again, there is no body of evidence supporting the conclusion that early education, preschool, or language training would show IQ gains in children from better-off families, where they already benefit from the advantages of a richer environment.[13]

Brain Training?

What about "brain training" games? We've seen a new kind of business emerge, pitching online games and videos promising to exercise your brain like a muscle, building your cognitive ability. These products are largely founded on the findings of one Swiss study, reported in 2008, which was very limited in scope and has not been replicated.[14] The study focused on improving "fluid intelligence": the facility for abstract reasoning, grasping unfamiliar relationships, and solving new kinds of problems. Fluid intelligence is one of two kinds of intelligence that make up IQ. The other is crystallized intelligence, the storehouse of knowledge we have accumulated through the years. It's clear that we can increase our crystallized intelligence through effective learning and memory strategies, but what about our fluid intelligence?

A key determiner of fluid intelligence is the capacity of a person's working memory—the number of new ideas and relationships that a person can hold in mind while working through a problem (especially with some amount of distraction). The focus of the Swiss study was to give participants tasks requiring increasingly difficult working memory challenges, holding two different stimuli in mind for progressively longer periods of distraction. One stimulus was a sequence of numerals. The other was a small square of light that appeared in varying locations on a screen. Both the numerals and the locations of the square changed every three seconds. The task was to decide—while viewing a sequence of changed numerals and repositioned squares—for each combination of numeral and square, whether it matched a combination that had been presented n items back in the series. The number n increased during the trials, making the challenge to working memory progressively more arduous.

All the participants were tested on fluid intelligence tasks at the outset of the study. Then they were given these increasingly difficult exercises of their working memory over periods ranging up to nineteen days. At the end of the training, they were retested for fluid intelligence. They all performed better than they had before the training, and those who had engaged in the training for the longest period showed the greatest improvement. These results showed for the first time that fluid intelligence can be increased through training.

What's the criticism?

The participants were few (only thirty-five) and were all recruited from a similar, highly intelligent population. Moreover, the study focused on only one training task, so it is unclear to what extent it might apply to other working-memory training tasks, or whether the results are really about working memory rather than some peculiarity of the particular training. Finally, the durability of the improved performance is unknown, and the results, as noted, have not been replicated by other studies. The ability to replicate empirical results is the bedrock of scientific theory. The website PsychFileDrawer .org keeps a list of the top twenty psychological research studies that the site's users would like to see replicated, and the Swiss study is the first on the list. A recent attempt whose results were published in 2013 failed to find any improvements to fluid intelligence as a result of replicating the exercises in the Swiss study. Interestingly, participants in the study believed that their mental capacities had been enhanced, a phenomenon the authors describe as illusory. However, the authors also acknowledge that an increased sense of self-efficacy can lead to greater persistence in solving difficult problems, encouraged by the belief that training has improved one's abilities.[15]

The brain is not a muscle, so strengthening one skill does not automatically strengthen others. Learning and memory strategies such as retrieval practice and the building of mental models are effective for enhancing intellectual abilities in the material or skills practiced, but the benefits don't extend to mastery of other material or skills. Studies of the brains of experts show enhanced myelination of the axons related to the area of expertise but not elsewhere in the brain. Observed myelination changes in piano virtuosos are specific to piano virtuosity. But the ability to make practice a habit *is* generalizable. To the extent that "brain training" improves one's efficacy and self-confidence, as the purveyors claim, the benefits are more likely the fruits of better habits, such as learning how to focus attention and persist at practice.

Richard Nisbett writes of environmental "multipliers" that can deliver a disproportionate effect from a small genetic predisposition—the kid who is genetically just a little bit more curious becomes significantly smarter if she's in an environment that feeds curiosity. Now stand that notion on its head. Since it's unlikely I'll be raising my IQ anytime soon, are there strategies or behaviors that can serve as *cognitive* "multipliers" to amp up the performance of the intelligence I've already got? Yes. Here are three: embracing a *growth mindset, practicing like an expert*, and *constructing memory cues*.

Growth Mindset

Let's return to the old saw "If you think you can, or you think you can't, you're right." If turns out there is more truth here than wit. Attitude counts for a lot. The studies of the psychologist Carol Dweck have gotten huge attention for showing just how big an impact one simple conviction can have on learning and performance: the belief that your level of intellectual ability is not fixed but rests to a large degree in your own hands.[16]

Dweck and her colleagues have replicated and expanded on their results in many studies. In one of the early experiments, she ran a workshop for low-performing seventh graders at a New York City junior high school, teaching them about the brain and about effective study techniques. Half the group also received a presentation on memory, but the other half were given an explanation of how the brain changes as a result of effortful learning: that when you try hard and learn something new, the brain forms new connections, and these new connections, over time, make you smarter. This group was told that intellectual development is not the natural unfolding of intelligence but results from the new connections that are formed through effort and learning. After the workshop, both groups of kids filtered back into their classwork. Their teachers were unaware that some had been taught that effortful learning changes the brain, but as the school year unfolded, those students adopted what Dweck calls a "growth mindset," a belief that their intelligence was largely within their own control, and they went on to become much more aggressive learners and higher achievers than students from the first group, who continued to hold the conventional view, what Dweck calls a "fixed mindset," that their intellectual ability was set at birth by the natural talents they were born with.

Dweck's research had been triggered by her curiosity over why some people become helpless when they encounter challenges and fail at them, whereas others respond to failure by trying new strategies and redoubling their effort. She found that a fundamental difference between the two responses lies in how a person attributes failure: those who attribute failure to their own inability—"I'm not intelligent"—become helpless. Those who interpret failure as the result of insufficient effort or an ineffective strategy dig deeper and try different approaches.

Dweck came to see that some students aim at *performance* goals, while others strive toward *learning* goals. In the first case, you're working to validate your ability. In the second, you're working to acquire new knowledge or skills. People with performance goals unconsciously limit their potential. If your focus is on validating or showing off your ability, you pick challenges you are confident you can meet. You want to look smart, so you do the same stunt over and over again. But if your goal is to increase your ability, you pick ever-increasing challenges, and you interpret setbacks as useful information that helps you to sharpen your focus, get more creative, and work harder. "If you want to demonstrate something over and over, 'ability' feels like something static that lies inside of you, whereas if you want to increase your ability, it feels dynamic and malleable," Dweck says. Learning goals trigger entirely different chains of thought and action from performance goals.[17]

Paradoxically, a focus on performance trips up some star athletes. Praised for being "naturals," they believe their performance is a result of innate gifts. If they're naturals, the idea goes, they shouldn't have to work hard to excel, and in fact many simply avoid practicing, because a need to practice is public evidence that their natural gifts are not good enough to cut the mustard after all. A focus on performance instead of on learning and growing causes people to hold back from risk taking or exposing their self-image to ridicule by putting themselves into situations where they have to break a sweat to deliver the critical outcome.

Dweck's work has extended into the realm of praise and the power it has in shaping the way people respond to challenges. Here's an example. A group of fifth grade students are individually given a puzzle to solve. Some of the students who solve the puzzle are praised for being smart; other students who solve it are praised for having worked hard. The students are then invited to choose another puzzle: either one of similar difficulty or one that's harder but that they would learn from by making the effort to try solving. A majority of the students who are praised for their smarts pick the easier puzzle; 90 percent of the kids praised for effort pick the harder one.

In a twist on this study, students get puzzles from two people, Tom and Bill. The puzzles Tom gives the students can be solved with effort, but the ones Bill gives them cannot be solved. Every student gets puzzles from both Tom and Bill. After working to solve the puzzles, some of the kids are praised for being smart, and some for their effort. In a second round, the kids get more puzzles from both Tom and Bill, and this time all the puzzles are solvable. Here's the surprise: of the students who were praised for being smart, few solved the puzzles they got from Bill, even though they were the same puzzles these students had solved earlier when they got them from Tom. For those who saw being considered smart as paramount, their failure to solve Bill's puzzles in the first round instilled a sense of defeat and helplessness.

When you praise for intelligence, kids get the message that being seen as smart is the name of the game. "Emphasizing effort gives a child a rare variable they can control," Dweck says. But "emphasizing natural intelligence takes it out of a child's control, and it provides no good recipe for responding to a failure."[18]

Paul Tough, in his recent book *How Children Succeed,* draws on Dweck's work and others' to make the case that our success is less dependent on IQ than on grit, curiosity, and persistence. The essential ingredient is encountering adversity in childhood and learning to overcome it. Tough writes that children in the lowest strata of society are so beset by challenges and starved of resources that they don't stand a chance of experiencing success. But, and here's another paradox, kids at the top of the heap, who are raised in cosseted settings, praised for being smart, bailed out of predicaments by helicopter parents, and never allowed to fail or overcome adversity on their own initiative, are also denied the character-building experiences essential for success later in life.[19] A kid who's born on third base and grows up thinking she hit a triple is unlikely to embrace the challenges that will enable her to discover her full potential. A focus on looking smart keeps a person from taking risks in life, the small ones that help people rise toward their aspirations, as well as the bold, visionary moves that lead to greatness. Failure, as Carol Dweck tells us, gives you useful information, and the opportunity to discover what you're capable of doing when you really set your mind to it.

The takeaway from Dweck, Tough, and their colleagues working in this field is that more than IQ, it's discipline, grit, and a growth mindset that imbue a person with the sense of possibility and the creativity and persistence needed for higher learning and success. "Study skills and learning skills are inert until they're powered by an active ingredient," Dweck says. The active ingredient is the simple but nonetheless profound realization that the power to increase your abilities lies largely within your own control.

Deliberate Practice

When you see stellar performances by an expert in any field—a pianist, chess player, golfer—perhaps you marvel at what natural talent must underlie their abilities, but expert performance does not usually rise out of some genetic predisposition or IQ advantage. It rises from thousands of hours of what Anders Ericsson calls sustained deliberate practice. If doing something repeatedly might be considered practice, deliberate practice is a different animal: it's goal directed, often solitary, and consists of repeated striving to reach beyond your current level of performance. Whatever the field, expert performance is thought to be garnered through the slow acquisition of a larger number of increasingly complex patterns, patterns that are used to store knowledge about which actions to take in a vast vocabulary of different situations. Witness a champion chess player. In studying the positions on a board, he can contemplate many alternative moves and the countless different directions each might precipitate. The striving, failure, problem solving, and renewed attempts that characterize deliberate practice build the new knowledge, physiological adaptations, and complex mental models required to attain ever higher levels.

When Michelangelo finally completed painting over 400 life size figures on the ceiling of the Sistine Chapel, he is reported to have written, "If people knew how hard I worked to get my mastery, it wouldn't seem so wonderful after all." What appeared to his admirers to have flowed from sheer genius had required four torturous years of work and dedication.[20]

Deliberate practice usually isn't enjoyable, and for most learners it requires a coach or trainer who can help identify areas of performance that need to be improved, help focus attention on specific aspects, and provide feedback to keep perception and judgment accurate. The effort and persistence of deliberate practice remodel the brain and physiology to accommodate higher performance, but achieving expertise in any field is particular to the field. It does not confer some kind of advantage or head start toward gaining expertise in another domain. A simple example of practice remodeling the brain is the treatment of focal hand dystonia, a syndrome affecting some guitarists and pianists whose repetitive playing has rewired their brains to think that two fingers have been fused into one. Through a series of challenging exercises, they can be helped gradually to retrain their fingers to move separately.

One reason that experts are sometimes perceived to possess an uncanny talent is that some can observe a complex performance in their field and later reconstruct from memory every aspect of that performance, in granular detail. Mozart was famous for being able to reconstruct complex musical scores after a single hearing. But this skill, Ericsson says, rises

not out of some sixth sense but from an expert's superior perception and memory within his domain, which are the result
of years of acquired skill and knowledge in that domain.
Most people who achieve expertise in a field are destined to
remain average performers in the other realms of life.

Ten thousand hours or ten years of practice was the average time the people Ericsson studied had invested to become
expert in their fields, and the best among them had spent the
larger percentage of those hours in solitary, deliberate practice. The central idea here is that expert performance is a
product of the quantity and the quality of practice, not of genetic predisposition, and that becoming expert is not beyond
the reach of normally gifted people who have the motivation,
time, and discipline to pursue it.

Memory Cues

Mnemonic devices, as we mentioned, are mental tools to help
hold material in memory, cued for ready recall. (Mnemosyne,
one of the nine Muses of Greek mythology, was the goddess
of memory.) Some examples of simple mnemonic devices are
acronyms, like "ROY G BIV" for the colors of the rainbow,
and reverse acronyms, as in "I Value Xylophones Like Cows
Dig Milk" for the ascending value of Roman numerals from
1 to 1000 (e.g., $V = 5$; $D = 500$).

A *memory palace* is a more complex type of mnemonic
device that is useful for organizing and holding larger volumes of material in memory. It's based on the *method of loci*,
which goes back to the ancient Greeks and involves associating mental images with a series of physical locations to help
cue memories. For example, you imagine yourself within a
space that is very familiar to you, like your home, and then
you associate prominent features of the space, like your easy

chair, with a visual image of something you want to remember. (When you think of your easy chair you may picture a limber yogi sitting there, to remind you to renew your yoga lessons.) The features of your home can be associated with a countless number of visual cues for retrieving memories later, when you simply take an imaginary walk through the house. If it's important to recall the material in a certain order, the cues can be sequenced along the route through your house. (The method of loci is also used to associate cues with features you encounter along a very familiar journey, like your walk to the corner store.)

As we write this passage, a group of students in Oxford, England, are constructing memory palaces to prepare for their A-level exams in psychology. Every week for six weeks, they and their instructor have visited a different café in town, where they have relaxed over coffee, familiarized themselves with the layout of the place, and discussed how they might imagine it occupied with vivid characters who will cue from memory important aspects of psychology that they will need to write about at exam time.

We'll come back to these students, but first a few more words about this technique, which is surprisingly effective and derives from the way imagery serves to contribute vividness and connective links to memory. Humans remember pictures more easily than words. (For example, the image of an elephant is easier to recall than the word "elephant.") So it stands to reason that associating vivid mental images with verbal or abstract material makes that material easier to retrieve from memory. A strong mental image can prove as secure and bountiful as a loaded stringer of fish. Tug on it, and a whole day's catch comes to the surface. When a friend is reminding you of a conversation with somebody the two of you met on a trip, you struggle to recall it. She tells you where the discussion happened, and you picture the place. Ah, yes, it all comes flooding back. Images cue memories.[21]

Mark Twain wrote about his personal experiences with this phenomenon in an article published by *Harper's*. In his days on the speaking circuit, Twain used a list of partial sentences to prompt himself through the different phases of his remarks, but he found the system unsatisfactory—when you glance at snippets of text, they all look alike. He experimented with alternatives, finally hitting on the idea of outlining his speech in a series of crude pencil sketches. The sketches did the job. A haystack with a snake under it told him where to start his story about his adventures in Nevada's Carson Valley. An umbrella tilted against a stiff wind took him to the next part of his story, the fierce winds that blew down out of the Sierras at about two o'clock every afternoon. And so on. The power of these sketches to evoke memory impressed Twain and gave rise one day to an idea for helping his children, who were still struggling to learn the kings and queens of England, despite long hours invested by their nanny in trying to hammer the names and dates into them through brute repetition. It dawned on Twain to try visualizing the successive reigns.

> We were at the farm then. From the house porch the grounds sloped gradually down to the lower fence and rose on the right to the high ground where my small work den stood. A carriage road wound through the grounds and up the hill. I staked it out with the English monarchs, beginning with [William] the Conqueror, and you could stand on the porch and clearly see every reign and its length, from the Conquest down to Victoria, then in the forty-sixth year of her reign—EIGHT HUNDRED AND SEVENTEEN YEARS of English history under your eye at once! . . .

I measured off 817 feet of the roadway, a foot representing a year, and at the beginning and end of each reign I drove a three-foot white-pine stake in the turf by the roadside and wrote the name and dates on it.

Twain and the children sketched icons for each of the monarchs: a whale for William the Conqueror, because both names begin with *W* and because "it is the biggest fish that swims, and William is the most conspicuous figure in English history"; a hen for Henry I, and so forth.

We got a good deal of fun out of the history road; and exercise, too. We trotted the course from the Conqueror to the study, the children calling out the names, dates, and length of reigns as we passed the stakes. . . . The children were encouraged to stop locating things as being "over by the arbor," or "in the oak [copse]," or "up at the stone steps," and say instead that the things were in Stephen, or in the Commonwealth, or in George III. They got the habit without trouble. To have the long road mapped out with such exactness was a great boon for me, for I had the habit of leaving books and other articles lying around everywhere, and had not previously been able to definitely name the place, and so had often been obliged to go to fetch them myself, to save time and failure; but now I could name the reign I left them in, and send the children.[22]

Rhyme schemes can also serve as mnemonic tools. The *peg method* is a rhyme scheme for remembering lists. Each number from 1 to 20 is paired with a rhyming, concrete image: 1 is *bun*, 2 is *shoe*, 3 is *tree*, 4 is *store*, 5 is *hive*, 6 is *tricks*, 7 is *heaven*, 8 is *gate*, 9 is *twine*, 10 is *pen*. (After 10 you add *penny-one* and start over with three-syllable cue words: 11 is *penny-one, setting sun*; 12 is *penny-two, airplane glue*; 13 is *penny-three, bumble bee*; and so on up to 20.) You use the rhyming concrete images as "pegs" on which to "hang" items you want to remember, such as the tasks you want to get done today. These twenty images stay with you, always at the ready whenever you need help to remember a list of things. So when you're running errands: *bun* gives you the image of a hairstyle and reminds you to buy a hat for your ski trip; *shoe* reminds you of being well dressed, prompting you to pick up the dry cleaning; *tree* reminds you of family tree, cuing that birthday card for your cousin. The rhyming images stay the same, while the associations they evoke change each time you need to hold a new list in mind.

A song that you know well can provide a mnemonic structure, linking the lyrics in each musical phrase to an image that will cue retrieval of the desired memory. According to the anthropologist Jack Weatherford, the preeminent historian of Genghis Khan and the Mongol Empire, traditional poems and songs seem to have been used as mnemonic devices for sending messages accurately over vast distances, from China at one end of the empire to Europe at the other end. The military were forbidden from sending written messages, and how they communicated remains a secret, but Weatherford thinks mnemonic devices were a likely method. He notes that the Mongol song known as the Long Song, for example, which describes the movement of a horse, can be sung in varying tones and trills so as to communicate movement through a particular location, like a crossing of the steppe or of the low mountains.

The versatility of mnemonic devices is almost endless. What they hold in common is a structure of some kind—number scheme, travel route, floor plan, song, poem, aphorism, acronym—that is deeply familiar and whose elements can be easily linked to the target information to be remembered.[23]

To return to the psychology students preparing for their A-level exams: In a classroom at Bellerbys College in Oxford, a dark-haired eighteen-year-old whom we'll call Marlys sits down to write her A2 exams in psychology. She will be asked to write five essays over the course of two testing sessions totaling three and a half hours. A-level courses are the British equivalent of Advanced Placement courses in the United States and are prerequisites for going on to university.

Marlys is under a lot of pressure. For one thing, her exam scores will make the difference in whether or not she gets into the university of her choice—she has applied to the London School of Economics. To be assured a spot in a top university in the United Kingdom, students are required to take A-levels in three subjects, and the grades they must earn are published in advance by the universities. It's not at all unusual that they are required to earn an A grade in each subject. If they earn less than the required grade, they must compete in a difficult clearing process by which the universities fill up their remaining spaces, a process that bears a lot in common with a lottery.

If that weren't stress-inducing enough, the scope of the material for which Marlys must be prepared to show mastery in the next hour and a half is enormous. She and her fellow psychology students have studied six major topics in their second year of A-level preparations: eating behavior, aggression, relationships, schizophrenia, anomalistic psychology, and the methods of psychological research. Within each of the first five topics she must be prepared to write essays on seven different questions. Each essay must illuminate the answer in twelve short paragraphs that describe, for instance, the thesis or condition, the extant research and its significance, the countervailing opinions, any biological treatments (say, for schizophrenia), and how these relate to the foundational concepts of psychology that she mastered for her first-year A-levels. So she faces: Five major topics, times seven essay questions for each topic, with a dozen succinct, well-argued paragraphs in each essay to show mastery of the subject. In other words, the universe of different essays she must master going into exams is a total of thirty-five—*plus* a series of short answers to questions on psychological research methods. Marlys knows which of the main topics will be the subject of today's exam, but she has no idea which essay questions will be assigned, so she's had to prepare herself to write on all of them.

Many students who reach this point simply freeze. Despite being well grounded in their material, the stakes at play can make their minds go blank the moment they confront the empty exam booklet and the proctor's ticking clock. That's where having taken the time to construct a memory palace proves as good as gold. It's not important that you understand the intricacies of British A-levels, just that they are difficult and highly consequential, which is why mnemonic devices are such a welcome tool at exam time.

Today, the three test topics turn out to be evolutionary explanations of human aggression, the psychological and biological treatments for schizophrenia, and the success and failure of dieting. Okay. For aggression, Marlys has got the she-wolf with her hungry pups at the window of the Krispy Kreme shop on Castle Street. For schizophrenia, she's got the over-caffeinated barista at the Starbucks on High Street. For dieting, that would be the extremely large and aggressive potted plant inside the café Pret-a-Manger on Cornmarket Street.

Excellent. She settles in her seat, sure of her knowledge and her ability to call it up. She tackles the dieting essay first. Pret-a-Manger is Marlys's memory palace for the safekeeping of what she has learned about the success and failure of dieting. Through a prior visit there, she has become thoroughly familiar with its spaces and furnishings and populated them with characters that are very familiar and vivid in her imagination. The names and actions of the characters now serve as cues to the dozen key points of her essay.

She enters the shop in her mind. La Fern (the man-eating plant in "Little Shop of Horrors," one of her favorite movies) is holding Marlys's friend *Herman* captive, her vines wrapped tightly around him, *restraining* him from a large dish of *mac* and cheese that sits just beyond his reach. Marlys opens her exam book and begins to write. "*Herman* and *Mack's restraint theory* suggests that attempting not to overeat may actually increase the probability of overeating. That is, in restrained eaters, it is the disinhibition (loss of control) that is the cause of overeating. . . ."

In this manner Marlys works her way through the café and the essay. Herman breaks free of his restraints with a mighty *roar* and makes a *bee* line for the plate, practically *inhaling* the pasta to the point of bursting. "Restraint theory received support in studies by *Wardle* and *Beale,* which found that obese women who restrained their eating *actually ate more* [inhaled the pasta] than obese women who took up exercise, and more than those who made no changes to their diet or lifestyle. However, Ogden argues . . ." and so on. Marlys moves mentally through the café clockwise, encountering her cues for the boundary model of hunger and satiety, biases arising from cultural inclinations to obesity, the problems with diet data based on anecdotal evidence, metabolic differences related to high levels of lipoprotein lipase levels ("little pink lemons"), and the rest.

From Pret-a-Manger she moves on to the Krispy Kreme shop, where a mental walk through the interior cues images that in turn cue what she's learned about the evolutionary explanations of aggression. Then on to Starbucks, where the crazed barista and the shop's floorplan and clientele cue her through twelve paragraphs on the biological treatments of schizophrenia.

Marlys's psychology teacher at Bellerbys College is none other than James Paterson, the boyish-looking Welshman who just happens to be a rising figure in world memory competitions.[24] When teachers at Bellerbys fill out the paperwork to take students on field trips, it's typically to a lecture at the Saïd Business School, or perhaps to the Ashmolean Museum or Bodleian Library in Oxford. Not so with James. His paperwork will more likely seek approval to take students to any of half a dozen different cafés around town, comfortable settings where they can tap into their imaginations and construct their mnemonic schemes. In order for the students to nail all thirty-five essays securely in memory, they divide the topics into several groupings. For one group they build memory palaces in cafés and at familiar locations around the Bellerbys campus. For another group they use the peg method. Still other groups they link to imagery in favorite songs and movies.

We should make one important point, though. Before Paterson takes students on their mnemonic outings to construct memory palaces, he has already thoroughly covered the material in class so that they understand it.

Among Paterson's former students who have graduated from Bellerbys and gone on to use the technique at university is Michela Seong-Hyun Kim, who described for us how she prepares for her university-level exams in psychology. First, she pulls together all her material from lecture slides, her outside reading, and her notes. She reduces this material to key ideas—not whole sentences. These form the plan for her essay. Next she selects the site for her memory palace. She ties each key idea to a location in the palace that she can visualize in her mind's eye. Then she populates each location with something crazy that will link her to one of the key ideas. When she sits in the exam hall and finds out the essay topics, she takes ten minutes to mentally walk through the relevant memory palaces and list the key ideas for each essay. If she's forgotten a point, she moves on to the next one and fills in the blank later. Once the plan is sketched out, she sets to work, free of the stressful anxiety that she won't remember what she's learned under the pressure of getting it right.[25] What she does is not so different from what Mark Twain did when he used sketches to remember his speeches.

Michela says that the idea of skipping a bullet point that she cannot remember but will fill in later would have been completely alien to her before learning to use mnemonics, but the techniques have given her the confidence to do this, knowing that the content will come to mind momentarily. The memory palace serves not as a learning tool but as a method to organize what's already been learned so as to be readily retrievable at essay time. This is a key point and helps to overcome the typical criticism that mnemonics are only useful in rote memorization. To the contrary, when used properly, mnemonics can help organize large bodies of knowledge to permit their ready retrieval. Michela's confidence that she can pull up what she knows when she needs it is a huge stress buster and a time saver, James says.

It's worth acknowledging that Krispy Kreme and Starbuck's shops are not often called palaces, but the mind is capable of wondrous things.

At Paterson's first World Memory Championships, that rookie year of 2006, he acquitted himself well by placing twelfth, narrowly edging out the American Joshua Foer, who later published an account of his experiences with mnemonics in the book *Moonwalking with Einstein*. Paterson can memorize the sequence of playing cards in a shuffled deck in less than two minutes, hand you the deck, and then recite them back to you with his eyes closed. Give him an hour, and he will memorize ten or twelve decks and recite them back without error. Top champs can memorize a single deck in thirty seconds or less and upward of twenty-five decks in an hour, so Paterson has a ways to go, but he's a dedicated competitor and coming on strong, building his skills and memory tools. For example, just as the peg method involves memorizing an image for the digits 1 through 10 (1 is *bun*, 2 is *shoe*, etc.), in order to remember much longer strings of digits, Paterson has committed to memory a unique image for every numeral from 0 to 1,000. This kind of achievement takes long hours of practice and intense focus—the kind of solitary striving that Anders Ericsson tells us characterizes the acquisition of expertise. The thousand images locked into memory took Paterson a year to master, fitted in between the other demands of family, work, and friends.

We caught up with Paterson in a school office and asked if he'd mind giving us a quick memory demonstration, to which he readily agreed. We recited, once, the random number string 615392611333517. Paterson listened closely and then said, "Okay. We'll use this space." He looked around at the fixtures. "I see this water cooler here becoming the space shuttle, which is taking off just as an underground train comes shooting out the bottom of the cooler. In the bookshelves there behind the cooler, I see the rapper Eminem having a gunfight with Leslie Nielsen from *Naked Gun*, while Lieutenant Columbo looks down on them."[26]

How to make sense of this? He remembers digits in groups of three. Every three-digit number is a distinct image. For example, the number 615 is always a space shuttle, 392 is always the Embankment tube station in London, 611 is Leslie Nielsen, 333 is Eminem, and 517 is Lieutenant Columbo. To make sense of these images, you need to understand another, underlying mnemonic: for each numeral 0 through 9, James has associated a sound of speech. The numeral 6 is always a *Sheh* or *Jeh* sound, the 1 is always a *Tuh* or *Duh* sound, and 5 is an *L* sound. So the image for the number 615 is *Sheh Tuh L*, or shuttle. Virtually every three-digit number from 000 to 999 lives in Paterson's mind as a unique image that is an embodiment of these sounds. For our spontaneous quiz, for example, he drew on these images in addition to the space shuttle:

392	3 = m, 9 = b, 2 = n	e*mb*ankme*n*t
611	6 = sh, 1 = t, 1 = t	*sh*oo*t*ou*t*
333	3 = m, 3 = m, 3 = m	E*m*ine*m*
517	5 = l, 1 = t, 7 = c	*Lt* Columbo

In the memory championship event of spoken numbers, which are read aloud to contestants at the rate of one per second, Paterson can memorize and recite back seventy-four without error, and, with much practice, he's raising that count. ("My wife calls herself a memory widow.") Without mnemonic tools, the maximum number of digits most people can hold in working memory is about seven. That is why local telephone numbers were designed to be no more than seven digits long. By the way, at the time of this writing the world record in spoken digits—what psychologists call memory span—is 364 digits (held by Johannes Mallow of Germany).

James is quick to acknowledge that he was first drawn to mnemonics as a shortcut for his studies. "Not the best of motives," he admits. He taught himself the techniques and became a bit of a slacker, walking into exams knowing he had all the names, dates, and related facts readily at hand.

What he didn't have, he discovered, was mastery of the concepts, relationships, and underlying principles. He had the mountaintops but not the mountain range, valleys, rivers, or the flora and fauna that compose the filled-in picture that constitutes knowledge.

Mnemonic devices are sometimes discounted as tricks of memory, not tools that fundamentally add to learning, and in a sense this is correct. The value of mnemonics to raise intellectual abilities comes *after* mastery of new material, as the students at Bellerbys are using them: as handy mental pockets for filing what they've learned, and linking the main ideas in each pocket to vivid memory cues so that they can readily bring them to mind and retrieve the associated concepts and details, in depth, at the unexpected moments that the need arises.

When Matt Brown, the jet pilot, describes his hours on the flight deck of a simulator drilling on the rhythm of the different hand movements required by potential emergencies, he reenacts distinct patterns he's memorized for different contingencies, choreographies of eye and hand, where the correct and complete sequence of instruments and switches is paramount. Each different choreography is a mnemonic for a corrective maneuver.

Karen Kim is a virtuoso violinist. When we spoke with her, Kim was second violin in the world-renowned string ensemble Parker Quartet, who play much of their material from memory, a rarity in classical music. Second violin is often largely accompanimental, and the mnemonic for memorizing the harmonies is the main melodic theme. "You sing the melody in your head," Kim says, "and you know that when the melody goes to this place, you change harmony." [27] The harmonies of some works, like fugues, with up to four themes that pass around the group in intricate ways, are especially challenging to memorize. "You need to know that while I'm playing the second theme, you're playing the first. Memorizing the fugues is very difficult. I need to learn everybody else's part better. Then I start to recognize patterns that I maybe knew intellectually before, but I wasn't listening out for them. Memorizing the harmonies is a big part of knowing the architecture of the piece, the map of it." When the quartet is mastering a new piece, they spend a lot of time playing through things slowly without the sheet music, and then gradually speeding it up. Think Vince Dooley gradually synchronizing the different positions on the Georgia Bulldogs football team as they tailor their plays to take on a new Saturday night opponent. Or the neurosurgeon Mike Ebersold, examining a gunshot victim in the emergency room and methodically rehearsing what he's likely to encounter in a brain surgery that he's about to perform.

Seeing the pattern of physical movements as a kind of choreography, visualizing a complex melody as it is handed off like a football from one player to another, "seeing the map of it": all are mnemonic cues to memory and performance.

With continued retrieval, complex material can become second nature to a person and the mnemonic cues are no longer needed: you consolidate concepts like Newton's 3 laws of motion into mental models that you use as a kind of shorthand. Through repeated use, your brain encodes and "chunks" sequences of motor and cognitive actions, and your ability to recall and apply them becomes as automatic as habit.

The Takeaway

It comes down to the simple but no less profound truth that *effortful learning changes the brain,* building new connections and capability. This single fact—that our intellectual abilities are not fixed from birth but are, to a considerable degree, ours to shape—is a resounding answer to the nagging voice that too often asks us "Why bother?" We make the effort because the effort itself extends the boundaries of our abilities. What we do shapes who we become and what we're capable of doing. The more we do, the more we can do. To embrace this principle and reap its benefits is to be sustained through life by a *growth mindset.*

And it comes down to the simple fact that the path to complex mastery or expert performance does not necessarily start from exceptional genes, but it most certainly entails *self-discipline, grit, and persistence;* with these qualities in healthy measure, if you want to become an expert, you probably can. And whatever you are striving to master, whether it's a poem you wrote for a friend's birthday, the concept of classical conditioning in psychology, or the second violin part in Hayden's Fifth Symphony, *conscious mnemonic devices* can help to organize and cue the learning for ready retrieval until sustained, deliberate practice and repeated use form the deeper encoding and subconscious mastery that characterize expert performance.

8

Make It Stick

NO MATTER WHAT YOU MAY set your sights on doing or becoming, if you want to be a contender, it's mastering the ability to learn that will get you in the game and keep you there.

In the preceding chapters, we resisted the temptation to become overtly prescriptive, feeling that if we laid out the big ideas from the empirical research and illustrated them well through examples, you could reach your own conclusions about how best to apply them. But early readers of those chapters urged us to get specific with practical advice. So we do that here.

We start with tips for students, thinking in particular of high school, college, and graduate school students. Then we speak to lifelong learners, to teachers, and finally to trainers. While the fundamental principles are consistent across these groups, the settings, life stages, and learning materials differ.

To help you envision how to apply these tips, we tell the stories of several people who, one way or another, have already found their way to these strategies and are using them to great effect.

Learning Tips for Students

Remember that the most successful students are those who take charge of their own learning and follow a simple but disciplined strategy. You may not have been taught how to do this, but you *can* do it, and you will likely surprise yourself with the results.

Embrace the fact that significant learning is often, or even usually, somewhat difficult. You will experience setbacks. These are signs of effort, not of failure. Setbacks come with striving, and striving builds expertise. Effortful learning changes your brain, making new connections, building mental models, increasing your capability. The implication of this is powerful: Your intellectual abilities lie to a large degree within your own control. Knowing that this is so makes the difficulties worth tackling.

Following are three keystone study strategies. Make a habit of them and structure your time so as to pursue them with regularity.

Practice Retrieving New Learning from Memory

What does this mean? "Retrieval practice" means self-quizzing. Retrieving knowledge and skill from memory should become your primary study strategy in place of rereading.

How to use retrieval practice as a study strategy: When you read a text or study lecture notes, pause periodically to ask yourself questions like these, without looking in the text: What are the key ideas? What terms or ideas are new to me? How would I define them? How do the ideas relate to what I already know?

Many textbooks have study questions at the ends of the chapters, and these are good fodder for self-quizzing. Generating questions for yourself and writing down the answers is also a good way to study.

Set aside a little time every week throughout the semester to quiz yourself on the material in a course, both the current week's work and material covered in prior weeks.

When you quiz yourself, check your answers to make sure that your judgments of what you know and don't know are accurate.

Use quizzing to identify areas of weak mastery, and focus your studying to make them strong.

The harder it is for you to recall new learning from memory, the greater the benefit of doing so. Making errors will not set you back, so long as you check your answers and correct your mistakes.

What your intuition tells you to do: Most studiers focus on underlining and highlighting text and lecture notes and slides. They dedicate their time to rereading these, becoming fluent in the text and terminology, because this feels like learning.

Why retrieval practice is better: After one or two reviews of a text, self-quizzing is far more potent for learning than additional rereading. Why might this be so? This is explained more fully in Chapter 2, but here are some of the high points.

The familiarity with a text that is gained from rereading creates illusions of knowing, but these are not reliable indicators of mastery of the material. Fluency with a text has two strikes against it: it is a misleading indicator of what you have learned, and it creates the false impression that you will remember the material.

By contrast, quizzing yourself on the main ideas and the meanings behind the terms helps you to focus on the central precepts rather than on peripheral material or on a professor's turn of phrase. Quizzing provides a reliable measure of what you've learned and what you haven't yet mastered. Moreover, quizzing arrests forgetting. Forgetting is human nature, but practice at recalling new learning secures it in memory and helps you recall it in the future.

Periodically practicing new knowledge and skills through self-quizzing strengthens your learning of it and your ability to connect it to prior knowledge.

A habit of regular retrieval practice throughout the duration of a course puts an end to cramming and all-nighters. You will need little studying at exam time. Reviewing the material the night before is much easier than learning it.

How it feels: Compared to rereading, self-quizzing can feel awkward and frustrating, especially when the new learning is hard to recall. It does not feel as productive as rereading your class notes and highlighted passages of text feels. But what you don't sense when you're struggling to retrieve new learning is the fact that every time you work hard to recall a memory, you actually strengthen it. If you restudy something after failing to recall it, you actually learn it better than if you had not tried to recall it. The effort of retrieving knowledge or skills strengthens its staying power and your ability to recall it in the future.

Space Out Your Retrieval Practice

What does this mean? Spaced practice means studying information more than once but leaving considerable time between practice sessions.

How to use spaced practice as a study strategy: Establish a schedule of self-quizzing that allows time to elapse between study sessions. How much time? It depends on the material. If you are learning a set of names and faces, you will need to review them within a few minutes of your first encounter, because these associations are forgotten quickly. New material in a text may need to be revisited within a day or so of your first encounter with it. Then, perhaps not again for several days or a week. When you are feeling more sure of your mastery of certain material, quiz yourself on it once a month. Over the course of a semester, as you quiz yourself on new material, also reach back to retrieve prior material and ask yourself how that knowledge relates to what you have subsequently learned.

If you use flashcards, don't stop quizzing yourself on the cards that you answer correctly a couple of times. Continue to shuffle them into the deck until they're well mastered. Only then set them aside—but in a pile that you revisit periodically, perhaps monthly. Anything you want to remember must be periodically recalled from memory.

Another way of spacing retrieval practice is to interleave the study of two or more topics, so that alternating between them requires that you continually refresh your mind on each topic as you return to it.

What your intuition tells you to do: Intuition persuades us to dedicate stretches of time to single-minded, repetitive practice of something we want to master, the massed "practice-practice-practice" regime we have been led to believe is essential for building mastery of a skill or learning new knowledge. These intuitions are compelling and hard to distrust for two reasons. First, as we practice a thing over and over we often see our performance improving, which serves as a powerful reinforcement of this strategy. Second, we fail to see that the gains made during single-minded repetitive practice come from short-term memory and quickly fade. Our failure to perceive how quickly the gains fade leaves us with the impression that massed practice is productive.

Moreover, most students, given their misplaced faith in massed practice, put off review until exam time nears, and then they bury themselves in the material, going over and over it, trying to burn it into memory.

Why spaced practice is better: It's a common but mistaken belief that you can burn something into memory through sheer repetition. Lots of practice works, but only if it's spaced.

If you use self-quizzing as your primary study strategy and space out your study sessions so that a little forgetting has happened since your last practice, you will have to work harder to reconstruct what you already studied. In effect, you're "reloading" it from long-term memory. This effort to reconstruct the learning makes the important ideas more salient and memorable and connects them more securely to other knowledge and to more recent learning. It's a powerful learning strategy. (How and why it works are discussed more thoroughly in Chapter 4.)

How it feels: Massed practice feels more productive than spaced practice, but it is not. Spaced practice feels more difficult, because you have gotten a little rusty and the material is harder to recall. It feels like you're not really getting on top of it, whereas in fact, quite the opposite is happening: As you reconstruct learning from long-term memory, as awkward as it feels, you are strengthening your mastery as well as the memory.

Interleave the Study of Different Problem Types

What does this mean? If you're trying to learn mathematical formulas, study more than one type at a time, so that you are alternating between different problems that call for different solutions. If you are studying biology specimens, Dutch painters, or the principles of macroeconomics, mix up the examples.

How to use interleaved practice as a study strategy: Many textbooks are structured in study blocks: They present the solution to a particular kind of problem, say, computing the volume of a spheroid, and supply many examples to solve before moving to another kind of problem (computing the volume of a cone). Blocked practice is not as effective as interleaved practice, so here's what to do.

When you structure your study regimen, once you reach the point where you understand a new problem type and its solution but your grasp of it is still rudimentary, scatter this problem type throughout your practice sequence so that you are alternately quizzing yourself on various problem types and retrieving the appropriate solutions for each.

If you find yourself falling into single-minded, repetitive practice of a particular topic or skill, change it up: mix in the practice of other subjects, other skills, constantly challenging your ability to recognize the problem type and select the right solution.

Harking back to an example from sports (Chapter 4), a baseball player who practices batting by swinging at fifteen fastballs, then at fifteen curveballs, and then at fifteen change-ups will perform better in practice than the player who mixes it up. But the player who asks for random pitches during practice builds his ability to decipher and respond to each pitch as it comes his way, and he becomes the better hitter.

What your intuition tells you to do: Most learners focus on many examples of one problem or specimen type at a time, wanting to master the type and "get it down cold" before moving on to study another type.

Why interleaved practice is better: Mixing up problem types and specimens improves your ability to discriminate between types, identify the unifying characteristics within a type, and improves your success in a later test or in real-world settings where you must discern the kind of problem you're trying to solve in order to apply the correct solution. (This is explained more fully in Chapter 3.)

How it feels: Blocked practice—that is, mastering all of one type of problem before progressing to practice another type—feels (and looks) like you're getting better mastery as you go, whereas interrupting the study of one type to practice a different type feels disruptive and counterproductive. Even when learners achieve superior mastery from interleaved practice, they persist in feeling that blocked practice serves them better. You may also experience this feeling, but you now have the advantage of knowing that studies show that this feeling is illusory.

Other Effective Study Strategies

ELABORATION improves your mastery of new material and multiplies the mental cues available to you for later recall and application of it (Chapter 4).

What is it? Elaboration is the process of finding additional layers of meaning in new material.

For instance: Examples include relating the material to what you already know, explaining it to somebody else in your own words, or explaining how it relates to your life outside of class.

A powerful form of elaboration is to discover a metaphor or visual image for the new material. For example, to better grasp the principles of angular momentum in physics, visualize how a figure skater's rotation speeds up as her arms are drawn into her body. When you study the principles of heat transfer, you may understand conduction better if you imagine warming your hands around a hot cup of cocoa. For radiation, visualize how the sun pools in the den on a wintry day. For convection, think of the life-saving blast of A/C as your uncle squires you slowly through his favorite back-alley haunts of Atlanta. When you learned about the structure of an atom, your physics teacher may have used the analogy of the solar system with the sun as the nucleus and electrons spinning around like planets. The more that you can elaborate on how new learning relates to what you already know, the stronger your grasp of the new learning will be, and the more connections you create to remember it later.

Later in this chapter, we tell how the biology professor Mary Pat Wenderoth encourages elaboration among her students by assigning them the task of creating large "summary sheets." Students are asked to illustrate on a single sheet the various biological systems studied during the week and to show graphically and through key words how the systems interrelate with each other. This is a form of elaboration that adds layers of meaning and promotes the learning of concepts, structures, and interrelationships. Students who lack the good fortune to be in Wenderoth's class could adopt such a strategy for themselves.

GENERATION has the effect of making the mind more receptive to new learning.

What is it? Generation is an attempt to answer a question or solve a problem before being shown the answer or the solution.

For instance: On a small level, the act of filling in a missing word in a text (that is, generating the word yourself rather than having it supplied by the writer) results in better learning and memory of the text than simply reading a complete text.

Many people perceive their learning is most effective when it is experiential—that is, learning by doing rather than by reading a text or hearing a lecture. Experiential learning is a form of generation: you set out to accomplish a task, you encounter a problem, and you consult your creativity and storehouse of knowledge to try to solve it. If necessary you seek answers from experts, texts, or the Web. By wading into the unknown first and puzzling through it, you are far more likely to learn and remember the solution than if somebody first sat you down to teach it to you. Bonnie Blodgett, an award-winning gardener and writer, provides a strong example of generative learning in Chapter 4.

You can practice generation when reading new class material by trying to explain beforehand the key ideas you expect to find in the material and how you expect they will relate to your prior knowledge. Then read the material to see if you were correct. As a result of having made the initial effort, you will be more astute at gleaning the substance and relevance of the reading material, even if it differs from your expectation.

If you're in a science or math course learning different types of solutions for different types of problems, try to solve the problems before you get to class. The Physics Department at Washington University in St. Louis now requires students to work problems before class. Some students take umbrage, arguing that it's the professor's job to teach the solution, but the professors understand that when students wrestle with content beforehand, classroom learning is stronger.

REFLECTION is a combination of retrieval practice and elaboration that adds layers to learning and strengthens skills.

What is it? Reflection is the act of taking a few minutes to review what has been learned in a recent class or experience and asking yourself questions. What went well? What could have gone better? What other knowledge or experiences does it remind you of? What might you need to learn for better mastery, or what strategies might you use the next time to get better results?

For instance: The biology professor Mary Pat Wenderoth assigns weekly low-stakes "learning paragraphs" in which students are asked to reflect on what they learned the previous week and to characterize how their class learning connects to life outside the class. This is a fine model for students to adopt for themselves and a more fruitful learning strategy than spending hours transcribing lecture slides or class notes verbatim into a notebook.

CALIBRATION is the act of aligning your judgments of what you know and don't know with objective feedback so as to avoid being carried off by the illusions of mastery that catch many learners by surprise at test time.

What is it? Everyone is subject to a host of cognitive illusions, some of which are described in Chapter 5. Mistaking fluency with a text for mastery of the underlying content is just one example. Calibration is simply the act of using an objective instrument to clear away illusions and adjust your judgment to better reflect reality. The aim is to be sure that your sense of what you know and can do is accurate.

For instance: Airline pilots use flight instruments to know when their perceptual systems are misleading them about critical factors like whether the airplane is flying level. Students use quizzes and practice tests to see whether they know as much as they think they do. It's worth being explicit here about the importance of answering the questions in the quizzes that you give yourself. Too often we will look at a question on a practice test and say to ourselves: Yup, I know that, and then move down the page without making the effort to write in the answer. If you don't supply the answer, you may be giving in to the illusion of knowing, when in fact you would have difficulty rendering an accurate or complete response. Treat practice tests as tests, check your answers, and focus your studying effort on the areas where you are not up to snuff.

MNEMONIC DEVICES help you to retrieve what you have learned and to hold arbitrary information in memory (Chapter 7).

What are they? "Mnemonic" is from the Greek word for memory, and mnemonic devices are like mental file cabinets. They give you handy ways to store information and find it again when you need it.

For instance: Here is a very simple mnemonic device that some schoolchildren are taught for remembering the US Great Lakes in geographic order, from east to west: Old Elephants Have Musty Skin. Mark Twain used mnemonics to teach his children the succession of kings and queens of England, staking the sequence and length of their reigns along the winding driveway of his estate, walking it with the children, and elaborating with images and storytelling. Psychology students at Bellerbys College in Oxford use mnemonic devices called memory palaces to organize what they have learned and must be prepared to expound upon in their A-level essay exams. Mnemonics are not tools for learning per se but for creating mental structures that make it easier to retrieve what you have learned.

Brief stories follow of two students who have used these strategies to rise to the top of their classes.

Michael Young, Medical Student

Michael Young is a high-achieving fourth-year medical student at Georgia Regents University who pulled himself up from rock bottom by changing the way he studies.

Young entered medical school without the usual foundation of premed coursework. His classmates all had backgrounds in biochemistry, pharmacology, and the like. Medical school is plenty tough under any circumstances, but in Young's case even more so for lack of a footing.

The scope of the challenge that lay before him became abruptly evident. Despite his spending every available minute studying his coursework, he barely eked out a 65 on his first exam. "Quite honestly, I got my butt kicked," he says. "I was blown away by that. I couldn't believe how hard it was. It was nothing like any kind of schooling I had done before. I mean, you come to class, and in a typical day you get about four hundred PowerPoint slides, and this is dense information."[1] Since spending more time studying wasn't an option, Young had to find a way to make studying more effective.

He started reading empirical studies on learning and became deeply interested in the testing effect. That's how we first learned of him: He emailed us with questions about the application of spaced retrieval practice in a medical school setting. Looking back on that stressful period, Young says, "I didn't just want to find somebody's opinion about how to study. Everybody has an opinion. I wanted real data, real research on the issue."

You might wonder how he got himself into medical school without premed coursework. He had earned a master's degree in psychology and worked in clinical settings, eventually as a drug addiction counselor. He teamed up with a lot of doctors, and he slowly began to wonder if he would be happier in medicine. Had he missed his calling? "I didn't think of myself as being especially intelligent, but I wanted to do more with my life and the idea wouldn't leave me." One day he went to the biology department of his local university, Columbus State in Columbus, Georgia, and asked what courses he would need to become a doctor. They laughed. "They said, 'Well, nobody from this school becomes a doctor. People at the University of Georgia and Georgia Tech go to medical school, we haven't had anybody go to medical school in a decade.'" Not to be put off, Young cobbled together some courses. For example, for the biology requirement, the only thing he could take at Columbus State was a fishing class. That was his biology course. Within a year he had gotten whatever medical background was available from the school, so he crammed for a month for the Medical College Admission Test and managed to score just well enough. He enrolled at Georgia Regents.

At which point he found himself very far indeed from being over the hump. As his first exam made all too clear, the road ahead went straight up. If he had any hope of climbing it, something about his study habits had to change. So what did change? He explains it this way:

> I was big into reading, but that's all I knew how to do for studying. I would just read the material and I wouldn't know what else to do with it. So if I read it and it didn't stick in my memory, then I didn't know what to do about that. What I learned from reading the research [on learning] is that you have to do something beyond just passively taking in the information.
>
> Of course the big thing is to figure out a way to retrieve the information from memory, because that's what you're going to be asked to do on the test. If you can't do it while you're studying, then you're not going to be able to do it on the test.

He became more mindful of that when he studied. "I would stop. 'Okay, what did I just read? What is this about?' I'd have to think about it. 'Well, I believe it happens this way: The enzyme does this, and then it does that.' And then I'd have to go back and check if I was way off base or on the right track."

The process was not a natural fit. "It makes you uncomfortable at first. If you stop and rehearse what you're reading and quiz yourself on it, it just takes a lot longer. If you have a test coming up in a week and so much to cover, slowing down makes you pretty nervous." But the only way he knew of to cover more material, his established habit of dedicating long hours to rereading, wasn't getting the results he needed. As hard as it was, he made himself stick to retrieval practice long enough at least to see if it worked. "You just have to trust the process, and that was really the biggest hurdle for me, was to get myself to trust it. And it ended up working out really well for me."

Really well. By the time he started his second year, Young had pulled his grades up from the bottom of his class of two hundred students to join the high performers, and he has remained there ever since.

Young spoke with us about how he adapted the principles of spaced retrieval practice and elaboration to medical school, where the challenges arise both from the sheer volume of material to be memorized and from the need to learn how complex systems work and how they interrelate with other systems. His comments are illuminating.

On deciding what's important: "If it's lecture material and you have four hundred PowerPoint slides, you don't have time to rehearse every little detail. So you have to say, 'Well this is important, and this isn't.' Medical school is all about figuring out how to spend your time."

On making yourself answer the question: "When you go back and review, instead of just rereading you need to see if you can recall the learning. Do I remember what this stuff was about? You always test yourself first. And if you don't remember, then that's when you go back and look at it and try again."

On finding the right spacing: "I was aware of the spacing effect, and I knew that the longer you wait to practice retrieval the better it is for memory, but there's also a trade-off with how successful you are when you try to recall it. When you have these long enzyme names, for example, and this step-by-step process of what the enzyme is doing, maybe if you learn ten steps of what the enzyme is doing, you need to stop and think, can I remember what those ten steps are? Once I found a good strategy for how much to space practice and I started seeing consistent results, it was easy to follow from there because then I could just trust the process and be confident that it was going to work."

On slowing down to find the meaning: Young has also slowed down the speed at which he reads material, thinking about meaning and using elaboration to better understand it and lodge it in memory. "When I read that dopamine is released from the ventral tegmental area, it didn't mean a lot to me." The idea is not to let words just "slide through your brain." To get meaning from the dopamine statement, he dug deeper, identified the structure within the brain and examined images of it, capturing the idea in his mind's eye. "Just having that kind of visualization of what it looks like and where it is [in the anatomy] really helps me to remember it." He says there's not enough time to learn everything about everything, but pausing to make it meaningful helps it stick.

Young's impressive performance has not been lost on his professors or his peers. He has been invited to tutor struggling students, an honor few are given. He has been teaching them these techniques, and they are pulling up their grades.

"What gets me is how interested people are in this. Like, in medical school, I've talked to all of my friends about it, and now they're really into it. People want to know how to learn."

Timothy Fellows, Intro Psych Student

Stephen Madigan, a professor at the University of Southern California, was astonished by the performance of a student in his Psych 100 course. "It's a tough course," Madigan says. "I use the most difficult, advanced textbook, and there's just a nonstop barrage of material. Three-quarters of the way through the class, I noticed this student named Timothy Fellows was getting 90 to 95 percent of the points on all the class activities— exams, papers, short-answer questions, multiple-choice questions. Those were just extraordinary grades. Students this good—well he's definitely an outlier. And so I just took him aside one day and said, 'Could you tell me about your study habits?' "[2]

The year was 2005. Madigan did not know Fellows outside class but saw him around campus and at football games enough to observe that he had a life beyond his academics. "Psychology wasn't his major, but it was a subject he cared about, and he just brought all his skills to bear." Madigan still has the list of study habit Fellows outlined, and he shares it with incoming students to this day.

Among the highlights were these:

- Always does the reading prior to a lecture
- Anticipates test questions and their answers as he reads
- Answers rhetorical questions in his head during lectures to test his retention of the reading
- Reviews study guides, finds terms he can't recall or doesn't know, and relearns those terms
- Copies bolded terms and their definitions into a reading notebook, making sure that he understands them
- Takes the practice test that is provided online by his professor; from this he discovers which concepts he doesn't know and makes a point to learn them

- Reorganizes the course information into a study guide of his design
- Writes out concepts that are detailed or important, posts them above his bed, and tests himself on them from time to time
- Spaces out his review and practice over the duration of the course

Fellows's study habits are a good example of doing what works and keeping at it, so that practice is spaced and the learning is solidly embedded come exam time.

Tips for Lifelong Learners

The learning strategies we have just outlined for students are effective for anyone at any age. But they are centered around classroom instruction. Lifelong learners are using the same principles in a variety of less-structured settings.

In a sense, of course, we're all lifelong learners. From the moment we're born we start learning about the world around us through experimentation, trial and error, and random encounters with challenges that require us to recall what we did the last time we found ourselves in a similar circumstance. In other words, the techniques of generation, spaced practice and the like that we present in this book are organic (even if counterintuitive), and it's not surprising that many people have already discovered their power in the pursuit of interests and careers that require continuous learning.

Retrieval Practice

Nathaniel Fuller is a professional actor with the Guthrie Theater in Minneapolis. We took an interest in him after a dinner party where the Guthrie's renowned artistic director, Joe Dowling, on hearing of our work, immediately suggested we interview Fuller. It seems that Fuller has the capacity to so fully learn the lines and movements of a role for which he is understudy that he can go onstage at the last moment with great success, despite not having had the benefit of learning and rehearsing it in the normal way.

Fuller is a consummate professional of the stage, having refined his techniques for learning roles over many years. He is often cast in a leading role; at other times, he may play several lesser characters in a play while also understudying the lead. How does he do it?

When he starts with a new script, Fuller puts it into a binder, goes through it, and highlights all of his lines. "I figure out how much I've got to learn. I try to estimate how much I can learn in a day, and then I try to start early enough to get that learned."[3] Highlighting his lines also makes them easy to find and gives him a sense of the construction, so this use of highlighting is rather different from what students do in class when they highlight merely for purposes of rereading. "You get the shape of the line, and how the back-and-forth works."

Fuller uses retrieval practice in various forms. First, he takes a blank sheet of paper and covers a page of the script. He draws it down, silently rendering the lines of the characters he's playing opposite, because those lines cue his own, and the emotion in them is reflected one way or another by his own character. He keeps his own line covered and attempts to speak it aloud from memory. He checks his accuracy. If he gets the line wrong, he covers it up and speaks it again. When he has spoken it correctly, he reveals the next passage and goes on.

"Half of knowing your part is not just what to say, but knowing when to say it. I don't have an exceptional brain for memorizing, but one of the keys I've found is, I need to try my best to say the line without looking at it. I need to have that struggle in order to make myself remember it.

"I'll work like crazy. When I get to where it feels like diminishing returns, I'll quit. Then I'll come back the next day, and I won't remember it. That's where a lot of my friends will panic. I just have faith now that it's in there, it's going to come back a little bit better the next time. Then I'll work on a new chunk, until I get to the end of the play."

As he progresses through the script, he's constantly moving from familiar pages and scenes into newer material, the play taking shape like threads added to a growing tapestry, each scene given meaning by those that came before and extending the story in turn. When he reaches the end, he practices in reverse order, moving from the less familiar last scene to practice the more familiar one that precedes it and then continuing on through the last scene again. Then he goes to the part preceding both of those scenes and practices through to the end. His practice continues reaching back in this way until he has come to the beginning of the play. This working backward and forward helps him stitch less familiar material to more familiar, deepening his mastery of the role as a whole.

Learning lines is visual (just as they are laid out in the script), but, he says, it's also "an act of the body, an act of the muscles, so I'm trying to say the lines in character, get how it *feels*." Fuller examines the language of the script, the textures of the words, and the figures of speech for how they reveal meaning. He works to discover the way the character carries himself, the way he moves across the stage, his facial expressions—all facets that reveal the underlying emotions that drive each scene. These forms of elaboration help him develop an emotional approach to the role and a deeper connection to the character.

He also notches up his retrieval practice. In place of the written script, he now speaks every line of the *other* actors in the play into a palm-sized digital recorder, voiced "in character" as best he can discern it. He tucks the recorder in his hand. His thumb knows where to find the controls. The thumb presses "play," and Fuller hears the characters' lines, then his cue; the thumb hits "pause," and he speaks his line from memory. If in doubt about his accuracy, he checks the script, replays the passage if need be, speaks his lines, and then goes on with the scene.

When he's understudying a role, before the director and cast have worked out the blocking (how the players move in relation to one another and the set), Fuller practices at home, imagining his living room as the stage and the way the blocking might be laid out. There, as he goes through scenes with his recorder, hearing others' lines and speaking his own, he is moving through the imagined scene, adding physicality to the part, reacting to imaginary props. When the actor he's understudying is in rehearsal, Fuller observes from behind the theater seats at the back of the hall, walking through the blocking himself as the actors rehearse on stage. He continues to practice later at home, adapting the imaginary stage within his living room to the now-established blocking.

Fuller's learning process is a seamless blend of desirable difficulties: retrieval practice, spacing, interleaving, generation (of his character's soul, carriage, motivations, and idiosyncrasies), and elaboration. Through these techniques, he learns the role and the many levels of meaning that make a performance come alive to himself and to his audience.

Generation

In 2013, John McPhee published a piece in the *New Yorker* about writer's block. Age eighty-two at the time, McPhee offered his remarks from the vantage of a high perch, atop an illustrious career that has earned him many awards and acknowledgment as a pioneer of the craft of creative nonfiction. Writer's block is the seemingly insurmountable barrier one must somehow clamber over if he is to have any hope of engaging his subject. Writing, like any art form, is an iterative process of creation and discovery. Many would-be writers fail to find their voices for the simple fact that, until they are clear about what they want to say, they cannot bring themselves to dive in. McPhee's solution to this problem? He writes a letter to his mother. He tells her how miserable he feels, what hopes he'd had for the subject about which he wants to write (a bear), but that he has no idea how to go about it and, really, it seems that he's not cut out to be a writer after all. He would like to put across the sheer size of the bear, and how utterly lazy it is, preferring to sleep fifteen hours a day, and so on. "And then you go back and delete the 'Dear Mother' and all the whimpering and whining, and just keep the bear."

McPhee's first draft is an "awful blurting." "Then you put the thing aside. You get in the car and drive home. On the way, your mind is still knitting at the words. You think of a better way to say something, a good phrase to correct a certain problem. Without the drafted version—if it did not exist— you obviously would not be thinking of ways to improve it. In short, you may actually be writing only two or three hours a day, but your mind, in one way or another, is working on it twenty-four hours a day—yes, while you sleep—but only if some sort of draft or earlier version exists. Until it exists, writing has not really begun."[4]

This is the crux: Learning works the same way as McPhee's "awful blurting." Your grasp of unfamiliar material often starts out feeling clumsy and approximate. But once you engage the mind in trying to make sense of something new, the mind begins to "knit" at the problem on its own. You don't engage the mind by reading a text over and over again or by passively watching PowerPoint slides. You engage it by making the effort to explain the material yourself, in your own words—connecting the facts, making it vivid, relating it to what you already know. Learning, like writing, is an act of engagement. Struggling with the puzzle stirs your creative juices, sets the mind to looking for parallels and metaphors from elsewhere in your experience, knowledge that can be transferred and applied here. It makes you hungry for the solution. And the solution, when you arrive at it, becomes more deeply embedded with your prior knowledge and abilities than anything pasted onto the surface of your brain by PowerPoint.

So take a page from McPhee: when you want to master something new, delete the whimpering and go wrestle the bear.

Reflection

In Chapter 2 we tell how the Mayo Clinic neurosurgeon Mike Ebersold uses the habit of reflection to improve his skills in the operating room. Reflection involves retrieval (What did I do? How did it work?) and generation (How could I do it better next time?), invoking imagery and mental rehearsal as well (What if I take a smaller bite with the needle?). It was this habit of reflection that brought him to devise a surgical solution for the repair of a delicate sinus structure in the back of the skull that cannot be tied off because the structure is somewhat flat and tears when you snug the suture.

Vince Dooley, Georgia Bulldogs football coach (Chapter 3), helped his players use reflection and mental rehearsal to learn their playbooks and their adjustments for next Saturday's game. The Minneapolis cop David Garman (Chapter 5) uses reflection to improve his undercover strategies. The power of reflection as a learning technique is apparent throughout the personal memoir *Highest Duty*, by Captain Chesley Sullenberger. "Sully" is the pilot who successfully and miraculously ditched US Airways Flight 1549 on the Hudson River in 2009. Time and again, in reading his autobiography, we see how he refined his understanding of flight and the control of his aircraft through training, personal experience, and the close observation of others. The process started from his earliest days at the stick of a single-engine crop duster, continued to his jet fighter days, his time investigating commercial airline disasters, and his granular analysis of the few available examples of the ditching of commercial aircraft, where he paid particular attention to the lessons for pitch, speed, and level wings. The evolution of Captain Sullenberger shows us that the habit of reflection is more than simply taking stock of a personal experience or the observed experiences of others. At its most powerful this habit involves engagement of the mind through generation, visualization, and mental rehearsal.

Elaboration

When we met the pianist Thelma Hunter, she was learning four new works for an upcoming concert performance: pieces by Mozart, Faure, Rachmaninoff, and William Bolcom. Hunter, who is eighty-eight, won her first prize as a pianist at age five in New York and has been performing ever since. She is not a prodigy, she insists, nor even particularly renowned, but she is accomplished. In addition to a busy life raising six kids with her husband, Sam, a heart surgeon, Hunter has enjoyed a long life of learning, teaching, and performing at the piano, and she is still in the game, sought after and bent to her life's pleasure at the keyboard.

Giving new learning multiple layers of meaning has been central to Hunter's methods and illustrates the way elaboration strengthens learning and memory. When she studies a new score, she learns it physically in the fingering, aurally in the sound, visually in the notes on the score, and intellectually in the way she coaches herself through transitions.

Hunter has made some concessions to age. She never used to warm up before playing, but now she does. "My stamina is not as great as it used to be. My reach is not as big. Now, if I memorize something, I have to *think* about it. I never used to have to do that, I just worked through all the aspects of it and the memorizing came."[5] She visualizes the score and makes mental marginalia. "When I'm practicing, sometimes I say it out loud, 'Up an octave, at this point,' but in my mind's eye I visualize the place on the sheet music, as well." In comments that resonate with John McPhee's observations about writing, Hunter says that at the point where a piece is almost memorized, "I'll be driving, and I can think about the whole piece, which I do. The shape of it, as though I were a conductor, thinking, 'Oh, that passage makes more sense if I speed it up. I have to practice that to get it faster.' Those are the large things that I can think about away from the piano."

Hunter's practice regimen is daily, working through new pieces, slowing down to parse the difficult passages, and then, because she now often performs with a cellist and violinist, the ensemble works through the pieces together to synchronize their individual interpretations.

In Chapter 7 we describe Anders Ericsson's research into how experts, through thousands of hours of solo, deliberate practice, build libraries of mental models that they can deploy to address a wide universe of situations they encounter in their area of expertise. Hunter describes experiences that would seem to manifest Ericsson's theory. At times she must sit at the keyboard and devise a fingering plan for playing a difficult passage. Oddly, she says, after having been away from the piece for a week, she will sit down and play it through, using a fingering pattern that she had not planned but feels entirely natural to her and familiar. It's a paradox, though perhaps not entirely surprising. She credits her subconscious, drawing from her long years of playing, with finding a more fluent solution than what she has devised by puzzling it out at the keyboard. But perhaps it has been the effort at the keys, like McPhee wrestling his bear, that has set her mind to sorting through the closets of her memory for something a little more elegant and natural to fit the occasion.

Tips for Teachers

Here again we are leery of being too prescriptive. Every teacher must find what's right in his or her classroom. Yet specifics can be helpful. So here are some basic strategies that in our judgment will go a long way toward helping students become stronger learners in the classroom. Brief descriptions follow of what some teachers are already doing along these lines. Between the recommendations and the examples, we hope you will find practical ideas you can adapt and put to work.

Explain to Students How Learning Works

Students labor under many myths and illusions about learning that cause them to make some unfortunate choices about intellectual risk taking and about when and how to study. It's the proper role of the teacher to explain what empirical studies have discovered about how people learn, so the student can better manage his or her own education.

In particular, students must be helped to understand such fundamental ideas as these:

- Some kinds of difficulties during learning help to make the learning stronger and better remembered.

- When learning is easy, it is often superficial and soon forgotten.
- Not all of our intellectual abilities are hardwired. In fact, when learning is effortful, it changes the brain, making new connections and increasing intellectual ability.
- You learn better when you wrestle with new problems before being shown the solution, rather than the other way around.
- To achieve excellence in any sphere, you must strive to surpass your current level of ability.
- Striving, by its nature, often results in setbacks, and setbacks are often what provide the essential information needed to adjust strategies to achieve mastery.

These topics, woven throughout the book, are discussed in depth in Chapters 4 and 7.

Teach Students How to Study

Students generally are not taught how to study, and when they are, they often get the wrong advice. As a result, they gravitate to activities that are far from optimal, like rereading, massed practice, and cramming.

At the beginning of this chapter we present effective study strategies. Students will benefit from teachers who help them understand these strategies and stick with them long enough to experience their benefits, which may initially appear doubtful.

Create Desirable Difficulties in the Classroom

Where practical, use *frequent quizzing* to help students consolidate learning and interrupt the process of forgetting. Make the ground rules acceptable to your students and yourself. Students find quizzing more acceptable when it is predictable and the stakes for any individual quiz are low. Teachers find quizzing more acceptable when it is simple, quick, and does not lead to negotiating makeup quizzes. (For one example, consider the way Kathleen McDermott, whose work we describe below, uses daily quizzing in her university class on human learning and memory.)

Create study tools that incorporate *retrieval practice, generation,* and *elaboration.* These might be exercises that require students to wrestle with trying to solve a new kind of problem before coming to the class where the solution is taught; practice tests that students can download and use to review material and to calibrate their judgments of what they know and don't know; writing exercises that require students to reflect on past lesson material and relate it to other knowledge or other aspects of their lives; exercises that require students to generate short statements that summarize the key ideas of recent material covered in a text or lecture.

Make quizzing and practice exercises count toward the course grade, even if for very low stakes. Students in classes where practice exercises carry consequences for the course grade learn better than those in classes where the exercises are the same but carry no consequences.

Design quizzing and exercises to *reach back to concepts and learning covered earlier* in the term, so that retrieval practice continues and the learning is cumulative, helping students to construct more complex mental models, strengthen conceptual learning, and develop deeper understanding of the relationships between ideas or systems. (For an example, read in Chapter 2 how Andy Sobel uses cumulative low-stakes quizzing in his university-level course in political economics.)

Space, interleave, and vary topics and problems covered in class so that students are frequently shifting gears as they have to "reload" what they already know about each topic in order to figure out how the new material relates or differs.

Be Transparent

Help your students understand the ways you have incorporated desirable difficulties into your lessons, and why. Be up front about some of the frustrations and difficulties this kind of learning entails and explain why it's worth persisting. Consider having them read the profile earlier in this chapter of the medical student Michael Young, who vividly describes the difficulties and ultimate benefits of using these strategies.

Mary Pat Wenderoth, Biology Professor, University of Washington

Mary Pat Wenderoth introduces desirable difficulties in her classes to help students master their coursework. She also works at helping students learn how to be effective at managing their own learning—to be the capable student within the professional that they envision becoming. Along that path she tackles yet another challenge, helping students learn to judge where their grasp of course material stands on Bloom's taxonomy of learning, and how to rise to the levels of synthesis and evaluation.

Bloom's taxonomy classifies cognitive learning on six levels. It was developed in 1956 by a committee of educators chaired by psychologist Benjamin Bloom. The six levels range from gaining *knowledge* (the most fundamental level) to developing *comprehension* of the underlying facts and ideas, being able to *apply* learning to solve problems, being able to *analyze* ideas and relationships so as to make inferences, being able to *synthesize* knowledge and ideas in new ways, and, at the most sophisticated level, being able to use learning to *evaluate* opinions and ideas and make judgments based on evidence and objective criteria.

Here are some of the main techniques Wenderoth uses.

Transparency. At the outset, Wenderoth teaches her students about the testing effect, the principle of desirable difficulties, and the perils of "illusions of knowing." She promises to make her instructional philosophy transparent and to model these principles in class. As she explained to us recently, "The whole idea of the testing effect is that you learn more by testing yourself than by rereading. Well, it's very hard to get students to do that because they've been trained for so long to keep reading and reading the book."[6]

I can't tell you how many times the students come to me and they show me their textbook and it's highlighted in four different colors. I say to them, "I can tell you have done a lot of work and that you really want to succeed in this class because you have blue and yellow and orange and green highlighter on your book." And then I have to try to tell them that any more time spent on this after the first time was a waste. They're, like, "How is that possible?" I say, "What you have to do is, you read a little bit and then you have to test yourself," but they don't quite know how to do that.

So I model it in class for them. Every five minutes or so I throw out a question on the material we just talked about, and I can see them start to look through their notes. I say, "Stop. Do not look at your notes. Just take a minute to think about it yourself." I tell them our brains are like a forest, and your memory is in there somewhere. You're here, and the memory is over there. The more times you make a path to that memory, the better the path is, so that the next time you need the memory, it's going to be easier to find it. But as soon as you get your notes out, you have short-circuited the path. You are not exploring for the path anymore, someone has told you the way.

At other times, Wenderoth will pose a question to the class and ask them to think about it. She has students write three possible answers on the whiteboard up front and then vote on which answer they think is correct by raising the number of fingers that corresponds with the answer on the board. She'll instruct students to find somebody with fingers "different from yours and talk to them and figure out who has the correct answer."

Wenderoth gives her students a new way to think about learning, and she gives them a new vocabulary for describing setbacks. When students trip over an exam question, they'll commonly accuse the test of containing trick questions. When the student blames the test, she says, it's not a good meeting ground for solving the problem. But now, students come to see her after a disappointing exam and say, "I have the illusion of knowing. How do I get better?" That's a problem Wenderoth can help with.

Testing groups. Wenderoth has transformed class "study groups" into "testing groups." In a study group, the person who knows the most talks and the others listen. The emphasis is on memorizing things. However, in a testing group, they all wrestle with a question together, without opening the textbook. "Everybody has bits of information, and you talk with your colleagues and figure it out." The emphasis is on exploration and understanding.

Wenderoth will ask students in a testing group what ideas they don't feel really clear on. Then she'll send one student to the whiteboard to try to explain the concept. As the student struggles, perhaps putting up the pieces of the answer she knows, the rest of the group are instructed to test her by asking questions whose answers will lead her to the larger concept. Throughout, all textbooks remain closed.

Free recall. Wenderoth assigns her students to spend ten minutes at the end of each day sitting with a blank piece of paper on which to write everything they can remember from class. They must sit for ten minutes. She warns that it will be uncomfortable, they will run out of ideas after two minutes, but they must stick it out. At the end of ten minutes, they're to go to their class notes and find out what they remembered and what they forgot, and to focus on the material they forgot. What they glean from this exercise guides their notes and questions for the next class. Wenderoth finds that the free recall exercise helps students pull learning forward and develop a more complex understanding of how the material interrelates.

Summary sheets. Every Monday, Wenderoth's students are required to turn in a single sheet of certain dimensions on which they have illustrated the prior week's material in drawings annotated with key ideas, arrows, and graphs. She's teaching physiology, which is about how things work, so the summaries take on the form of large cartoons dense with callouts, blowups, directional arrows, and the like. The sheets help her students synthesize a week's information, thinking through how systems are connected: "This is causing *this,* which causes *this,* which feeds back on *those.* We use a lot of arrows in physiology. The students can work with each other, I don't care. The sheet they bring in just has to be their own."

Learning paragraphs. From time to time, on a Friday, if she doesn't feel she's overburdening them, Wenderoth will assign students to write low-stakes "learning paragraphs" for which she poses a question and asks students to prepare a five- or six-sentence response. A question might be "How is the GI tract like the respiratory system?" Or "You just got your tests back; what would you do differently next time?" The point is to stimulate retrieval and reflection and to capture a week's learning before it is lost to the countless other concerns and diversions of college life. "What I found over the years is, if I don't do anything before the test, they don't do anything until the day before the test." The learning paragraphs also give her science majors practice in writing a passage of clear prose. She reads through the responses and makes a point to comment on them in class so that students know they're being read.

Bloom's taxonomy of learning. To remove some of the abstraction from Bloom's taxonomy, Wenderoth has translated her class material into the different levels of the taxonomy on an answer key to her tests. That is, for any given question, she provides a different answer for each level of the taxonomy: one that reflects learning at the level of knowledge, a more thorough answer that reflects understanding, a yet more complex answer that reflects analysis, and so on. When students get their tests back, they also receive the answer key and are asked to identify where their answers fell on the taxonomy and to think about what they need to know in order to respond at a higher level of learning.

Closing the achievement gap in the sciences. Wenderoth and her colleagues have experimented with class structure and the principles of active learning to help close the achievement gap in the sciences. Poorly prepared students seldom survive entry-level science courses. As a result, even students whose interests and aptitudes might lead them to successful science careers never get through the door. For whatever reason, these students do not have a history from high school or family life of learning how to succeed in these highly challenging academic settings.

"For most of us who have found our way in the sciences," Wenderoth says, "any time we fell, there was somebody around to help us up, or to say, 'This is how you get up.' You were taught that when things don't go well, you keep working anyway. You persevere."

In their experiments, Wenderoth and her colleagues have compared the results of "low-structure" classes (traditional lecturing and high-stakes midterm and final exams) with "high-structure" classes (daily and weekly low-stakes exercises to provide constant practice in the analytical skills necessary to do well on exams). They also teach students the importance of having a "growth mindset" (see the work of Carol Dweck, discussed in Chapter 7)—that is, that learning is hard work and that struggle increases intellectual abilities.

The results? High-structure classes in a gateway biology course significantly reduced student failure rates compared to low-structure classes—narrowing the gap between poorly prepared students and their better prepared peers while at the same time showing exam results at higher levels on Bloom's taxonomy. Moreover, it's not just whether the student completes the practice exercises that matters. In the classes where exercises count toward the course grade, even at very low stakes, students achieve higher success over the course of the term compared to students in classes where the exercises are the same but carry no consequences for the grade.

"We talk to the students about how these are the habits of mind," Wenderoth says. "This is the discipline that you have to have in order to succeed in the sciences. They've never thought about that, that every discipline has a culture. We teach them to think like the professionals they want to become. And when they fall, we show them how to get up again."[7]

Michael D. Matthews, Psychology Professor, U.S. Military Academy at West Point

The pedagogical philosophy at West Point is founded on an instructional system called the Thayer method, developed almost two hundred years ago by an early superintendent of the academy named Sylvanus Thayer. The method provides very specific learning objectives for every course, puts the responsibility for meeting those objectives on the student, and incorporates quizzing and recitation in every class meeting.

Students' grades at the academy rest on three pillars of training: academic, military, and physical. Mike Matthews, a professor of engineering psychology at the academy, says the load on students is enormous, greater than the hours available to them. In order to survive at the academy, West Point cadets must develop an ability to zero in on what's essential and let the rest fall by the wayside. "This is about having very high expectations across multiple dimensions and keeping them real busy," Matthews, says. In fact, as stunning as it sounds, Matthews will tell a student, "If you've read every word of this chapter, you're not being very efficient." The point is not to "slide your eyes over the words." You start with questions, and you read for answers.[8]

There's little or no lecturing in Matthews's courses. Class opens with a quiz on the learning objectives from the assigned reading. From there, on many days, students "take to the boards." The classrooms have slate on all four walls, and a group of students are sent to each blackboard to collaborate on answering a question given by the professor. These are higher-order questions than are given in the daily quiz, requiring the students to integrate ideas from the reading and apply them at a conceptual level. It's a form of retrieval practice, generation, and peer instruction. One student is selected from each group to give a recitation to the class explaining how the group has answered the question, and then the group's work is critiqued. All class meetings focus on constructs, not specific facts, and on the days the students do not take to the boards, they are engaged in other forms of exercise, demonstration, or group work aimed at understanding and articulating the larger concepts underlying the matter at hand.

Clear learning objectives prior to each class, coupled with daily quizzing and active problem solving with feedback, keep students focused, awake, and working hard.

One of the most important skills taught at West Point is something learned outside the classroom: how to shoot an azimuth. It's a skill used for keeping your bearings in unfamiliar territory. You climb a tree or a height of land and sight a distant landmark in the direction you're headed. Compass in hand, you note how many degrees your landmark lies off of due north. Then you descend into the bush and keep working your way in that direction. Periodically, you pause to shoot an azimuth and make sure you're on course. Quizzing is a way of shooting an azimuth in the classroom: are you gaining the mastery you need to get where you're trying to go?

Matthews has had the privilege of seeing two of his students win Rhodes Scholarships. The most recent was Cadet Kiley Hunkler (now Second Lieutenant Hunkler). Hunkler will be spending the next two years at Oxford University, and then matriculating at Johns Hopkins Medical School. It was Hunkler who spoke to us of shooting an azimuth. "Everything at the academy is about self-responsibility, taking ownership for finding your own way to the objective," she said.[9] The Medical College Admission Test, for example, encompasses four major course blocks: reading, chemistry, physiology, and writing. For each of these blocks, Hunkler created the learning objectives in her head that she deemed most important and then set out to answer them as she studied. "I took a practice test every three days, saw what I got wrong, and adjusted." Shooting her azimuth. "A lot of students get hung up studying for months, trying to memorize everything, but for me it was more about understanding the concepts. So my azimuth check would be, Okay, what is this question asking, what's the broader theme here, and does that match up with what I've outlined for this section."

One of this book's authors (Roediger) attended Riverside Military Academy in Gainesville, Georgia, for high school. Riverside used a form of the Thayer method, with students having daily quizzes, problem sets, or assignments to be completed in class. The range of ability of these younger cadets was much more varied than at the elite US Military Academy at West Point, but the Thayer method worked well. In fact, such methods that include daily participation are especially likely to help students who are not prone to work hard on their own outside of class. The Thayer method is a strong encouragement for them to keep at it, and echoes what Mary Pat Wenderoth (above) has found in her empirical studies: that high-structure classes help students who lack a history of using effective learning techniques and habits to develop them and succeed in rigorous settings.

Kathleen McDermott, Psychology Professor, Washington University at St. Louis

Kathleen McDermott administers daily low-stakes quizzes in a university course on human learning and memory. It's a class of twenty-five students that meets twice a week for fourteen weeks, minus midterms and a final exam. She gives a four-item quiz in the last three to five minutes of every class. The questions hit the high points of the lecture, the readings, or both. If students have understood the material, they will get all four answers right, but they'll have to think in order to do it. Anything covered in the course to date is fair game for a quiz, and she will sometimes draw from past material that she feels the students haven't fully grasped and need to review.

McDermott sets the ground rules very clearly at the start of the term. She lays out the research on learning and the testing effect and explains why the quizzes are helpful, even if they don't feel helpful. Students are allowed to drop four quizzes across the semester. In exchange, absences need not be justified, and no missed quizzes will be made up.

Students initially are not happy about the quiz regime, and in the first few weeks of the term McDermott will get email from students explaining why they had a legitimate excuse for an absence and should be allowed to make up a missed quiz. She reiterates the terms: four free absences, no makeups.

McDermott says the quizzes provide an incentive for students to attend class and give students a way to contribute to their grade on a daily basis if they answer four out of four questions correctly. By the end of the semester, her students say that the quizzes have helped them keep up with the course and discover when they are getting off track and need to bone up.

"The key with quizzes is to establish very clear ground rules for the student, and make them manageable for the professor," McDermott says. "As a student, you're either there and you take it, or you're not. For the professor, no hassling over makeup tests."[10]

The quizzes in totality count for 20 percent of a student's grade in the course. In addition, McDermott gives two midterm exams and a final. The last two exams are cumulative. Having cumulative exams reinforces learning by requiring students to engage in spaced review.

Columbia, Illinois, Public School District

As recounted in Chapter 2, we have worked with teachers in a middle school in Columbia, Illinois, to test the effects of integrating low-stakes quizzing into the curriculum. Regular quizzing and other forms of retrieval practice have been adopted by teachers in the school who were a part of the research study and by others who were not but who observed the beneficial results. The initial research project has since been extended into history and science classes in the district's high school, where frequent retrieval practice is being used both to bolster learning and to help teachers focus instruction on areas where student understanding and performance need to be improved.

The Illinois State Board of Education has adopted new math and English language arts standards for K–12 education in line with the Common Core State Standards Initiative led by the National Governors Association and endorsed by the nation's secretary of education. Common Core establishes standards for college and career readiness that students should be able to meet on graduation from high school. The Columbia School District, like others, is redesigning its curriculum and its tests to be more rigorous and to engage students in more writing and analysis work, with the aim of promoting the higher-level skills of conceptual understanding, reasoning, and problem solving that will enable students to meet the standards established by the state. As one example of this overhaul, the sciences curriculum is being vertically aligned so that students are reexposed to a subject at various stages of their school careers. The result is more spaced and interleaved instruction. In physical sciences, for instance, middle school students may learn to identify the six basic machines (inclined plane, wedge, screw, lever, wheel and axle, and pulley) and how they work, and then may return to these concepts in subsequent grades, delving into the underlying physics and how these basic tools can be combined and applied to solve different problems.

Tips for Trainers

Here are some ways trainers are using the same principles as those who teach in schools, in a variety of less structured and nonclassroom settings.

In-Service Training

Licensed professionals in many fields must earn continuing education credits to keep their skills current and maintain their licenses. As the pediatric neurologist Doug Larsen describes in Chapter 3, this kind of training for doctors is typically compressed into a weekend symposium, out of respect for participants' busy schedules, set at a hotel or resort, and structured around meals and PowerPoint lectures. In other words, the strategies of retrieval practice, spacing, and interleaving are nowhere to be seen. Participants are lucky to retain much of what they learn.

If you see yourself in this scenario, there are a few things you might consider doing. One, get a copy of the presentation materials and use them to quiz yourself on the key ideas, much as Nathaniel Fuller quizzes himself on the arc of a play, his lines, the many layers of character. Two, schedule follow-up emails to appear in your inbox every month or so with questions that require you to retrieve the critical learning you gained from the seminar. Three, contact your professional association and ask them to consider revamping their approach to training along the lines outlined in this book.

The testing effect forms the basis of a new commercial training platform called Qstream that helps trainers send learners periodic quizzes via their mobile devices to strengthen learning through spaced retrieval practice. Similarly, an emerging platform called Osmosis uses mobile and Web based software to provide learners access to thousands of crowdsourced practice questions and explanations. Osmosis combines the testing effect, spacing, and social networking to facilitate what its developers call "student-driven social learning." Qstream (qstream.com) and Osmosis (osmose-it.com) suggest interesting possibilities for redesigning in-service training for professionals. Many other companies are developing similar programs.

Kathy Maixner, Business Coach

The Maixner Group is a consulting shop based in Portland, Oregon, that helps companies identify growth strategies and improve their sales tactics. Kathy Maixner fries big fish and little. One of the big fish added $21 million to its annual revenue as a result of hooking up with Maixner. One of the small ones, Inner Gate Acupuncture (profiled at the close of this chapter), learned how to establish a solid business management footing under a clinical practice whose growth was outpacing its control systems.

We're interested in Maixner because the coaching techniques she has developed over her career line up so well with the learning principles described in this book. In short, Maixner sees her role as helping the client dig past the symptoms of a problem to discover its root causes, and then to generate possible solutions and play out the implications of different strategies before committing to them.

Maixner told us: "If you hand people the solution, they don't need to explore how you got to that solution. If they generate the solution, then they're the ones who are traveling down that road. Should they go left or right? We discuss the options."[11]

Maixner's years of experience working with clients in many different fields helps her see around corners, where the hazards lie. She often uses role-playing to simulate problems, getting her clients to generate solutions, try them out, get feedback, and practice what works. In other words, she introduces the difficulties that make the learning stronger and more accurately reflect what the client will encounter out in the marketplace.

Farmers Insurance

Corporate sales training can be complicated. Typically, it's about corporate culture, beliefs and behavior, and learning to promote and protect the brand. It's also technical, learning the features and advantages of the products. And it's partly strategic, learning about the target market and how to generate prospects and make sales. At Farmers Insurance, whose principal sales force is a cadre of about fourteen thousand exclusive independent agents, training must also equip the company's reps to become successful as entrepreneurs, building and managing their own agency.

Farmers sells property and casualty policies and investment products like annuities and mutual funds to the tune of about $20 billion a year. Describing the full scope of their training could fill volumes, but we'll focus on the way Farmers brings new agents on board, training them in the four areas of sales, marketing systems, business planning, and advocacy of the brand. The company's new-agent training is an excellent example of interleaving the learning and practice of different but related topics so that each adds meaning to the other, broadening and deepening competency.

The company recruits upward of two thousand new agents annually. Many leave traditional jobs elsewhere, drawn to the rewards of running their own business and the opportunity to represent an established product line. Newly appointed agents arrive at one of two training campuses for an intensive weeklong program of learning exercises that spiral upward in sophistication.

At the start, participants are given a pile of magazines, scissors, and marking pens with which to illustrate on posterboard what being a successful Farmers agent would look like to them personally, five years down the road. For some, the poster shows fancy houses and cars. For others, kids are being sent to college and aging parents are being cared for. The point is simple: if your definition of success requires, say, $250,000 a year in revenues and twenty-five hundred policies in force, we can help you work backward to set the metrics for where you need to be in four years, in three years, and even three months from now. The image on the poster shows where you're headed, the metrics are your road map, and the skills that are learned over the coming days and months are the tools that will enable you to make the journey.

From here, the week is not so much about teaching from the top down—there are no PowerPoint lectures as such—but about learning from the bottom up, as in: "What knowledge and skills do I need in order to succeed?"

The learning unfolds through a series of exercises that cycle through the principal topics of sales, marketing systems, business planning, and advocacy of the company's values and its brands—returning time and again to each, requiring that participants recall what they have learned earlier and apply it in a new, enlarged context.

For example, when participants first arrive, they're assigned to a red, blue, or green group. The red group is instructed to go *meet* people in the room. The blue group is instructed to go *learn three things* about somebody in the room. The green group is instructed to ask another member of the class about his or her *family,* prior *occupation,* favorite forms of *recreation,* and what he or she *enjoys* most. When the class reconvenes, they share what they have learned about others, and it is quickly evident that the green group, which had a structure for talking to others, learned much more than did their peers.

When talking about sales later in the week the question comes up, what's an effective way to learn about a prospective customer? Somebody will recall the initial get-acquainted exercise that proved so fruitful: asking about one's family, occupation, recreation, and enjoyment. That icebreaker now morphs into a handy tool for getting to know a prospective client and it gets an acronym: FORE.

Throughout the week the four principal training topics are repeatedly touched on, a point is made, and the exercises shift to related questions. In one session, participants brainstorm what kinds of marketing and development strategies might generate the flow of leads they need in order to meet sales targets. An effective sales and marketing system has a structure called 5-4-3-2-1. Five new business marketing initiatives every month, four cross-marketing and four retention programs in place, three appointments scheduled every day, two appointments kept (prospects often have to reschedule), one new customer sold on average two policies per sale. At twenty-two working days a month, that's about five hundred new policies in a year, making twenty-five hundred over the five-year horizon of the agent's vision.

Practice is a central learning strategy. For example, they practice how to respond to a sales lead. Trying to sell the company's products is how they learn about selling, but it's also how they learn about the products they're selling—not by sitting in front of PowerPoint slides gazing at long lists of product features. You be the agent, I'll be the customer. Then we'll switch.

Interwoven with these exercises are others that help the new agents learn about the company's history, what it stands for, and the value of its products in people's lives, for instance through stories of how it has helped people recover from catastrophes like Hurricane Katrina.

Given the emphasis on marketing and the limited resources new agents have to invest, how does an agent determine which strategies will pay? The question goes out: What's a reasonable return to expect from a direct mail campaign? The agents mull it over and hazard guesses. Usually, one or more of the agents will have had direct-mail marketing experience and offer the sobering answer: returns are closer to 1 percent than the 50 percent many had guessed.

Once you turn up a lead, how do you discover needs he or she has that the company's products can meet? They return to the handy acronym FORE. Now, the habit of asking about one's family, occupation, recreation, and enjoyment becomes something even more potent than a tool for getting acquainted. It provides an opening into four of the most important realms of a prospect's life where insurance and financial products can help that person protect his or her assets and achieve his or her financial goals. At each pivot from one subject back to another, understanding deepens, and new skills take form.

In this way, through generation, spaced practice, and interleaving of the essential core curriculum, with an eye always to the five-year vision and road map, new agents learn what they need to do, and how, in order to thrive as a part of the Farmers Insurance family.

Jiffy Lube

If you don't expect innovations in training to spring from your local service garage, Jiffy Lube may surprise you. An integrated suite of educational courses under the felicitous name Jiffy Lube University is helping the company's franchisees win customers, reduce employee turnover, broaden their service offerings, and boost sales.

Jiffy Lube is a network of more than two thousand service centers in the United States and Canada that provide oil changes, tire rotation, and other automotive services. Although the company is a subsidiary of Shell Oil Company, every outlet is owned and operated by an independent franchisee, who hires employees to serve customers.

The rapid-oil-change business, like most others, has had to adjust to changes in the marketplace and advances in technology. Synthetic lubricants have made oil changes less frequent, and because cars have become more complicated, garage employees need higher levels of training to understand diagnostic codes and provide appropriate services.

No employee may work on a customer's car until he or she has been certified as proficient. For this, they enter Jiffy Lube University, a Web-based learning platform. Certification starts with interactive e-learning, with frequent quizzing and feedback to learn what a particular job entails and how it's to be performed. When employees score 80 percent or better on an exam, they are eligible to begin training on the job, practicing new skills by following a written guide that breaks each service activity into its component steps. The steps may number as many as thirty and are performed as a part of a team, often involving call and response (for example, between a technician working from the top side of an engine and another underneath). A supervisor coaches the employee and rates his or her performance on each step. When the technician demonstrates mastery, certification is recorded in his or her permanent file, signed by the supervisor. Technicians must recertify every two years to keep their mastery up to snuff and adapt to operational and technical changes. Higher-level jobs for advanced services like brake repair or running engine diagnostics are trained in the same manner.

The e-learning and on-the-job training are active learning strategies that incorporate various forms of quizzing, feedback, and spaced and interleaved practice. All progress is displayed by computer on a virtual "dashboard" that provides an individualized learning plan, enabling an employee to track his or her performance, focus on skills that need to be raised, and monitor his or her progress against the company's completion schedule. Jiffy Lube employees are typically eighteen to twenty-five years old and filling their first job. As a technician is certified in one job, he or she begins training in another, until he or she has trained in all store positions, including management.

Ken Barber, Jiffy Lube International's manager of learning and development, says training has to be engaging in order to hold employees' attention. At the time we spoke, Barber was putting the finishing touches on a computer-based simulation game for company managers called "A Day in the Life of a Store Manager." The service center manager is confronted with various challenges and is required to select among a range of possible strategies for resolving them. The manager's choices determine how the game unfolds, providing feedback and the opportunity to strive for better outcomes, sharpening decision-making skill.

In the six years since Jiffy Lube University was launched, it has received many accolades from the training profession and earned accreditation by the American Council on Education.

Employees who progress through training in all job certifications can enroll at a postsecondary institution with seven hours of college credit under their belts. Since the program's beginning, employee turnover has dropped and customer satisfaction has increased.

"For most employees of a Jiffy Lube franchisee, this is a way into the workforce, and the training curriculum helps them to continue to grow and expand their knowledge," Barber says. "It helps them find a path to success."[12]

Andersen Windows and Doors

At Andersen Windows and Doors, a culture of continuous improvement turns learning on its head: the production workers teach the managers how to make the plant more efficient.

This story is a little different from the others in this chapter in two respects. It's partly about creating a learning culture in the workplace, and partly about empowering employees to use what they learn to change the workplace. By encouraging employees to identify problems on the job and propose improvements, the company is supporting one of the most powerful learning techniques we have discussed, wrestling to solve a problem.

A good place to focus is on the company's division called Renewal by Andersen, which produces replacement windows of all types and sizes: double-hung, casement, gliding, picture windows, and specialty windows in nontraditional shapes.

At Renewal by Andersen's facility in Cottage Grove, Minnesota, their double-hung production line employs thirty-six people during an eight-hour shift that is divided into three work cells, one for sash fabrication, another for frame fabrication, and one for final assembly. Each work cell has four work stations and is led by a crew leader who is responsible for safety, quality, cost, and delivery within that cell. Workers change jobs every two hours to minimize repetitive stress injuries and broaden cross-training. Like interleaving the practice of two or more different but related topics, frequent switching between jobs builds an understanding of the integrated process for which their unit is responsible and equips workers to respond more broadly to unexpected events that arise.

It probably won't surprise you to learn that every job is performed to a written standard that describes each step and the way it is to be taken. The written standard is essential for uniformity of product and quality. Without it, plant manager Rick Wynveen says, four different people will perform the job in four different ways, and produce four different versions of the product.

When a new employee comes on board, he or she is trained following an instructional sequence of practice and feedback that Wynveen calls "tell—show—do—review." The new worker is paired with an experienced worker, practice is on-the-job, and feedback brings learning and performance in line with the written standard.

How do the workers train the managers? When a worker has an idea for improving productivity and management endorses it, for instance revamping the way parts arrive at a work station to make life easier for the worker and assembly faster, the worker who offered it takes leave from production to help implement the new standard. "Everyone's idea is valuable," Wynveen told us, "whether you're an engineer, a maintenance technician, or a production worker."[13] Likewise, when one of the production line teams comes up short in meeting its targets, it's the workers who are asked to identify the problem and redesign the production process to solve it.

The instructional role of employees is most dramatically illustrated in what Wynveen calls a Kaizen event. *Kaizen* is a

Japanese term for improvement. It has been central to Toyota Motor Company's success and has been adopted by many other companies to help create a culture of continuous improvement.

When Wynveen wanted to effect a major increase in the productivity of the plant's double-hung window line, he recruited a design team to engage in a Kaizen event. The team consisted of an engineer, a maintenance technician, a crew leader from the production line, and five production workers. They were given the stretch goals of reducing the line's space requirement by 40 percent and doubling production. (Stretch goals are ones that cannot be reached through incremental improvement but require significant restructuring of methods.) The team met in a conference room eight hours a day for a week, in effect teaching each other the elements, capacities, and constraints of the production process and asking themselves how to make it smaller and better. The following week they came back to Wynveen saying "Here's what we think we can do."

Wynveen took their plan to each of the twelve work stations on the line with a simple question: What changes are needed to make this plan work? Production workers and their crew leaders put their heads together and redesigned the components to fit the new plan. The line was disassembled and rebuilt in two halves, over two weekends, restarted, and fine-tuned over subsequent months, a process that generated yet an additional two hundred improvements suggested by production workers: a learning process of testing, feedback, and correction.

The result? After five months, the plant had met Wynveen's stretch goals and cut costs in half. During the conversion and shakedown, the production teams never missed a shipment and never had a quality issue. The principle of engagement—actively seeking the ideas of employees from all levels of the plant—is central to the company's culture of continuous improvement. "Engagement is a management style of trust and a willingness to talk," Wynveen says. The production employees learned how to refine the design as they worked, and the company provided a way for suggestions to be heard and for employees to participate in their implementation.

A learning culture places the responsibility for learning with the employees and empowers them to change the system. Problems become information rather than failures. And learning by solving the problems (generation) and by teaching others (elaboration) becomes an engine for continuous improvement of performance by individuals and by the production line that they compose.

Inner Gate Acupuncture

There are times when getting learning and teaching right can shape the trajectory of an entire life. Consider Erik Isaacman, a thirty-something husband, father of two, and passionate practitioner of traditional Chinese medicine: acupuncture, massage, and herbal therapy. We close this chapter with the story of a turning point in Erik's fledgling practice, Inner Gate Acupuncture in Portland, Oregon. It's the story of a clinic that was succeeding in its therapeutic mission but struggling as a business.

Erik and his business partner, Oliver Leonetti, opened Inner Gate in 2005, after earning graduate degrees in traditional Chinese medicine. Through networking and creative marketing, they began to build a stream of clients. Portland is fertile territory for alternative therapies. The business grew, and so did expenses: They leased larger space, hired an assistant to schedule appointments and manage the office, brought in a third clinician, and hired a back-office employee. "We were growing 35 to 50 percent every year," Erik recalled when we spoke. "The growth covered up a lot that was missing: We didn't have the systems in place to manage costs. We didn't have clear goals or a management hierarchy. It was fast becoming clear that we had no idea how to run a business."[14]

One of Erik's patients is the Oregon business coach Kathy Maixner. Maixner offered to help. "Unmanaged growth is scary," she told us. "You jump ahead, then you flounder." She asked a lot of questions that quickly focused Erik's and Oliver's thinking on critical gaps in their systems. The three then set out a schedule of frequent coaching sessions, between which Erik and Oliver generated elements of the missing infrastructure: operating manual, job descriptions, financial goals, metrics for measuring the performance of their clinicians.

Every business serves two masters, its customer and its bottom line. "Our clinicians need to understand more than how to practice traditional Chinese medicine," Erik said, as he reflected on his and Oliver's learning curve. "They need to understand how to turn a patient visit into a relationship, and how to help the patient understand his insurance coverage. Satisfying our customers is our highest priority. But we have to pay the bills, too."

Maixner used generation, reflection, elaboration, and rehearsal in her coaching sessions, asking questions that exposed gaps in thinking or that invited the partners to strengthen their understanding of the behavior and tools they needed to adopt in order to be effective managers who delegate and empower their employees.

They developed a system to track clinic metrics, like the number of patient visits, patient disappearance rates, and referral sources. They learned how to ensure they were paid appropriately by insurance companies, raising reimbursements from as little as 30 cents on the dollar. They drafted a uniform protocol, or template, for clinicians to follow in seeing a new patient. They role-played conversations between themselves and their employees.

Central to putting the clinic on sound footing has been Erik's becoming an effective coach and teacher of his coworkers. "We're not just letting it be intuitive," he said. For example, the new protocol for clinicians to follow in a patient's initial session helps to clarify what brought the patient in, the therapies that might be useful, how to describe these therapies in terms the patient would be likely to understand, how to discuss fees and insurance reimbursement options, and how to recommend a treatment plan.

"If you're the clinician, we'll role-play: You are now the patient, and I'm the clinician. We raise questions, objections, and we practice how to respond and end up at the right place for the patient and for the clinic. Then we'll switch roles. We record the role playing, and we listen to the differences: how you have responded to the patient, and how I have responded."

In other words, learning through simulation, generation, testing, feedback, and practice.

As we write this, Inner Gate is in its eighth year, supporting four clinicians and two and a half administrative staff. A fifth clinician is coming up to speed, and the partners are looking to open a second location. By dedicating themselves to being learners as well as teachers, Erik and Oliver have turned their passion into a solid enterprise, and a top-rated acupuncture clinic in Portland.

We have talked throughout this book about learning, not about education. The responsibility for learning rests with every individual, whereas the responsibility for education (and training, too) rests with the institutions of society. Education embraces a world of difficult questions. Are we teaching the right things? Do we reach children young enough? How should we measure outcomes? Are our young people mortgaging their futures to pay for a college degree?

These are urgent issues, and we need to wrestle through them. But while we're doing that, the techniques for highly effective learning that are outlined in this book can be put to use right now everywhere learners, teachers, and trainers are at work. They come at no cost, they require no structural reform, and the benefits they promise are both real and long-lasting.

NOTES

SUGGESTED READING

ACKNOWLEDGMENTS

INDEX

Notes

1. Learning Is Misunderstood

1. The term mental model was first coined to refer to complex conceptual representations, such as understanding the workings of an electrical grid or an automobile engine. We extend the use here to motor skills, referring to what are sometimes called motor schemas.

2. The data about student study strategies come from a survey by J.D. Karpicke, A.C. Butler, & H.L. Roediger, Metacognitive strategies in student learning: Do students practice retrieval when they study on their own?, *Memory* 17 (2010), 471–479.

3. Peter Brown interview of Matt Brown, March 28, 2011, Hastings, MN. All quotes of Matt Brown are from this interview.

4. Find this advice online at http://caps.gmu.edu/educational programs/pamphlets/StudyStrategies.pdf, accessed November 1, 2013.

5. Find this advice online at www.dartmouth.edu/~acskills/docs /study_actively.doc, accessed November 1, 2013.

6. The study advice cited from the St. Louis Post-Dispatch is distributed by Newspapers in Education and can be seen online in "Testing 1, 2, 3! How to Study and Take Tests," p14, at http://nieonline.com/includes/hottopics/Testing%20Testing%20123.pdf, accessed November 2, 2013.

7. The studies showing the futility of mere repetition in recalling the details of what a penny looks like or where a fire extinguisher is located in a building are in R.S. Nickerson & M.J. Adams, Long term memory of a common object, *Cognitive Psychology* 11 (1979), 287–307, and A.D. Castel, M. Vendetti, & K.J. Holyoak, Inattentional blindness and the location of fire extinguishers, *Attention, Perception and Performance* 74 (2012), 1391–1396.

8. The experiment referred to by Tulving was reported in E. Tulving, Subjective organization and the effects of repetition in multi-trial free recall learning, *Journal of Verbal Learning and Verbal Behavior* 5 (1966), 193–197.

9. The experiment on how rereading does not produce much benefit in later retention is from A.A. Callender & M.A. McDaniel, The limited benefits of rereading educational texts, *Contemporary Educational Psychology* 34 (2009), 30–41.

10. The survey showing that students prefer to reread as a study strategy is from Karpicke et al., Metacognitive strategies. Data were also taken from J. McCabe, Metacognitive awareness of learning strategies in undergraduates, *Memory & Cognition* 39 (2010), 462–476.

11. Illusions of knowing will be a theme throughout this book. A general reference is Thomas Gilovich, *How We Know What Isn't So: The Fallibility of Human Reason in Everyday Life* (New York: Free Press, 1991).

12. R.J. Sternberg, E.L. Grigorenko, & L. Zhang, Styles of learning and thinking matter in instruction and assessment, *Perspectives on Psychological Science* 3 (2008), 486–506.

13. The project at Columbia Middle School is reported in M.A. McDaniel, P.K. Agarwal, B.J. Huelser, K.B. McDermott, & H.L. Roediger (2011). Test-enhanced learning in a middle school science classroom: The effects of quiz frequency and placement. *Journal of Educational Psychology, 103*, 399–414.

14. The concept of testing as a learning tool is described in detail in Chapter 2. A general reference on material in this chapter (and other educational applications of cognitive psychology to education) is M.A. McDaniel & A.A. Callender, Cognition, memory, and education, in H.L. Roediger, *Cognitive Psychology of Memory*, vol. 2 of *Learning and Memory: A Comprehensive Reference* (Oxford: Elsevier, 2008), pp. 819–844.

2. To Learn, Retrieve

1. Peter Brown interview of Michael Ebersold, December 31, 2011, Wabasha, MN. All quotes from Ebersold are from this interview.

2. The early work on forgetting curves was published by Hermann Ebbinghaus in 1885 in a book translated into English as *On Memory* in 1913. The most recent version is H. Ebbinghaus, *Memory: A contribution to experimental psychology* (New York: Dover, 1964). Ebbinghaus is often viewed as the "father" of the scientific study of memory.

3. The quotes from Aristotle and Bacon are from H.L. Roediger & J.D. Karpicke, The power of testing memory: Basic research and implications for educational practice, *Perspectives on Psychological Science* 1 (2006), 181–210.

4. Benedict Carey, "Forget what you know about good study habits," *New York Times*, September 7, 2010. The study reported in this article was H.L. Roediger & J.D. Karpicke, Test-enhanced learning: Taking memory tests improves long-term retention, *Psychological Science* 17 (2006), 249–255.

5. A.I. Gates, Recitation as a factor in memorizing, *Archives of Psychology* 6 (1917) and H.F. Spitzer, Studies in retention, *Journal of Educational Psychology* 30 (1939), 641–656. These two large-scale studies with children in elementary and middle school were among the first to document that taking a test or reciting material appearing in didactic texts improved retention for that material.

6. The study involving repeated testing versus repeated studying was E. Tulving, The effects of presentation and recall of material

in free-recall learning, *Journal of Verbal Learning and Verbal Behavior* 6 (1967), 175–184. The study involving amounts of forgetting being reduced from testing is M.A. Wheeler & H.L. Roediger, Disparate effects of repeated testing: Reconciling Ballard's (1913) and Bartlett's (1932) results, *Psychological Science* 3 (1992), 240–245.

7. The positive effects of generation appear in L.L. Jacoby, On interpreting the effects of repetition: Solving a problem versus remembering a solution, *Journal of Verbal Learning and Verbal Behavior* 17 (1978), 649–667. This laboratory experiment demonstrated that generation of target information does not have to be exceptionally challenging in order for generation to produce better retention relative to reviewing information to be learned.

8. Two papers describing the research at Columbia Middle School are H.L. Roediger, P.K. Agarwal, M.A. McDaniel, & K. McDermott, Test-enhanced learning in the classroom: Long-term improvements from quizzing, *Journal of Experimental Psychology: Applied* 17 (2011), 382–395, and M.A. McDaniel, P.K. Agarwal, B.J. Huelser, K.B. McDermott, & H.L. Roediger, Test-enhanced learning in a middle school science classroom: The effects of quiz frequency and placement, *Journal of Educational Psychology* 103 (2011), 399–414. These companion papers were the first to report well-controlled experiments on the benefits of quizzing for middle school students' performances on classroom exams in social studies and science. The findings demonstrated that quizzing produced a significant improvement relative to no-quizzing or directed review of target concepts on unit exams and on cumulative semester and end-of-year exams. In addition, in some cases a single well-placed review quiz produced benefits on the exams that were as robust as several repeated quizzes. For an interesting view of this project by one of the lead researchers, the first teacher and the first principal involved, see P.K. Agarwal, P.M. Bain, & R.W. Chamberlain, The value of applied research: Retrieval practice improves classroom learning and recommendations from a teacher, a principal, and a scientist. *Educational Psychology Review* 24 (2012), 437–448.

9. Peter Brown interview of Roger Chamberlain, October 27, 2011, Columbia Middle School, Illinois. All quotes from Chamberlain are from this interview.

10. Peter Brown interview of Andrew Sobel, December 22, 2011, St. Louis, Missouri. All quotes from Sobel are from this interview.

11. The experiments described here are by H.L. Roediger & J.D. Karpicke, Test-enhanced learning: Taking memory tests improves long-term retention, *Psychological Science* 17 (2006), 249–255. Experiments showing that recall of studied prose passages produced better 2-day and one-week retention than did restudy of the passages. For an earlier study with the same outcome using word lists, see C.P. Thompson, S.K. Wenger, & C.A. Bartling, How recall facilitates subsequent recall: A reappraisal. *Journal of Experimental Psychology: Human Learning and Memory* 4 (1978), 210–221. This experiment showed that massing study was better than practicing retrieval on an immediate test but not a delayed test.

12. Many studies exist on the effects of feedback. One is A.C. Butler & H.L. Roediger, Feedback enhances the positive effects and reduces the negative effects of multiple-choice testing. *Memory & Cognition* 36 (2008), 604–616. The experiments show that feedback strengthens the effects of testing alone, and that feedback may be more beneficial when it's slightly delayed. The authors also showed that that feedback enhances the positive effects and reduces the negative effects of multiple-choice testing. For motor skills, a classic reference is A.W. Salmoni, R.A. Schmidt, and C.B. Walter, Knowledge of results and motor learning: A review and critical reappraisal. *Psychological Bulletin* 95 (1984), 355–386. The authors proposed the guidance hypothesis of feedback effects on motor learning: Frequent immediate feedback can be detrimental to long-term learning—even though it helps immediate performance—because it provides a crutch during practice that is no longer present on a delayed test.

13. The open-book test study was P.K. Agarwal, J.D. Karpicke, S.H.K. Kang, H.L. Roediger, & K.B. McDermott, Examining

the testing effect with open- and closed-book tests, *Applied Cognitive Psychology* 22 (2008), 861–876.

14. Studies comparing the types of tests are S.H. Kang, K.B. Mc-Dermott, H.L. Roediger, Test format and corrective feedback modify the effect of testing on long-term retention. *European Journal of Cognitive Psychology* 19 (2007), 528–558, and M.A. McDaniel, J.L. Anderson, M.H. Derbish, & N. Morrisette, Testing the testing effect in the classroom. *European Journal of Cognitive Psychology* 19 (2007), 494–513. These parallel experiments, one conducted in the laboratory and one in a college course, showed that a short-answer quiz with feedback produced better gains on final tests than a recognition quiz with feedback. The implication is that the testing effect is more robust when more effort is required for retrieval, as it typically is for short-answer questions than for multiple choice questions. However, some studies have shown that multiple choice tests, especially when given repeatedly, can have as much positive effect in the classroom as a short-answer test; see K.B. McDermott, P.K. Agarwal, L. D'Antonio, H.L. Roediger, & M.A. McDaniel, Both multiple-choice and short-answer quizzes enhance later exam performance in middle and high school classes, *Journal of Experimental Psychology: Applied* (in press).

15. These studies examined students' use of testing as a study strategy: J. D. Karpicke, A. C. Butler, & H. L. Roediger, III, Metacognitive strategies in student learning: Do students practice retrieval when they study on their own?, *Memory* 17 (2009), 471–479, and N. Kornell & R. A. Bjork, The promise and perils of self regulated study, *Psychonomic Bulletin & Review* 14 (2007), 219–224. These studies reported the surveys of college students' use of retrieval practice as study technique.

16. Taking a test—even when one fails to correctly recall information on it—enhances learning from a new study episode. See K. M. Arnold & K. B. McDermott, Test-potentiated learning: Distinguishing between the direct and indirect effects of tests, *Journal of Experimental Psychology: Learning, Memory and Cognition* 39 (2013), 940–945.

17. This is a study of frequent low-stakes testing: F.C. Leeming, The exam-a-day procedure improves performance in psychology classes, *Teaching of Psychology* 29 (2002), 210–212. The author found that in sections in which he gave students a short test at the start of every class the students attended class more often and felt that they studied more and learned more than students in classes with only four tests throughout the semester. Final test performance for the different sections (quiz a day or no quiz a day) confirmed students' impressions. Another interesting study conducted in a classroom is K. B. Lyle & N. A. Crawford, Retrieving essential material at the end of lectures improves performance on statistics exams, *Teaching of Psychology* 38 (2011), 94–97.

    Two reviews of research on retrieval practice and testing appear in H. L. Roediger & J. D. Karpicke, The power of testing memory: Basic research and implications for educational practice, *Perspectives on Psychological Science* 1 (2006), 181–210. This paper represents a comprehensive review of laboratory and classroom studies over nearly one hundred years of research, showing that testing can be a powerful learning tool. A more recent review points to many benefits of frequent testing in addition to the direct benefit from retrieval practice: H. L. Roediger, M. A. Smith, & A. L. Putnam, Ten benefits of testing and their applications to educational practice, in J. Mestre & B. H. Ross (eds.), *Psychology of Learning and Motivation* (San Diego: Elsevier Academic Press, 2012). This chapter provides a summary of the host of potential benefits of using testing as a learning technique.

3. Mix Up Your Practice

1. The report of the beanbag study can be found in R. Kerr & B. Booth, Specific and varied practice of motor skill, *Perceptual and Motor Skills* 46 (1978), 395–401.

2. Many well-controlled experiments conducted with a variety of materials and training tasks provide solid evidence that massed practice (doing the same thing over and over repeatedly, a strategy often preferred by learners) is inferior to spacing and

interleaving of practice for learning and retention. A review of the literature on the spacing effect in memory can be found in N. J. Cepeda, H. Pashler, E. Vul, J. T. Wixted, & D. Rohrer, Distributed practice in verbal recall tasks: A review and quantitative synthesis, *Psychological Bulletin* 132 (2006), 354–380.

3. The surgery study is C-A. E. Moulton, A. Dubrowski, H. Mac-Rae, B. Graham, E. Grober, & R. Reznick, Teaching surgical skills: What kind of practice makes perfect?, *Annals of Surgery* 244 (2006), 400–409. This study randomly assigned surgical residents to either a normal daylong intensive lesson on a surgical procedure or to an experimental lesson that spaced four short periods of instruction over several weeks. The findings, showing better retention and application of the surgical techniques after spaced instruction, prompted the medical school to reexamine their standard instructional procedure of cramming instruction on a particular surgical technique into one intensive session.

4. The study showing the benefit of interleaving in mathematics problems is D. Rohrer & K. Taylor, The shuffling of mathematics problems improves learning, *Instructional Science* 35 (2007), 481–498. The standard practice in mathematics textbooks is to cluster practice problems by problem type. This laboratory experiment demonstrated that this standard practice produced inferior performance on a final test in which new problems of each problem type were given relative to a practice procedure in which the practice problems from different problem types were shuffled (interleaved).

5. The study relating differences in practice strategies to differences in motor-memory consolidation was by S. S. Kantak, K. J. Sullivan, B. E. Fisher, B. J. Knowlton, & C. J. Winstein, Neural substrates of motor memory consolidation depend on practice structure, Nature Neuroscience 13 (2010), 923–925.

6. The anagram study was by M. K. Goode, L. Geraci, & H. L. Roediger, Superiority of variable to repeated practice in transfer on anagram solution, *Psychonomic Bulletin & Review* 15 (2008), 662–666. These researchers gave subjects practice on solving anagrams for a set of words: one group was given the same anagram for a particular target word on every practice

trial (massed practice), whereas another group was given a different anagram for a particular target word on each practice trial (varied practice). Surprisingly, varied practice produced better performance on a final trial in which the anagrams were the very ones that were practiced in the other group that had practiced the tested anagram repeatedly.

7. The study about learning of artists' styles was by N. Kornell & R. A. Bjork, Learning concepts and categories: Is spacing the "enemy of induction"?, *Psychological Science* 19 (2008), 585–592. In these experiments, college students attempted to learn the painting style of a number of relatively unknown artists. Students learned the styles better when the paintings of the artists were interleaved compared to when each artist's paintings were massed during learning. Yet, at odds with the objective learning outcomes, most of the learners insisted that they learned better with the massed presentations. Another informative study is S.H.K. Kang & H. Pashler, Learning painting styles: Spacing is advantageous when it promotes discriminative contrast, *Applied Cognitive Psychology* 26 (2012), 97–103, which showed that mixing the examples of paintings helped to highlight the differences among painters' styles (what we are calling discriminative contrast).

8. The finding that improving discrimination among examples contributes to conceptual learning is from L. L. Jacoby, C. N. Wahlheim, & J. H. Coane, Test-enhanced learning of natural concepts: effects on recognition memory, classification, and metacognition, *Journal of Experimental Psychology: Learning, Memory, and Cognition* 36 (2010), 1441–1442.

9. Peter Brown interview of Doulas Larsen, December 23, 2011, St. Louis, MO. All quotes from Larsen are from this interview.

10. Doug Larsen's work can be found in D.P. Larsen, A. C. Butler, & H. L. Roediger, Repeated testing improves long-term retention relative to repeated study: a randomized controlled trial. *Medical Education* 43 (2009), 1174–1181; D.P. Larsen, A. C. Butler, A.L. Lawson, & H. L. Roediger, The importance of seeing the patient: Test-enhanced learning with standardized patients and written tests improves clinical application of knowledge, *Advances in Health Science Education* 18 (2012), 1–17; and

D.P. Larsen, A. C. Butler, & H. L. Roediger, Comparative effects of test-enhanced learning and self-explanation on long-term retention, *Medical Education* 47, 7 (2013), 674–682.

11. Peter Brown interview of Vince Dooley, February 18, 2012, Athens, GA. All quotes of Dooley are from this interview.

12. Psychologists interested in learning have long distinguished between momentary performance and underlying learning (as measured after a delay with intervening reminders). As a simple example, someone might tell you that James Monroe was the fifth US president. You would probably be able to answer correctly if asked about the fifth president for the rest of the day or the week. That would be due to having just heard it (thus boosting the momentary strength or what the psychologists Robert and Elizabeth Bjork call retrieval strength). However, if someone asks you a year later about the fifth president, this would be a measure of habit strength or, as the Bjorks call it, storage strength. See R. A. Bjork & E. L. Bjork, A new theory of disuse and an old theory of stimulus fluctuation, in A.F. Healy, S.M. Kosslyn, & R.M. Shiffrin (eds.), *From learning processes to cognitive processes: Essays in honor of William K. Estes* (vol. 2, pp. 35–67) (Hillsdale, NJ: Erlbaum, 1992). For a recent discussion, see N.C. Soderstrom & R. A. Bjork, Learning versus performance, in D.S. Dunn (ed.), Oxford Bibliographies online: Psychology (New York: Oxford University Press, 2013) doi 10. 1093/obo/9780199828340-0081.

4. Embrace Difficulties

1. All quotes of Mia Blundetto are from telephone conversations between Peter Brown, in Austin, TX, and Blundetto, at Camp Fuji, Japan, on February 9 and March 2, 2013.

2. The phrase "desirable difficulties in learning" originated in the article R. A. Bjork & E. L. Bjork, A new theory of disuse and an old theory of stimulus fluctuation, in A.F. Healy, S.M. Kosslyn, & R.M. Shiffrin (eds.), *From learning processes to cognitive processes: Essays in honor of William K. Estes* (vol. 2, pp. 35–67) (Hillsdale, NJ: Erlbaum, 1992). The idea seems counterintuitive—how can making a task more difficult lead

to it's being learned better and retained longer? The rest of this chapter explains this puzzle and why it seems to arise.

3. Psychologists distinguish among three stages in the learning /memory process: Encoding (or acquisition of information); storage (persistence of information over time); and retrieval (later use of the information). Any time you successfully remembered an event, all three stages were intact. Forgetting (or the occurrence of false memories—retrieving a wrong "memory" of some event but believing it to be right) can occur at any stage.

4. For a classic article on consolidation, see J.L. McGaugh, Memory—a century of consolidation, *Science* 287 (2000), 248–251. For a somewhat more recent and lengthy review, see Y. Dudai, The neurobiology of consolidations, or, how stable is the engram?, *Annual Review of Psychology* 55 (2004), 51–86. For evidence that sleep and dreaming helps with memory consolidation, see E.J. Wamsley, M. Tucker, J.D. Payne, J.A. Benavides, & R. Stickgold, Dreaming of a learning task is associated with enhanced sleep-dependent memory consolidation, *Current Biology* 20 (2010), 850–855.

5. Endel Tulving emphasized the critical role of retrieval cues in remembering by stressing that remembering is always a product of both the information stored (the memory trace) and the cues in the environment that might remind you of the information. With stronger cues, even weaker traces become accessible for recall. See E. Tulving, Cue dependent forgetting, *American Scientist* 62 (1974), 74–82.

6. Robert Bjork has emphasized the role of forgetting of an original event to some degree as aiding the amount of learning from a second presentation of the same event. The power of spacing of events on memory (the spacing effect) is one example. For examples see N.C. Soderstrom & R.A. Bjork, Learning versus performance, in D.S. Dunn (ed.), Oxford Bibliographies in Psychology (New York: Oxford University Press, in press).

7. The problem of old learning interfering with new learning is called negative transfer in psychology. For evidence on how forgetting of old information can help in learning of new

information, see R. A. Bjork, On the symbiosis of remembering, forgetting, and learning, in A. S. Benjamin (ed.), *Successful Remembering and Successful Forgetting: A Festschrift in
Honor of Robert A. Bjork* (pp. 1–22) (New York: Psychology
Press, 2010).

8. The situation where information still exists in memory yet
cannot be actively recalled has been emphasized as a key problem in remembering (Tulving, Cue dependent forgetting). Stored
information is said to be *available,* whereas retrievable information is *accessible.* The instance we give in this chapter of an old
address that a person cannot recall but could easily recognize
among several possibilities is an example of the power of retrieval cues in making available memories accessible to conscious awareness. Recognition tests usually provide more powerful cues than recall tests.

9. The study of baseball players practicing hitting was reported
in K. G. Hall, D. A. Domingues, & R. Cavazos, Contextual interference effects with skilled baseball players, *Perceptual and
Motor Skills* 78 (1994), 835–841.

10. "Reload" is the term the Bjorks use to indicate reconstruction
of a concept or skill after some delay. A good, accessible source
for these ideas is E. L. Bjork & R. A. Bjork, Making things
hard on yourself, but in a good way: Creating desirable difficulties to enhance learning, in M. A. Gernsbacher, R. W. Pew,
L. M. Hough, & J. R. Pomerantz (eds.), *Psychology and the real
world: Essays illustrating fundamental contributions to society* (pp. 56–64) (New York: Worth, 2009).

11. The term *reconsolidation* has several different uses in psychology and neuroscience. The core meaning is the reviving of
an original memory and then having it consolidate again (as
in retrieval practice). However, the original memory can be
changed by reconsolidation if new information is introduced
when the original memory is revived. Reconsolidation has been
studied by both neurobiologists and cognitive psychologists.
Some entry points into this literature are D. Schiller, M. H.
Monfils, C. M. Raio, D. C. Johnson, J. E. LeDoux, & E. A.
Phelps, Preventing the return of fear in humans using reconsolidation update mechanisms, *Nature* 463 (2010), 49–53,

and B. Finn & H. L. Roediger, Enhancing retention through reconsolidation: Negative emotional arousal following retrieval enhances later recall, *Psychological Science* 22 (2011), 781–786.

12. For the research on interleaving, see M. S. Birnbaum, N. Kornell, E. L. Bjork, & R. A. Bjork, Why interleaving enhances inductive learning: The roles of discrimination and retrieval, *Memory & Cognition* 41 (2013), 392–402.

13. Several studies have shown that although making text more difficult to read by leaving out letters or using an unusual typography may slow reading, readers remember more. See M. A. McDaniel, G. O. Einstein, P. K. Dunay, & R. Cobb, Encoding difficulty and memory: Toward a unifying theory, *Journal of Memory and Language* 25 (1986), 645–656, and C. Diemand-Yauman, D. Oppenheimer, & E. B. Vaughn, Fortune favors the **bold** *(and the italicized):* Effects of disfluency on educational outcomes, *Cognition* 118 (2010), 111–115. The study in which the outline either matched or mismatched the chapter is S. M. Mannes & W. Kintsch, Knowledge organization and text organization, *Cognition and Instruction* 4 (1987), 91–115.

14. Studies showing that generation can improve retention include L. L. Jacoby, On interpreting the effects of repetition: Solving a problem versus remembering a solution, *Journal of Verbal Learning and Verbal Behavior* 17 (1978), 649–667, and N. J. Slamecka & P. Graf, The generation effect: Delineation of a phenomenon, *Journal of Experimental Psychology: Human Learning and Memory* 4 (1978), 592–604. More recently, the act of generation before a learning episode has also been shown to enhance performance; see L. E. Richland, N. Kornell, & L. S. Kao, The pretesting effect: Do unsuccessful retrieval attempts enhance learning? *Journal of Experimental Psychology: Applied* 15 (2009), 243–257.

15. The cited study of write-to-learn is K. J. Gingerich, J. M. Bugg, S. R. Doe, C. A. Rowland, T. L. Richards, S. A. Tompkins, & M. A. McDaniel, Active processing via write-to-learn assignments: Learning and retention benefits in introductory psychology, *Teaching of Psychology*, (in press).

16. B.F. Skinner had many influential and interesting ideas about learning in schools as well as on other topics in American society. His important book *Science and Human Behavior* can be downloaded at no cost from the website of the B.F. Skinner Foundation. See also B.F. Skinner, Teaching machines, *Science* 128 (1958), 969–977. Errorless learning does seem important in teaching memory-impaired people, but for most educational situations, errors (so long as they are corrected with feedback) do not hurt and may even aid learning. For example, see B.J. Huelser & J. Metcalfe, Making related errors facilitates learning, but learners do not know it, *Memory & Cognition* 40 (2012), 514–527.

17. The French study on schoolchildren solving anagrams appears in F. Autin & J.C. Croziet, Improving working memory efficiency by reframing metacognitive interpretation of task difficulty, *Journal of Experimental Psychology: General* 141 (2012), 610–618. For a story on the Festival of Errors, see Lizzy Davis, "Paris Stages 'Festival of Errors' to Teach French Schoolchildren How to Think," *Guardian*, July 21, 2010, http://www.guardian .co.uk/world/2010/jul/21/france-paris-festival-of-errors, accessed October 22, 2013.

18. Peter Brown telephone interview of Bonnie Blodgett, March 10, 2013, St. Paul, MN. All quotes of Blodgett are from this interview.

19. The quote from the Bjorks comes from E.L. Bjork & R.A. Bjork, Making things hard on yourself, but in a good way: Creating desirable difficulties to enhance learning, in M.A. Gernsbacher, R.W. Pew, L.M. Hough, and J.R. Pomerantz (eds.), *Psychology and the real world: Essays illustrating fundamental contributions to society* (pp. 56–64) (New York: Worth, 2009).

5. Avoid Illusions of Knowing

1. The field of metacognition—what we know about what we know and how we assess our performance—is a burgeoning one in psychology. A good general reference about metacognition is John Dunlosky and Janet Metcalfe, *Metacognition*

(Los Angeles: Sage, 2009). Daniel Kahneman, *Thinking Fast and Slow* (New York: Farrar, Strauss and Giroux, 2011), also includes a discussion of many illusions to which the mind falls prey. For an earlier discussion of many illusions, see Thomas Gilovich, *How We Know What Isn't So: The Fallibility of Human Reason in Everyday Life* (New York: Free Press, 1991). For a briefer review, see H. L. Roediger, III, & A. C. Butler, Paradoxes of remembering and knowing, in N. Kapur, A. Pascual-Leone, & V. Ramachandran (eds.), *The Paradoxical Brain* (pp. 151–176) (Cambridge: Cambridge University Press, 2011).

2. Peter Brown interview of David Garman, December 12, 2011, Minneapolis, MN. All quotes of Garman are from this interview.

3. The China Airlines incident is reported in: National Transportation Safety Board, "Aircraft Accident report–China Airlines Boeing 747-SP N4522V, 300 Nautical Miles Northwest of San Francisco, California, February 19, 1985," March 29, 1986, and can be found at http://www.rvs.uni-bielefeld.de/publications /Incidents/DOCS/ComAndRep/ChinaAir/AAR8603.html, accessed October 24, 2013.

   The report of the National Transportation Safety Board's investigation into the Carnahan accident is reported by: D. A. Lombardo, "'Spatial disorientation' caused Carnahan crash," *Aviation International News*, AINonline, July 2002, and can be found at: http://www.ainonline.com/aviation-news/aviation -international-news/2008-04-16/spatial-disorientation-caused -carnahan-crash, accessed October 24, 2013.

   The report of the National Transportation Safety Board's investigation into the J. F. Kennedy Jr. accident is reported by: N. Sigelman, "NTSB says spatial disorientation caused Cape Air crash," *Martha's Vineyard Times*, mntimes.com, and can be found at http://www.mvtimes.com/ntsb-says-spatial -disorientation-caused-cape-air-crash-960/, accessed October 24, 2013.

4. E. Morris, "The anosognosic's dilemma: Something's wrong but you'll never know what it is" (pt. 5), *New York Times*, June 24, 2010.

5. L.L. Jacoby, R. A. Bjork, & C.M. Kelley, Illusions of comprehension, competence, and remembering, in D. Druckman & R.A. Bjork (eds.), *Learning, remembering, believing: Enhancing human performance* (pp.57–80) (Washington, DC: National Academy Press, 1994).

6. The Carol Harris/Helen Keller study is reported in R.A. Sulin & D.J. Dooling, Intrusion of a thematic idea in retention of prose, *Journal of Experimental Psycholog* 103 (1974), 255–262. For an overview on memory illusions, see H. L. Roediger & K. B. McDermott, Distortions of memory, in F.I.M. Craik & E. Tulving (eds.), *The Oxford Handbook of Memory* (pp.149–164) (Oxford: Oxford University Press, 2000).

7. Imagination inflation has been shown both in studies of memories from early life and in laboratory studies. Two of the original references for each type of study are M. Garry, C.G. Manning, E.F. Loftus, & S.J. Sherman, Imagination inflation: Imagining a childhood event inflates confidence that it occurred, *Psychonomic Bulletin & Review* 3 (1996), 208–214, and L.M. Goff & H. L. Roediger, Imagination inflation for action events: Repeated imaginings lead to illusory recollections, *Memory & Cognition* 26 (1998), 20–33.

8. The leading questions experiment is E. F. Loftus & J.C. Palmer, Reconstruction of automobile destruction: An example of the interaction between language and memory, *Journal of Verbal Learning and Verbal Behavior* 13 (1974), 585–589.

9. One article on the dangers of hypnosis on memory is P.A. Register & J.F. Kihlstrom, Hypnosis and interrogative suggestibility, *Personality and Individual Differences* 9 (1988), 549–558. For an overview of issues in memory relevant to legal situations, see H. L. Roediger & D.A. Gallo, Processes affecting accuracy and distortion in memory: An overview, in M.L. Eisen, G.S. Goodman, & J.A. Quas (eds.), *Memory and Suggestibility in the Forensic Interview* (pp.3–28) (Mahwah, NJ: Erlbaum, 2002).

10. The story about Don Thomson can be found in B. Bower, Gone but not forgotten: Scientists uncover pervasive unconscious influences on memory, *Science News* 138, 20 (1990), 312–314.

11. The curse of knowledge, hindsight bias, and other topics are covered in Jacoby, Bjork, & Kelley, Illusions of comprehension, competence, and remembering, and in many other places. A relatively recent review of the effects of fluency can be found in D.M. Oppenheimer, The secret life of fluency, *Trends in Cognitive Science* 12 (2008), 237–241.

12. Social contagion of memory: H. L. Roediger, M.L. Meade, & E. Bergman, Social contagion of memory, *Psychonomic Bulletin & Review* 8 (2001), 365–371

13. Two important reviews of the false consensus effect are found in L. Ross, The false consensus effect: An egocentric bias in social perception and attribution processes, *Journal of Experimental Social Psychology* 13 (1977), 279–301, and G. Marks, N. Miller, Ten years of research on the false-consensus effect: An empirical and theoretical review, *Psychological Bulletin* 102 (1987), 72–90.

14. Flashbulb memories of 9/11: J.M. Talarico & D.C. Rubin, Confidence, not consistency, characterizes flashbulb memories, *Psychological Science* 14 (2003), 455–461, and W. Hirst, E.A. Phelps, R.L. Buckner, A. Cue, D.E. Gabrieli & M.K. Johnson Long-term memory for the terrorist attack of September 11: Flashbulb memories, event memories and the factors that influence their retention, *Journal of Experimental Psychology: General* 138 (2009), 161–176.

15. Eric Mazur material comes from his YouTube lecture "Confessions of a converted lecturer," available at www.youtube.com /watch?v=WwslBPj8GgI, accessed October 23, 2013.

16. The curse of knowledge study about guessing tunes tapped out is from L. Newton, Overconfidence in the communication of intent: Heard and unheard melodies (Ph.D. diss., Stanford University, 1990).

17. The Dunning-Kruger effect originated with Justin Kruger & David Dunning, Unskilled and unaware of it: How difficulties in recognizing one's own incompetence lead to inflated self-assessments, *Journal of Personality and Social Psychology* 77 (1999), 1121–1134. Many later experimental studies and articles have been based on this one. See D. Dunning, *Self-Insight: Roadblocks and Detours on the Path to Knowing Thyself* (New York: Psychology Press, 2005).

18. Stories on student-directed learning: Susan Dominus, "Play-Dough? Calculus? At the Manhattan Free School, Anything Goes," *New York Times,* October 4, 2010, and Asha Anchan, "The DIY Approach to Education," *Minneapolis StarTribune,* July 8, 2012.

19. Studies showing that students drop flashcards sooner than they should for long-term learning include N. Kornell & R. A. Bjork, Optimizing self-regulated study: The benefits—and costs—of dropping flashcards, *Memory* 16 (2008), 125–136, and J. D. Karpicke, Metacognitive control and strategy selection: Deciding to practice retrieval during learning, *Journal of Experimental Psychology: General* 138 (2009), 469–486.

20. Eric Mazur has published *Peer Instruction: A User's Manual,* about his approach to teaching. (Upper Saddle River, NJ: Prentice-Hall, 1997). In addition, he exemplifies his approach in an engaging YouTube lecture, "Confessions of a converted lecturer," described in Note 15. Again, it is http://www.youtube .com/watch?v=WwslBPj8GgI, accessed October 23, 2013.

21. The Dunning quote comes from E. Morris, "The anosognosic's dilemma: Something's wrong but you'll never know what it is" (pt. 5), *New York Times,* June 24, 2010.

22. Peter Brown interview of Catherine Johnson, December 13, 2011, Minneapolis, MN.

23. Much of this chapter is about how to regulate one's learning while avoiding various illusions and biases based on fluency, hindsight bias, and the like. An excellent recent article on self-regulated learning that would prove useful to anyone seeking more knowledge on these topics is R. A. Bjork, J. Dunlosky, & N. Kornell, Self-regulated learning: Beliefs, techniques, and illusions, *Annual Review of Psychology* 64 (2013), 417–444.

6. Get Beyond Learning Styles

1. Francis Bacon (1561–1626) was an English philosopher and statesman. The full quote is "All rising a to great place is by a winding stair; and if there be factions, it is good to side a man's self, whilst he is in the rising, and to balance himself when he is placed." From Bacon's essay *Of Great Place.*

2. Peter Brown interview of Bruce Hendry, August 27, 2012, St. Paul, MN. All quotes of Hendry are from this interview.

3. Betsy Morris, Lisa Munoz, and Patricia Neering, "Overcoming dyslexia," *Fortune*, May, 2002, 54–70.

4. Annie Murphy Paul, "The upside of dyslexia," *New York Times,* February 4, 2012. The work by Geiger and Lettvin is described in G. Geiger & J. Y. Lettvin, Developmental dyslexia: A different perceptual strategy and how to learn a new strategy for reading, *Saggi: Child Development and Disabilities* 26 (2000), 73–89.

5. Survey is listed in F. Coffield, D. Moseley, E. Hall, Learning styles and pedagogy in post-16 learning, a systematic and critical review, 2004, Learning and Skills Research Centre, London; the quote by the student ("there's no point in me reading a book") is from same source, p. 137. The quote "a bedlam of contradictory claims" is from Michael Reynolds, Learning styles: a critique, *Management Learning*, June 1997, vol. 28 no. 2, p. 116.

6. The material about learning styles is drawn largely from H. Pashler, M.A. McDaniel, D. Rohrer, & R. A. Bjork, Learning styles: A critical review of concepts and evidence, *Psychological Science in the Public Interest* 9 (2009), 105–119. This article reviewed the published evidence bearing on whether learning is improved when the instructional method is matched to students' learning styles relative to when the instructional method is not matched. Two important findings were that (1) there are very few studies that adopted the gold standard of performing controlled experiments, and (2) the few published experiments consistently found that matching instruction to learning style did not improve learning. One key conclusion is that more experimental research on this issue is needed, but at the moment there is little evidence for the existence of commonly postulated learning styles.

7. An excellent text on classic views of intelligence is Earl Hunt, *Human intelligence* (Cambridge: Cambridge University Press, 2010).

8. Howard Gardner's theory is described in his book *Multiple Intelligences: New Horizons* (New York: Basic Books, 2006), among other venues.

9. The material on work by Robert Sternberg, Elena Grigorenko, and their colleagues comes from several sources. For a nice presentation of the theory, see R. J. Sternberg, Grigorenko, E. L., & Zhang, L., Styles of learning and thinking in instruction and assessment, *Perspectives on Psychological Science* (2008) 486–506. Another interesting study by Sternberg, Grigorenko and colleagues identified college students who showed much higher skill in either analytical, creative, or practical ability (relative to the other two abilities), and assigned them to different classes that focused on analytic instruction, creative instruction, or practical instruction. Students receiving instruction that matched their strongest ability tended to perform better on certain class-performance assessments than students who received mismatched instruction; see R. J. Sternberg, E. L. Grigorenko, M. Ferrari, & P. Clinkenbeard, A triarchic analysis of an aptitude–treatment interaction, *European Journal of Psychological Assessment* 15 (1999), 1–11.

10. The study of Brazilian children was T. N. Carraher, D. W. Carraher, & A. D. Schliemann, Mathematics in the streets and in the schools, *British Journal of Developmental Psychology* 3 (1985), 21–29. This fascinating study focused on five children from very poor backgrounds who were working on street corners or markets in Brazil. Performance was compared for similar multiplication problems presented in different contexts: the natural context in which the child was expert (e.g., selling coconuts, but role-played in the experiment), word problems phrased within a different context (e.g., selling bananas), or formal math problems without context. The children solved nearly 100 percent of the problems when presented in the natural context, fewer in the different context, and only about a third when presented as a formal problem. A key point is that the children used concrete grouping strategies to solve the natural context problems, but then switched to school-taught strategies (not yet well learned) when presented with the formal problems. The mathematical strategies the children had developed were not evident on an academically oriented test.

11. The study of race handicappers is S. J. Ceci & J. K. Liker, A day at the races: A study of IQ, expertise, and cognitive complex-

ity, *Journal of Experimental Psychology: General* 115 (1986), 255–266. This study sampled harness racing fans, with some classified as expert and some as less expert. The expert group and less expert group were evenly matched on IQ, yet the expert group showed much better success at predicting outcomes of actual races and experimenter-contrived races. The experts' success was related to their using an extremely complex system of weighting and combining the range of information related to the horses and the race conditions.

12. Dynamic testing: Robert Sternberg and Elena Grigorenko discuss this concept in *Dynamic Testing: The Nature and Measurement of Learning Potential* (Cambridge: Cambridge University Press, 2002).

13. The fundamental work on structure building was begun by M. A. Gernsbacher, K. R. Varner, & M. E. Faust, Investigating differences in general comprehension skills, *Journal of Experimental Psychology: Learning, Memory, and Cognition* 16 (1990), 430–445. This article provides some of the elegant experimental work that contributed to the development of the structure-building theory—the idea that good comprehenders are able to construct a coherent, organized representation of a narrative from many sources (either read, listened to, or seen in pictures), whereas less able comprehenders tend to construct many, somewhat fractionated representations of the narratives. This research further suggested that poor structure-builders, but not good structure-builders, have trouble inhibiting irrelevant information, which likely contributes to their fractionated (ineffective) representations. Another relevant article is A. A. Callender & M. A. McDaniel, The benefits of embedded question adjuncts for low and high structure builders, *Journal of Educational Psychology* 99 (2007), 339–348. They demonstrated that low structure-builders achieve less learning from standard school materials (textbook chapters) than do high structure-builders. However, embedding questions into chapters to focus the low structure-builders on the important concepts (and requiring them to answer the questions) boosted the low structure-builders to levels of learning enjoyed by high structure-builders.

14. The discussion of learning concepts here relies on two studies: T. Pachur, & H. Olsson, Type of learning task impacts performance and strategy selection in decision making, *Cognitive Psychology* 65 (2012), 207–240. The typical approach to studying conceptual learning in the laboratory is to provide one example at a time, with learners attempting to learn the likely classification of this example (e.g., given a case with a particular set of symptoms, what is the likely disease?). This experiment modified that procedure by presenting two examples simultaneously (e.g., two cases) and requiring learners to select which of the two would be most likely to reflect a particular classification. This comparative approach stimulated less focus on memorizing the examples and better extraction of the underlying rule by which the examples were classified. A similar theme to the one above, except that the focus was on transfer in problem solving, appears in M.L. Gick & K.J. Holyoak, Schema induction and analogical transfer, *Cognitive Psychology* 15 (1983), 1–38. Learners either studied one example of how to solve a particular problem or were required to contrast two different kinds of problems to figure out the common elements of their solutions. The learners who contrasted two problems were more likely to extract a general solution scheme and transfer that scheme to successfully solve new problems than were the learners who studied only one problem.

15. The reference on rule learners and example learners is M.A. McDaniel, M.J. Cahill, M. Robbins, & C. Wiener, Individual differences in learning and transfer: Stable tendencies for learning exemplars versus abstracting rules, *Journal of Experimental Psychology: General* 143 (2014). Using laboratory learning tasks, this novel study revealed that some people tend to learn concepts by focusing on memorizing the particular examples and responses associated with the examples that are used to illustrate the concept (termed *exemplar learners*), whereas other learners focus on the underlying abstraction reflected in the particular exemplars used to illustrate the concept (termed *abstractors*). Further, a particular individual's concept-learning tendency persisted across quite different laboratory concept-

learning tasks, suggesting that individuals may have a fairly stable predisposition toward exemplar learning versus abstraction across a range of conceptual-learning tasks. Of interest, an initial result was that the abstractors on average achieved higher grades in an introductory college chemistry course than did the exemplar learners.

7. Increase Your Abilities

1. A good introduction to Walter Mischel's classic research on delay in gratification in children is W. Mischel, Y. Shoda, & M.L. Rodriguez, Delay of gratification in children, *Science* 244 (1989), 933–938. For an accessible introduction for nonpsychologists, see Jonah Lehrer, "Don't! The secret of self-control," *New Yorker,* May 18, 2009, 26–32. For a 2011 update, see W. Mischel & O. Ayduk, Willpower in a cognitive-affective processing system: The dynamics of delay of gratification, in K.D. Vohs & R.F. Baumeister (eds.), *Handbook of Self-Regulation: Research, Theory, and Applications* (2nd ed., pp.83–105) (New York: Guilford, 2011).

2. Accounts of Carson are reprinted at the website maintained by historian Bob Graham, whose antecedents were among the original American settlers in California, www.longcamp.com /kit_bio.html, accessed October 30, 2013, and are drawn from material published originally in the *Washington Union* in the summer of 1847 and reprinted in *Supplement to the Connecticut Courant,* July 3, 1847. Hampton Sides, *Blood and Thunder* (New York: Anchor Books, 2006), 125–126, relates Fremont's directing Carson on this journey.

3. Research on brain plasticity: J.T. Bruer, Neural connections: Some you use, some you lose, *Phi Delta Kappan* 81, 4 (1999), 264–277. The Goldman-Rakic quote comes from Bruer's article, which quotes from remarks she made before the Education Commission of the States. Further research on brain plasticity, with an emphasis on treatment of brain damage, may be found in D.G. Stein & S.W. Hoffman, Concepts of CNS plasticity in the context of brain damage and repair, *Journal of Head Trauma Rehabilitation* 18 (2003), 317–341.

4. H.T. Chugani, M.E. Phelps, & J.C. Mazziotta, Positron emission tomography study of human brain function development, *Annals of Neurology* 22 (1987), 487–497.

5. J. Cromby, T. Newton, and S.J. Williams, Neuroscience and subjectivity, *Subjectivity* 4 (2011), 215–226.

6. An accessible introduction to this work is Sandra Blakeslee, "New tools to help patients reclaim damaged senses," *New York Times,* November 23, 2004.

7. P. Bach-y-Rita, Tactile sensory substitution studies, *Annals of the New York Academy of Sciences* 1013 (2004), 83–91.

8. For work on myelination, see R.D. Fields, White matter matters, *Scientific American* 298 (2008), 42–49, and R.D. Fields, Myelination: An overlooked mechanism of synaptic plasticity?, *Neuroscientist* 11 (December 2005), 528–531. For a more popular exposition, see Daniel Coyle, *The Talent Code* (New York: Bantam, 2009).

9. Some references on neurogenesis: P.S. Eriksson, E. Perfilieva, T. Björk-Eriksson, A.M. Alborn, C. Nordborg, D.A. Peterson, & F.H. Gage, Neurogenesis in the adult human hippocampus, *Nature Medicine* 4 (1998), 1313–1317; P. Taupin, Adult neurogenesis and neuroplasticity, *Restorative Neurology and Neuroscience* 24 (2006), 9–15.

10. The quote comes from Ann B. Barnet & Richard J. Barnet, *The Youngest Minds: Parenting and Genes in the Development of Intellect and Emotion* (New York: Simon and Schuster, 1998), 10.

11. The Flynn effect is named for James Flynn, who first reported on the trend for increased IQs in the twentieth century in developed nations in J.R. Flynn, Massive IQ gains in 14 nations: What IQ tests really measure, *Psychological Bulletin* 101 (1987), 171–191.

12. This section draws heavily on Richard E. Nisbett, *Intelligence and How to Get It* (New York: Norton, 2009.)

13. The study cited is J. Protzko, J. Aronson, & C. Blair, How to make a young child smarter: Evidence from the database of raising intelligence, *Perspectives in Psychological Science* 8 (2013), 25–40.

14. The cited study is S.M. Jaeggi, M. Buschkuehl, J. Jonides, & W.J. Perrig, Improving fluid intelligence with training on working memory, *Proceedings of the National Academy of Sciences* 105 (2008), 6829–6833.

15. The failure to replicate the working memory training result appears in T.S. Redick, Z. Shipstead, T.L. Harrison, K.L. Hicks, D.E. Fried, D.Z. Hambrick, M.J. Kane, & R.W. Engle, No evidence of intelligence improvement after working memory training: A randomized, placebo-controlled study, *Journal of Experimental Psychology: General* 142, 2013), 359–379.

16. Carol Dweck's research on growth mindsets is summarized in many places. See a nice summary by Marina Krakovsky, "The effort effect," *Stanford Magazine*, March/April 2007. For two articles by Dweck, see H. Grant & C.S. Dweck, Clarifying achievement goals and their impact, *Journal of Personality and Social Psychology* 85 (2003), 541–553, and C.S. Dweck, The perils and promise of praise, *Educational Leadership* 65 (2007), 34–39. She also has a book, *Mindset: The New Psychology of Success* (New York: Ballantine Books, 2006).

17. Dweck quote is from Krakovsky, "Effort effect."

18. The Dweck quotes are from Po Bronson, "How not to talk to your kids," *New York Times Magazine*, February 11, 2007.

19. Paul Tough, *How Children Succeed* (New York: Houghton Mifflin Harcourt, 2012).

20. Anders Ericsson's work on deliberate practice has been described in many places, including Malcolm Gladwell, *Outliers: The Story of Success* (New York: Little, Brown, 2008). For accessible introductions to the work by Ericsson, see K.A. Ericsson & P. Ward, Capturing the naturally occurring superior performance of experts in the laboratory: Toward a science of expert and exceptional performance, *Current Directions in Psychological Science* 16 (2007), 346–350.

21. Mental imagery and its power as an aid to learning and memory has been appreciated since the time of the ancient Greeks. However, psychologists only began studying the topic in experimental studies in the 1960s. Allan Paivio's research showed the power of imagery in controlled studies. A summary of his

early research appears in A. Paivio, *Imagery and Verbal Processes* (New York: Holt, Rinehart, and Winston, 1971).

22. Mark Twain, "How to Make History Dates Stick," *Harper's,* December 1914, available at www.twainquotes.com/History Dates/HistoryDates.html, accessed October 30, 2013.

23. In the history of mnemonic devices (and psychologists' and educators' attitudes toward them), they have suffered various reversals of fortune over the centuries. They were valued from Greek and Roman times and throughout the Middle Ages by educated people who needed to remember large amounts of information (e.g., to make a two-hour speech in the Roman Senate). In recent years, educators have dismissed them as useful merely for rote learning. However, as we show in this chapter, this charge is not fair. Mnemonics, as used by James Paterson and his students, can serve (as they did for the ancient Greeks and Romans) as organizing systems for retrieving information. To put it simply, mnemonic devices are not necessarily good for comprehending complex information, but using a mnemonic system to help to retrieve learned information can be invaluable. James Worthy and Reed Hunt provide an excellent introduction to the history of and psychological research on mnemonic devices in their book *Mnemonology: Mnemonics for the 21st Century* (New York: Psychology Press, 2011).

24. James Paterson is a "memory athlete," partaking in a growing sport in Europe, China, and to some extent the United States. Joshua Foer wrote about this emerging subculture in his bestselling book *Moonwalking with Einstein: The Art and Science of Remembering Everything* (New York: Penguin, 2011). How long might it take a person to remember a shuffled deck of cards in order? For you, a long time. For a memory athlete in the top rungs, under two minutes. A video of Simon Reinhard memorizing a deck of cards in 21.9 seconds is available at www.youtube.com/watch?v=sbinQ6GdOVk, accessed October 30, 2013. This was a world record at the time, but Reinhard has since broken it (21.1 seconds is the record as of this writing). Reinhard has broken twenty seconds in practice sessions but not yet in a timed public event (Simon Reinhard,

personal communication in the form of a conversation over dinner in St. Louis, MO, on May 8, 2013, with Roddy Roediger and several other people).

25. Michela Seong-Hyun Kim's description of her experience using mnemonics was relayed to Peter Brown by James Paterson in private correspondence, February 8, 2013.

26. Peter Brown and Roddy Roediger interview of James Paterson, January 4, 2013, St. Louis, MO.

27. Peter Brown interview of Karen Kim, April 18, 2013, St. Paul, MN.

8. Make It Stick

1. Peter Brown telephone interview of Michael Young, May 21, 2013. All quotes of Young are from this interview.

2. Peter Brown telephone interview of Stephen Madigan, May 20, 2013.

3. Peter Brown interview of Nathaniel Fuller, April 29, 2013, Minneapolis, MN.

4. John McPhee, "Draft no. 4," *New Yorker,* April 29, 2013, 32–38.

5. Peter Brown interview of Thelma Hunter, April 30, 2013, St. Paul, MN.

6. Peter Brown interview of Mary Pat Wenderoth, May 7, 2013, Seattle, WA.

7. The empirical studies aimed at testing the effects of high-structure classes in reducing student attrition in gateway science classes are S. Freeman, D. Haak, & M. P. Wenderoth, Increased course structure improves performance in introductory biology, *CBE Life Sciences Education* 10 (Summer 2011), 175–186; also S. Freeman, E. O'Connor, J. W. Parks, D. H. Cunningham, D. Haak, C. Dirks, & M. P. Wenderoth, Prescribed active learning increases performance in introductory biology, *CBE Life Sciences Education* 6 (Summer 2007), 132–139.

8. Peter Brown telephone interview of Michael Matthews, May 2, 2013.

9. Peter Brown telephone interview of Kiley Hunkler, May 21, 2013.

10. Peter Brown interview of Kathleen McDermott, June 20, 2013, Folly Beach, SC.
11. Peter Brown telephone interview of Kathy Maixner, July 18, 2013.
12. Peter Brown telephone interview of Kenneth Barber, July 1, 2013.
13. Peter Brown telephone interview of Richard Wynveen, July 17, 2013.
14. Peter Brown telephone interview of Erik Isaacman, June 2, 2013.

Suggested Reading

Following are some readings to provide underpinnings for and to further illustrate the principles we have described in this book. These readings are just the tip of the iceberg; in the scientific literature there are hundreds of papers addressing these techniques. In the notes section, we provide references for studies and quotes that are included in the text so that readers may delve deeper. We have tried to balance the need for more information without afflicting the reader with paralyzing detail about the studies.

Scholarly Articles

Crouch, C. H., Fagen, A. P., Callan, J. P., & Mazur, E. (2004). Classroom demonstrations: Learning tools or entertainment? *American Journal of Physics, 72,* 835–838. An interesting use of generation to enhance learning from classroom demonstrations.

Dunlosky, J., Rawson, K. A., Marsh, E. J., Nathan, M. J., & Willingham, D. T. (2013). Improving students' learning with effective learning techniques: Promising directions from cognitive and educational psychology. *Psychological Science in the Public Interest* 14, 4–58. Describes techniques that research has shown to work in improving educational practice in both laboratory and field (educational) settings, as well as other techniques that do not work. Provides a thorough discussion of the research literature supporting (or not) each technique.

McDaniel, M. A. (2012). Put the SPRINT in knowledge training: Training with SPacing, Retrieval, and INTerleaving. In A. F. Healy & L. E. Bourne Jr. (eds.), *Training Cognition: Optimizing Efficiency, Durability, and Generalizability* (pp. 267–286). New York: Psychology Press. This chapter points out that many training situations, from business to medicine to continuing education, tend to cram training into an intensive several day "course." Evidence that spacing and interleaving would be more effective for promoting learning and retention is summarized and some ideas are provided for how to incorporate these techniques into training.

McDaniel, M. A., & Donnelly, C. M. (1996). Learning with analogy and elaborative interrogation. *Journal of Educational Psychology* 88, 508–519. These experiments illustrate the use of several elaborative techniques for learning technical material, including visual imagery and self-questioning techniques. This article is more technical than the others in this list.

Richland, L. E., Linn, M. C., & Bjork, R. A. (2007). Instruction. In F. Durso, R. Nickerson, S. Dumais, S. Lewandowsky, & T. Perfect (eds.), *Handbook of Applied Cognition* (2nd ed., pp. 553–583). Chichester: Wiley. Provides examples of how desirable difficulties, including generation, might be implemented in instructional settings.

Roediger, H. L., Smith, M. A., & Putnam, A. L. (2011). Ten benefits of testing and their applications to educational practice. In B. H. Ross (ed.), *Psychology of Learning and Motivation.* San Diego: Elsevier Academic Press. Provides a summary of the host of potential benefits of practicing retrieving as a learning technique.

Books

Brooks, D. *The Social Animal: The Hidden Sources Love, Character, and Achievement.* New York: Random House, 2011.

Coyle, D. *The Talent Code: Greatness Isn't Born. It's Grown. Here's How.* New York: Bantam Dell, 2009.

Doidge, N. *The Brain the Changes Itself: Stories of Personal Triumph from the Frontiers of Brain Science.* New York: Penguin Books, 2007.

Duhigg, C. *The Power of Habit: Why We Do What We Do in Life and Business.* New York: Random House, 2012.

Dunlosky, J., & Metcalfe, J. *Metacognition.* Los Angeles: Sage Publications, 2009.

Dunning, D. *Self-Insight: Roadblocks and Detours on the Path to Knowing Thyself (Essays in Social Psychology).* New York: Psychology Press, 2005.

Dweck, C. S. *Mindset: The New Psychology of Success.* New York: Ballantine Books, 2008.

Foer, J. *Moonwalking with Einstein: The Art and Science of Remembering Everything.* New York: Penguin, 2011.

Gilovich, T. *How We Know What Isn't So: The Fallibility of Human Reason in Everyday Life.* New York: Free Press, 1991.

Gladwell, M. *Blink: The Power of Thinking Without Thinking.* New York: Little, Brown & Co., 2005.

——. *Outliers: The Story of Success.* New York: Little Brown & Co, 2008.

Healy, A. F. & Bourne, L. E., Jr. (Eds.). *Training Cognition: Optimizing Efficiency, Durability, and Generalizability.* New York: Psychology Press, 2012.

Kahneman, D. *Thinking Fast and Slow.* New York: Farrar, Straus and Giroux, 2011.

Mayer, R. E. *Applying the Science of Learning.* Upper Saddle River, NJ: Pearson, 2010.

Nisbett, R. E. *Intelligence and How to Get It.* New York: W. W. Norton & Company, 2009.

Sternberg, R. J., & Grigorenko, E. L. *Dynamic Testing: The Nature and Measurement of Learning Potential.* Cambridge: University of Cambridge, 2002.

Tough, P. *How Children Succeed: Grit, Curiosity, and the Hidden Power of Character.* Boston: Houghton Mifflin Harcourt, 2012.

Willingham, D. T. *When Can You Trust the Experts: How to Tell Good Science from Bad in Education.* San Francisco: Jossey-Bass, 2012.

Worthen, J. B., & Hunt, R. R. *Mnemonology: Mnemonics for the 21st Century (Essays in Cognitive Psychology).* New York: Psychology Press, 2011.

Acknowledgments

Writing this book was truly a joint enterprise. The authors collaborated over a three year period in a most productive way. Many people and organizations contributed helpful support and insights.

We acknowledge the James S. McDonnell Foundation of St. Louis, Missouri, for their grant "Applying Cognitive Psychology to Enhance Educational Practice" awarded to Henry Roediger and Mark McDaniel, with Henry Roediger as the principal investigator. This grant supported eleven researchers who collaborated for ten years on research to translate cognitive science into educational science. Many points in our book come from the research the McDonnell Foundation supported. We thank the other nine members of our group, from whom we have learned much: Robert and Elizabeth Bjork of the University of California at Los Angeles, John Dunlosky and Katherine Rawson at Kent State University, Larry Jacoby of

Washington University, Elizabeth Marsh of Duke University, Kathleen McDermott of Washington University, Janet Metcalfe at Columbia University, and Hal Pashler at the University of California at San Diego. We particularly thank John Bruer, president of the McDonnell Foundation, and Susan Fitzpatrick, vice president, for their guidance and support, as well as the James S. McDonnell family.

We would also like to thank the Cognition and Student Learning Program of the Institute for Education Sciences (U.S. Department of Education) for a series of grants that have aided research by Roediger and McDaniel in school settings, in collaboration with Kathleen McDermott. The work we conducted in Illinois at Columbia Middle School and Columbia High School would not have been possible without this support. We thank our program officers at CASL, Elizabeth Albro, Carol O'Donnell, and Erin Higgins. In addition, we thank teachers, principals, and students at the Columbia Schools, in particular, Roger Chamberlain (principal at Columbia Middle School when we began our research there) and Patrice Bain, the first teacher who pioneered implementation of our research in a classroom. Other teachers who permitted us to conduct experiments in their classrooms include Teresa Fehrenz, Andria Matzenbacher, Michelle Spivey, Ammie Koch, Kelly Landgraf, Carleigh Ottwell, Cindy McMullan, Missie Steve, Neal O'Donnell and Linda Malone. A great group of research assistants has helped with this research, including Kristy Duprey, Lindsay Brockmeier, Barbie Huelser, Lisa Cressey, Marco Chacon, Anna Dinndorf, Laura D'Antonio, Jessye Brick, Allison Obenhaus, Meghan McDoniel, and Aaron Theby. Pooja Agarwal has been instrumental in this project every step of the way, leading the research on a day-to-day basis while she was a graduate student at Washington University and then overseeing the project as a postdoctoral fellow. Many of the practical suggestions in the book came from our classroom experiments.

Dart NeuroScience of San Diego, California, supported our research on memory athletes through a generous grant. Roediger served as principal investigator and was joined by David Balota, Kathleen McDermott, and Mary Pyc. We tested several memory athletes in this project, and we appreciate James Paterson for letting us use his story in the book. We are especially grateful for the support of Tim Tully, Dart's chief scientific officer, who first approached us with the idea of identifying individuals with highly superior memory abilities.

Our granting agencies were generous in their support, but we provide the usual disclaimer that the opinions expressed in this book are those of the authors and do not represent the views of the James S. McDonnell Foundation, the Institute of Education Sciences, the U.S. Department of Education, or Dart NeuroScience.

Roediger and McDaniel would like to thank the many students and postdoctoral fellows who worked with us and helped with the projects described in this book. Graduate students who worked with Roediger on relevant projects during this period are Pooja Agarwal, Andrew Butler, Andy DeSoto, Michael Goode, Jeff Karpicke, Adam Putnam, Megan Smith, Victor Sungkhasettee, and Franklin Zaromb. Postdoctoral fellows included Pooja Agarwal, Jason Finley, Bridgid Finn, Lisa Geraci, Keith Lyle, David McCabe, Mary Pyc, and Yana Weinstein. Research staff that worked on the project include Jane McConnell, Jean Ortmann-Sotomayor, Brittany Butler, and Julie Gray. Mark McDaniel would like to thank his students who worked on research pertinent to this book: Aimee

Calendar, Cynthia Fadler, Dan Howard, Khuyen Nguyen, Mathew Robbins, and Kathy Wildman, and his research-assistant staff, Michael Cahill, Mary Derbish, Yiyi Liu, and Amanda Meyer. His postdoctoral fellows who worked on related projects were Jeri Little, Keith Lyle, Anaya Thomas, and Ruthann Thomas.

We are indebted to those individuals from many walks of life who shared their stories of learning and remembering to help us illustrate the important ideas in this book. We thank Ken Barber at Jiffy Lube International, Bonnie Blodgett, Mia Blundetto, Derwin Brown, Matt Brown, Patrick Castillo, Vince Dooley, Mike Ebersold, Nathaniel Fuller, Catherine Johnson, Sarah Flanagan, Bob Fletcher, Alex Ford, Steve Ford, David Garman, Jean Germain, Lucy Gerold, Bruce Hendry, Michael Hoffman, Peter Howard, Kiley Hunkler, Thelma Hunter, Erik Isaacman, Karen Kim, Young Nam Kim, Nancy Lageson, Douglas Larsen, Stephen Madigan, Kathy Maixner, Michael Matthews, Kathleen McDermott, Michael McMurchie and Rick Wynveen at Renewal by Andersen, Jeff Moseley, James Paterson and his students at Bellerbys College (Stephanie Ong, Victoria Gevorkova, and Michela Seong-Hyun Kim), Bill Sands, Andy Sobel, Annette Thompson and Dave Nystrom at Farmers Insurance, Jon Wehrenberg, Mary Pat Wenderoth, and Michael Young. We thank Lorri Freifeld at *Training* magazine for introducing us to the leaders of exemplary corporate training programs.

Several people kindly read earlier drafts of the book or selected chapters. We thank Ellen Brown, Kathleen McDermott, Henry Moyers, Thomas Moyers, and Steve Nelson. As is customary in the sciences, five of our peers from the scientific community were recruited by our publisher to review the book anonymously in manuscript: we thank the three who have subsequently identified themselves–Bob Bjork, Dan Schacter, and Dan Willingham–and the two whose identities remain unknown to us.

Finally, we thank Elizabeth Knoll, our editor, and the professional staff at Harvard University Press for their insights, guidance, and devotion to the quality of this book.

Index

Accessible information, compared to available information, 268n8

Achievement: attributions on, 180–182; in science courses, class structure affecting, 232–234, 283n7

Achievement gap in the sciences, on closing, 232–234, 283n7

Acquired skill, learning as, 2

Agarwal, Pooja, 34

Alzheimer's disease, 164

Ambiguity, hunger for narrative in, 109–112

Anagram solving: difficulty and working memory in, 91–92, 270n17; distraction of one-sided conversation affecting, 109–110; varied practice in, 52–53, 264–265n6

Analogical transfer, 278n14

Analytical skills: and achievement in science courses, 233; in Bloom's taxonomy of learning, 228; and intelligence, 148, 150

Andersen Windows and Doors, 247–250

Anxiety in test taking, 91–92

Application of learning, in Bloom's taxonomy of learning, 228

Apprentice model in training, 127

Aristotle, 28

Artists, learning painting styles of, 53–54, 84, 265n7

Associative learning, 172

Culture of continuous improvement in Andersen Windows and Doors, 247–250
Cumulative learning: fostered by cumulative quizzing, 38–39; 238; in Columbia Public School District, 238–239; as teaching strategy, 227; testing on, 238
Curse of knowledge, 115–116, 119, 273n11, 273n16

Dartmouth College, 12, 257n5
Darwin Awards, 104
Delay of gratification, 162–163, 279n1
Deliberate practice, 183–185, 281n20
Dellis, Nelson, 164, 166
Dendrites, 166, 169–170
Desirable difficulties in learning, 68–69, 98, 160, 226–228, 229, 266–267n2
Developmental psychology, 8
Difficulty of learning, 7, 67–101; as desirable, 68–69, 98, 160, 226–228, 229, 266–267n2; in jump school training, 68–78; in spaced practice, 4, 47, 49, 81, 82, 205; and strength and duration of memory, 9; for students, 201; as teaching strategy, 225–228, 229; as undesirable, 92, 98–99
Discrimination skills, 65, 101; in identification of artists' painting styles, 53–54, 84,

265n7; in identification of birds, 54–55, 84–85; fostered by interleaved and varied practice , 53–55, 65, 84–85, 101
Disraeli, Benjamin, 109
Distortions of memory, 109–118; in false consensus effect, 117, 273n13; in familiarity, 116; in flashbulb memories, 117–118, 273n14; in hindsight bias, 115–116, 273n11; in hunger for narratives, 109–112; in hypnosis, 114, 272n9; in imagination inflation, 113, 272n7; in interference, 114–115; in social influences, 116–117; in suggestion, 113–114
Doidge, Norman, 168
Donahue, Barney, 136–137
Dooley, Vince, 60–62, 120, 198, 222, 266n11
Dowling, Joe, 217
Dreaming, consolidation of memory in, 267n4
Dunn, Kenneth, 144
Dunn, Rita, 144
Dunning, David, 109, 121, 122, 126, 273n17
Dunning-Kruger effect, 121, 273n17
Dweck, Carol, 92, 139, 179–183, 233, 281n16
Dynamic testing, 151–152, 159, 277n12; steps in, 152
Dyslexia, 139–140, 141–143, 159, 275nn3–4